THE NATIONAL EDUCATION GOALS REPORT

Building a Nation of Learners

1994

NATIONAL
EDUCATION
GOALS
PANEL

3.79.2
United

For sale by the U.S. Government Printing Office
Superintendent of Documents, Mail Stop: SSOP, Washington, DC 20402-9328
ISBN 0-16-045194-9

Foreword

On behalf of the National Education Goals Panel, I am pleased to present the *1994 National Education Goals Report*, the fourth in a series of annual reports to measure progress toward the National Education Goals through the year 2000. Not only does 1994 mark the fifth anniversary of the 1989 Education Summit in Charlottesville, Virginia, which spurred the creation of the National Education Goals, but 1994 also brings significant changes and exciting new challenges to the Goals Panel.

Earlier this year, Congress adopted and the President enacted the *Goals 2000: Educate America Act*, which significantly expanded the role of the Goals Panel. While reporting the amount of educational progress the nation and states are making continues to be one of the Panel's main responsibilities, the Goals Panel is also responsible for:

- building a national consensus for education improvement;
- accelerating progress by reporting on promising or effective actions being taken at the national, state, and local levels to achieve the Goals;
- identifying actions that federal, state, and local governments should take to enhance progress toward achieving the Goals and to provide all students with a fair opportunity to learn; and
- working in partnership with the newly created National Education Standards and Improvement Council to review the criteria for voluntary content, performance, and opportunity-to-learn standards reflecting high expectations for all students.

The *1994 Goals Report* consists of three documents. The *National* and *State Data Volumes* include comprehensive sets of measures to describe our educational progress at the national level and the amount of progress that individual states have made against their own baselines. The central document, the *1994 Goals Report*, focuses on sixteen policy-actionable core indicators to convey to parents, educators, and policymakers how far we are from where we should be and what we must do in order to reach our destination.

Attainment of the National Education Goals will require commitment on the part of all Americans, and we encourage all states and local communities to become active participants in the "Goals Process" by adopting education goals, setting ambitious standards, and improving data collection systems so that we can regularly monitor and share results.

Sincerely,

John R. McKernan, Jr., Chair
(August 1993-August 1994)
National Education Goals Panel, and
Governor of Maine

Governors

Evan Bayh, Chair
(August 1994-August 1995)
National Education Goals Panel, and
Governor of Indiana

Arne H. Carlson,
Governor of Minnesota

Jim Edgar,
Governor of Illinois

John Engler,
Governor of Michigan

Michael Leavitt,
Governor of Utah

E. Benjamin Nelson,
Governor of Nebraska

Roy Romer,
Governor of Colorado

**Members of
the Administration**

Carol H. Rasco,
Assistant to the President
for Domestic Policy

Richard W. Riley,
Secretary of Education

Members of Congress

Jeff Bingaman,
U.S. Senator, New Mexico

Thad Cochran,
U.S. Senator, Mississippi

William F. Goodling,
U.S. Representative, Pennsylvania

Dale E. Kildee,
U.S. Representative, Michigan

State Legislators

Anne C. Barnes,
State Representative, North Carolina

G. Spencer Coggs,
State Representative, Wisconsin

Robert T. Connor,
State Senator, Delaware

Doug Jones,
State Representative, Idaho

Preface

Planning, design, and production of the *1994 National Education Goals Report* and the accompanying *National* and *State Data Volumes* were the responsibility of Cynthia Prince, Associate Director for Analysis and Reporting, and Leslie Lawrence, Education Associate, of the National Education Goals Panel.

Justin Boesel, Babette Gutmann, and Allison Henderson of Westat, Inc., supplied invaluable technical assistance and statistical support services. Jim Page and Kelli Sechrist of Impact Design, Inc., contributed expertise in graphic design, layout, and report production. Additional graphics were designed by Ogilvy, Adams and Rinehart and by the National Geographic Society.

Portions of the text were written by Cynthia Prince, Anne Lewis, and Leslie Lawrence, with assistance from Emily Wurtz. Scott Miller of Editorial Experts, Inc., contributed essential editorial support.

Special thanks go to members of the National Education Goals Panel's Working Group for helpful critiques of earlier drafts of the Report, especially members of the Reporting Committee: Patricia Brown, John Burkett, Alison Englund, Lori Gremel, W. Davis Lackey, Leo Martin, Mary Rollefson, Marjorie Steinberg, Susan Traiman, and Georgia Jackson VanAdestine.

The *1994 Goals Report* would not have been possible without the hard work, thoughtful planning, and careful review provided by all of these individuals. Their dedication and assistance are gratefully acknowledged.

Ken Nelson
Executive Director
National Education Goals Panel

TABLE OF CONTENTS

The National Education Goals

GOAL 1: Ready to Learn

By the year 2000, all children in America will start school ready to learn.

Objectives:

- All children will have access to high-quality and developmentally appropriate preschool programs that help prepare children for school.

- Every parent in the United States will be a child's first teacher and devote time each day to helping such parent's preschool child learn, and parents will have access to the training and support parents need.

- Children will receive the nutrition, physical activity experiences, and health care needed to arrive at school with healthy minds and bodies, and to maintain the mental alertness necessary to be prepared to learn, and the number of low-birthweight babies will be significantly reduced through enhanced prenatal health systems.

Goal 2: School Completion

By the year 2000, the high school graduation rate will increase to at least 90 percent.

Objectives:

- The Nation must dramatically reduce its school dropout rate, and 75 percent of the students who do drop out will successfully complete a high school degree or its equivalent.

- The gap in high school graduation rates between American students from minority backgrounds and their non-minority counterparts will be eliminated.

Goal 3: Student Achievement and Citizenship

By the year 2000, all students will leave grades 4, 8, and 12 having demonstrated competency over challenging subject matter including English, mathematics, science, foreign languages, civics and government, economics, arts, history, and geography, and every school in America will ensure that all students learn to use their minds well, so they may be prepared for responsible citizenship, further learning, and productive employment in our Nation's modern economy.

Objectives:

- The academic performance of all students at the elementary and secondary level will increase significantly in every quartile, and the distribution of minority students in each quartile will more closely reflect the student population as a whole.

- The percentage of all students who demonstrate the ability to reason, solve problems, apply knowledge, and write and communicate effectively will increase substantially.

- All students will be involved in activities that promote and demonstrate good citizenship, good health, community service, and personal responsibility.

- All students will have access to physical education and health education to ensure they are healthy and fit.

- The percentage of all students who are competent in more than one language will substantially increase.

- All students will be knowledgeable about the diverse cultural heritage of this Nation and about the world community.

Goal 4: Teacher Education and Professional Development

By the year 2000, the Nation's teaching force will have access to programs for the continued improvement of their professional skills and the opportunity to acquire the knowledge and skills needed to instruct and prepare all American students for the next century.

Objectives:

- All teachers will have access to preservice teacher education and continuing professional development activities that will provide such teachers with the knowledge and skills needed to teach to an increasingly diverse student population with a variety of educational, social, and health needs.

- All teachers will have continuing opportunities to acquire additional knowledge and skills needed to teach challenging subject matter and to use emerging new methods, forms of assessment, and technologies.

- States and school districts will create integrated strategies to attract, recruit, prepare, retrain, and support the continued professional development of teachers, administrators, and other educators, so that there is a highly talented work force of professional educators to teach challenging subject matter.

- Partnerships will be established, whenever possible, among local educational agencies, institutions of higher education, parents, and local labor, business, and professional associations to provide and support programs for the professional development of educators.

Goal 5: Mathematics and Science

By the year 2000, United States students will be first in the world in mathematics and science achievement.

Objectives:

- Mathematics and science education, including the metric system of measurement, will be strengthened throughout the system, especially in the early grades.

- The number of teachers with a substantive background in mathematics and science, including the metric system of measurement, will increase by 50 percent.

- The number of United States undergraduate and graduate students, especially women and minorities, who complete degrees in mathematics, science, and engineering will increase significantly.

Goal 6: Adult Literacy and Lifelong Learning

By the year 2000, every adult American will be literate and will possess the knowledge and skills necessary to compete in a global economy and exercise the rights and responsibilities of citizenship.

Objectives:

- Every major American business will be involved in strengthening the connection between education and work.

- All workers will have the opportunity to acquire the knowledge and skills, from basic to highly technical, needed to adapt to emerging new technologies, work methods, and markets through public and private educational, vocational, technical, workplace, or other programs.

- The number of quality programs, including those at libraries, that are designed to serve more effectively the needs of the growing number of part-time and midcareer students will increase substantially.

- The proportion of the qualified students, especially minorities, who enter college, who complete at least two years, and who complete their degree programs will increase substantially.

- The proportion of college graduates who demonstrate an advanced ability to think critically, communicate effectively, and solve problems will increase substantially.

- Schools, in implementing comprehensive parent involvement programs, will offer more adult literacy, parent training and lifelong learning opportunities to improve the ties between home and school, and enhance parents' work and home lives.

Goal 7: Safe, Disciplined, and Alcohol- and Drug-free Schools

By the year 2000, every school in the United States will be free of drugs, violence, and the unauthorized presence of firearms and alcohol and will offer a disciplined environment conducive to learning.

Objectives:

- Every school will implement a firm and fair policy on use, possession, and distribution of drugs and alcohol.

- Parents, businesses, governmental and community organizations will work together to ensure the rights of students to study in a safe and secure environment that is free of drugs and crime, and that schools provide a healthy environment and are a safe haven for all children.

- Every local educational agency will develop and implement a policy to ensure that all schools are free of violence and the unauthorized presence of weapons.

- Every local educational agency will develop a sequential, comprehensive kindergarten through twelfth grade drug and alcohol prevention education program.

- Drug and alcohol curriculum should be taught as an integral part of sequential, comprehensive health education.

- Community-based teams should be organized to provide students and teachers with needed support.

- Every school should work to eliminate sexual harassment.

Goal 8: Parental Participation

By the year 2000, every school will promote partnerships that will increase parental involvement and participation in promoting the social, emotional, and academic growth of children.

Objectives:

- Every State will develop policies to assist local schools and local educational agencies to establish programs for increasing partnerships that respond to the varying needs of parents and the home, including parents of children who are disadvantaged or bilingual, or parents of children with disabilities.

- Every school will actively engage parents and families in a partnership which supports the academic work of children at home and shared educational decisionmaking at school.

- Parents and families will help to ensure that schools are adequately supported and will hold schools and teachers to high standards of accountability.

Chapter 1: Introduction

"If you're not keeping score, you're just practicing."

Vince Lombardi

In any sport, it is difficult to determine how well your team is doing unless you have complete, accurate, and up-to-date information on the team's performance. If you want to determine your team's standing and see how far you are from first place, you also need measures that allow you to compare your team to the very best in the league. Most important, if you expect to win, then all players must work cooperatively to achieve common goals.

Until recently, it was not possible for the United States to apply these same principles to our education system to determine whether we were making the kind of progress needed to remain internationally competitive. As recently as five years ago, the United States had no nationwide goals to provide focus and consistency in order to determine whether we were all working toward high-performance education results. With the exception of mathematics, no voluntary nationwide standards existed to determine what students should know and be able to do in any of the core subjects. In a number of key areas, we lacked the necessary data to judge whether we were making sufficient progress or falling further behind.

Public dissatisfaction with low levels of student performance, increasing global economic competition, and consistently poor showings on international assessments led policymakers to conclude five years ago that the United States had been spending too much time merely practicing and had not devoted sufficient attention to improving performance. The National Education Goals were created in 1990 to reverse that trend. This fourth annual report of the National Education Goals Panel is designed to help parents, educators, and policymakers score our education performance by reporting where the nation and the states stand with respect to each of the National Education Goals, where we *should* be if we expect to reach the Goals by the year 2000, and which actions are necessary in order for us to reach our destination.

The National Education Goals

In 1989, the nation's Governors and the President reached agreement at an education summit convened in Charlottesville, Virginia, that unless the nation established clear education goals and all citizens worked cooperatively to achieve them, the United States would be woefully unprepared to face the technological, scientific, and economic challenges of the 21st century. The 1989 Education Summit led to the adoption of six National Education Goals which set high expectations for education performance at every stage of a learner's life, from the preschool years through adulthood. In 1994, Congress adopted the six Goals and expanded the number to eight, underscoring the critical roles that teachers and parents play in improving the nation's education performance. The Goals state that by the year 2000:

1. **All children in America will start school ready to learn.**

2. **The high school graduation rate will increase to at least 90 percent.**

3. **All students will leave grades 4, 8, and 12 having demonstrated competency over challenging subject matter including English, mathematics, science, foreign languages, civics and government, economics, arts, history, and geography, and every school in America will ensure that all students learn**

to use their minds well, so they may be prepared for responsible citizenship, further learning, and productive employment in our Nation's modern economy.

4. The Nation's teaching force will have access to programs for the continued improvement of their professional skills and the opportunity to acquire the knowledge and skills needed to instruct and prepare all American students for the next century.

5. United States students will be first in the world in mathematics and science achievement.

6. Every adult American will be literate and will possess the knowledge and skills necessary to compete in a global economy and exercise the rights and responsibilities of citizenship.

7. Every school in the United States will be free of drugs, violence, and the unauthorized presence of firearms and alcohol and will offer a disciplined environment conducive to learning.

8. Every school will promote partnerships that will increase parental involvement and participation in promoting the social, emotional, and academic growth of children.

The National Education Goals Panel

Following the adoption of the National Education Goals, the White House and the National Governors' Association established the National Education Goals Panel. Its primary purpose at that time was to monitor and report annual progress toward the Goals at the national and state levels. In March of 1994, Congress codified the National Education Goals and established the Goals Panel as an independent federal agency by enacting the *Goals 2000: Educate America Act*. The eighteen-member bipartisan Goals Panel now consists of eight Governors, four members of Congress, four State Legislators, the U.S. Secretary of Education, and the Assistant to the President for Domestic Policy.

Congress also considerably expanded the Goals Panel's charge in the new legislation. While monitoring and reporting progress toward the Goals continues to be one of the primary duties of the Goals Panel, the Panel is also responsible for:

• building a national consensus for the reforms necessary to achieve education improvement;

• reporting on promising or effective actions being taken at the national, state, and local levels to achieve the Goals;

• identifying actions that federal, state, and local governments should take to enhance progress toward achieving the Goals and to provide all students with a fair opportunity to learn; and

• collaborating with the newly created National Education Standards and Improvement Council to review the criteria for voluntary content, performance, and opportunity-to-learn standards.

The 1994 National Education Goals Report

For the past three years the Goals Panel has measured progress toward each of the Goals by establishing baseline performance measures around the time of the Charlottesville Summit, and by updating the baselines as new data become available. While this information does tell us where we currently stand, the Goals Panel has never set specific targets to determine where we *should* be each year if we expect to reach the National Education Goals by the year 2000. This year the Panel begins that process by making four fundamental changes to the annual Goals Report so that it is more useful and more understandable.

As was the case last year, the 1994 Report consists of three documents. The *National* and *State Data Volumes* contain comprehensive sets of indicators to describe our educational progress at the national level and the amount of progress made by individual states against their own baselines. However, this central document, the *1994 National Education Goals Report*, has been expanded and revised so that it:

1. Focuses on a limited set of core education indicators to measure progress. If policymakers, educators, and the public focus on improving performance on these core indicators, the nation should be able to raise its overall level of "educational health" over time.

2. Focuses on indicators that are policy-actionable, so that policymakers and the public will have a better understanding of what they can do to improve education performance.

3. Begins the process of setting challenging, yet meaningful, benchmarks for performance so that the American public clearly understands how far we are from where we should be.

4. Identifies data gaps at both the national and state levels that impede the Panel's ability to measure progress toward the Goals, so that the Panel and its partners can design short- and long-term strategies for filling these gaps.

Core Indicators

Sixteen core indicators are the central focus of the *1994 Goals Report*. They were selected with the assistance of members of the Goals Panel's Resource and Technical Planning Groups, who were asked to recommend a small set of indicators for the core that were, to the extent possible:

• comprehensive across the Goals;

• most critical in determining whether the Goals are actually achieved;

• policy-actionable; and

• updated at frequent intervals, so that the Panel can provide regular progress reports.

The core indicators are discussed in detail in Chapter 2 of this Report. The sixteen are:

GOAL 1: READY TO LEARN
1. Children's Health Index
2. Immunizations
3. Family-child reading and storytelling
4. Preschool participation

GOAL 2: SCHOOL COMPLETION
5. High school completion

GOAL 3: STUDENT ACHIEVEMENT AND CITIZENSHIP
6. Mathematics achievement
7. Reading achievement

GOAL 4: TEACHER EDUCATION AND PROFESSIONAL DEVELOPMENT
(No core indicators have been selected for this new Goal yet. They will be addressed in future Goals Reports.)

GOAL 5: MATHEMATICS AND SCIENCE
8. International mathematics achievement comparisons
9. International science achievement comparisons

GOAL 6: ADULT LITERACY AND LIFELONG LEARNING
10. Adult literacy
11. Participation in adult education
12. Participation in higher education

GOAL 7: SAFE, DISCIPLINED, AND ALCOHOL- AND DRUG-FREE SCHOOLS
13. Overall student drug and alcohol use
14. Sale of drugs at school
15. Student and teacher victimization
16. Disruptions in class by students

GOAL 8: PARENTAL PARTICIPATION
(No core indicators have been selected for this new Goal yet. They will be addressed in future Goals Reports.)

It is important to understand that the indicators selected for the core are not necessarily the ideal measures of progress, nor are they all policy-actionable. They do represent, however, the best currently available measures. The list will be expanded as other central measures become available for the original six Goals (e.g., new student achievement levels in science), and for the two new Goals on Teacher Education and Professional Development, and Parental Participation.

While this small core of indicators has the distinct advantage of bringing greater focus to our discussions about national and state progress, the Panel acknowledges that sixteen indicators cannot possibly capture the breadth or depth of the educational needs that we face. Therefore, a much broader range of indicators for each Goal is presented in the accompanying *National* and *State Data Volumes*.

The Goals Process

Meeting the challenges of the next century will require the involvement of all Americans: public officials, educators, parents, business and community leaders, and students. Becoming active participants and improving our ability to gauge our education performance will enable us to make better decisions that will benefit our schools. One of the most important roles that the Goals Panel plays is encouraging collaborative efforts to improve education that are taking place at all levels of governance and, hopefully, in every community.

The heart of the Goals Process is *informed* decision-making. Citizens need accurate, reliable information to determine the strengths and weaknesses of their education systems and to make decisions that will allow those systems to perform at more ambitious levels. The Goals Process can help communities determine how well they are doing, where they would like to be, and what they will have to do to move their results in the desired direction. It involves three essential steps:

- adopting and adapting the National Education Goals to reflect high expectations for all learners and cover a lifetime of learning, from the preschool years through adulthood;

- assessing current strengths and weaknesses, and building a strong accountability system to measure and report progress regularly toward all of the goals; and

- setting performance milestones to serve as checkpoints along the way.

Once these steps have been taken and the community has made a long-term commitment to evaluate its progress, it will need to identify potential barriers to success, develop strategies to overcome them, and use the information it is collecting along the way to fine-tune its own approach to education improvement.

A new product created by the Goals Panel, the Community Action Toolkit, is designed to help communities implement the Goals Process. The Toolkit includes a handbook which outlines the steps required to collect reliable data so that informed decisionmaking can take place at the local level. The Toolkit also includes advice on organizing community leaders and communicating educational strengths, weaknesses, and priorities to the general public. Information about the Toolkit can be obtained by returning the questionnaire located in the back of this document to the Goals Panel.

Next Steps

Five years ago the White House and the nation's Governors, later joined by Congress and State Legislators, began a process intended to result in a rapid rebuilding of the nation's education system. By the end of the century, they agreed, the commitment made by policymakers, communities, educators, students, and parents should be turning those ambitious goals into reality.

That process is nearly at midpoint. A permanent foundation has been laid and considerable information has been gathered on progress, though it will require continued improvements before it can be considered complete in all areas. This *1994 National Education Goals Report* introduces the essential areas in which policymakers need to act and the public needs to be involved. In the pages that follow, the Goals Panel presents a status report on each of these indicators, shows how much improvement we have made and have yet to make, and addresses the level of commitment and collaboration that will be needed during the crucial next six years if we are serious about keeping score, not simply practicing.

UNITED STATES

	Baseline	Most Recent Update	Overall Progress
1. Children's Health Index: Has the U.S. reduced the percentage of infants born with 2 or more health and developmental risks? *(1990, 1991)* ▲	14%	13%	↑
2. Immunizations: Has the U.S. increased the percentage of 2-year-olds who have been fully immunized against preventable childhood diseases? *(1992)*	55%	—	
3. Family-Child Reading and Storytelling: Has the U.S. increased the percentage of 3- to 5-year-olds whose parents read to them or tell them stories regularly? *(1993)*	66%	—	
4. Preschool Participation: Has the U.S. reduced the gap in preschool participation between 3- to 5-year-olds from high- and low-income families? *(1991, 1993)*	28 points	28 points	↔
5. High School Completion: Has the U.S. increased the percentage of 19- to 20-year-olds who have a high school credential? *(1992, 1993)*	87%	86% ns	↔
6. Mathematics Achievement: Has the U.S. increased the percentage of students who meet the Goals Panel's performance standard in mathematics? ▼			
• Grade 4 *(1990, 1992)*	13%	18%	↑
• Grade 8 *(1990, 1992)*	20%	25%	↑
• Grade 12 *(1990, 1992)*	13%	16% ns	↔
7. Reading Achievement: Has the U.S. increased the percentage of students who meet the Goals Panel's performance standard in reading? ▼			
• Grade 4 *(1992)*	25%	—	
• Grade 8 *(1992)*	28%	—	
• Grade 12 *(1992)*	37%	—	
8. International Mathematics Achievement: Has the U.S. improved its standing on international mathematics assessments of 13-year-olds? *(1991)* ●	U.S. below 5 out of 5 countries	—	
9. International Science Achievement: Has the U.S. improved its standing on international science assessments of 13-year-olds? *(1991)* ●	U.S. below 3 out of 5 countries	—	
10. Adult Literacy: Has the U.S. increased the percentage of adults who score at or above Level 3 in prose literacy? *(1992)* ■	52%	—	
11. Participation in Adult Education: Has the U.S. reduced the gap in adult education participation between adults who have a high school diploma or less, and those who have additional post-secondary education or technical training? *(1991)*	27 points	—	
12. Participation in Higher Education: Has the U.S. reduced the gap between White and Black high school graduates who:			
• enroll in college? *(1990, 1992)*	14 points	14 points	↔
• complete a college degree? *(1992, 1993)*	16 points	17 points ns	↔
Has the U.S. reduced the gap between White and Hispanic high school graduates who:			
• enroll in college? *(1990, 1992)*	11 points	6 points ns	↔
• complete a college degree? *(1992, 1993)*	12 points	18 points ns	↔
13. Overall Student Drug and Alcohol Use: Has the U.S. reduced the percentage of 10th graders reporting doing the following during the previous year:			
• using any illicit drug? *(1991, 1993)* ■	24%	27%	↓
• using alcohol? *(1991, 1993)*	72%	69%	↑
14. Sale of Drugs at School: Has the U.S. reduced the percentage of 10th graders reporting that someone offered to sell or give them an illegal drug at school during the previous year? *(1992, 1993)*	18%	20% ns	↔
15. Student and Teacher Victimization: Has the U.S. reduced the percentage of students and teachers reporting that they were threatened or injured at school during the previous year?			
• 10th graders *(1991, 1993)*	40%	35%	↑
• public school teachers *(1991)*	10%	—	
16. Disruptions in Class by Students: Has the U.S. reduced the percentage of students and teachers reporting that disruptions often interfere with teaching and learning?			
• 10th grade students *(1992, 1993)*	17%	18% ns	↔
• high school teachers *(1991)*	33%	—	

— Data not available.
ns Interpret with caution. Change was not statistically significant.

▲ See technical note on page 133.
▼ See technical note on pages 134-135.
● See technical note on pages 135-136.

■ See technical note on page 136.
■ See technical note on page 137.

Chapter 2: How Much Progress Have We Made?

America's 1994 scorecard, which summarizes national progress on the sixteen core education indicators, is presented on the preceding page. Baseline measures of progress, which appear in the first column, were established as close as possible to 1990, the year that the National Education Goals were adopted. These serve as our starting points. For some of the indicators, such as student achievement in mathematics and reading, we hope to increase the baseline to 100% by the year 2000. For others, such as student drug and alcohol use, we hope to decrease the baseline to 0%. The most recent measures of performance for each indicator appear in the second column.

The arrows in the third column show our overall progress on each indicator:

↑ Arrows which point upward indicate where we have made significant* progress.

↓ Arrows which point downward indicate where we have fallen further behind.

↔ Horizontal arrows indicate where we have seen no discernible change in our performance.

(No arrows are shown in cases where we do not yet have a second data point to determine whether performance has improved or declined since the baseline.)

Summaries of individual state progress on the sixteen core indicators are presented in Appendix A, beginning on page 72. A more detailed guide to reading the information on the national and state pages appears on page 73. At present, lack of comparable state data for many of the core indicators seriously constrains the Panel's ability to provide full progress reports for individual states. In addition, regular collection of data for a number of core indicators at both the national and state levels cannot be confirmed beyond 1996, further impeding the Panel's ability to provide regular updates. These data gaps and the steps that must be taken in order to remedy them are discussed in detail in Chapter 3 of this Report.

> National performance has improved in four areas, has gotten worse in one, and has not changed significantly in six. In the remaining areas, we cannot tell whether performance has improved or declined until data are collected a second time.

How Are We Doing?

In four areas, national performance has gotten significantly better:

• The general health and developmental status of the nation's infants has improved.

• Mathematics achievement at Grades 4 and 8 has increased.

• Student alcohol use has declined.

---

* In this report, "significance" refers to statistical significance and indicates that the observed differences are not likely to have occurred by chance.

• Incidents of threats and injuries to students at school have declined.

In one area, national performance has gotten significantly worse:

• Student drug use has increased.

In six areas, no significant changes in national performance have occurred. We have made no discernible progress toward:

• reducing the gap in preschool participation between rich and poor;

• improving the high school completion rate;

• increasing mathematics achievement at Grade 12;

• reducing the gap in college enrollment and completion rates between White and minority students;

Within the next three years we should be able to add history, geography, science, and arts achievement to the list of core indicators.

• reducing the sale of drugs at school; or

• reducing classroom disruptions that interfere with students' learning.

In eight areas we cannot determine whether national performance has improved or fallen further behind, because at present we do not have a second data point to compare against our baseline performance. The good news is that we should be able to fill in most of these blanks next year in the *1995 Goals Report*. Next year we should know:

• whether the proportion of fully immunized 2-year-olds has increased;

• whether the proportion of preschoolers who are regularly read to and told stories has increased;

• whether reading achievement at Grades 4, 8, and 12 has improved;

• whether the gap in adult education participation has been reduced between adults with a high school diploma or less, and those with additional post-secondary education or technical training;

• whether incidents of threats and injuries to teachers at school have been reduced; and

• whether classroom disruptions that interfere with teaching have declined.

Next year we should be able to add history and geography achievement to the list of core indicators and report national baselines for students in Grades 4, 8, and 12.

Furthermore, within the next two years we should know:

• whether our international standing in mathematics and science achievement has improved.

Within the next three years we should be able to add science and arts achievement to the list of core indicators and report national baselines for students in Grades 4, 8, and 12.

In several areas (e.g., student achievement in foreign languages, civics and government, and economics) we simply do not know, and will not know, how we are doing because no baseline data will be collected before the year 2000. In several other areas (e.g., adult literacy, and student achievement in science, arts, history, geography), we will have a baseline, but we will be unable to tell whether performance has improved by the end of the decade because no updates are presently planned. These data needs are fully discussed in Chapter 3.

Determining Where We Should Be

On the whole, our progress toward the National Education Goals has been modest, at best. Even in areas where we have made significant progress from where we started, such as mathematics achievement at Grades 4 and 8, our current rate of progress will simply not be sufficient to reach the ambitious levels specified in the National Education Goals.

The amount of accelerated progress that must be made if we expect to reach our targets is explicitly shown in sixteen exhibits which appear throughout this chapter. In order to interpret the graphs correctly, the reader should take note of the following:

1. For some of the core indicators, baselines could not be established until 1992 or 1993, either because data were not collected prior to that time, or because changes in survey questions or methodology yielded non-comparable data.

2. Most of the core indicators are not updated annually. Footnotes on each graph indicate when data will be collected again.

3. Although this Report includes the most recent data available, there is sometimes a lag of several years between the time that data are collected and the time that they are available for inclusion in the annual Goals Report. For example, the most recent birth certificate data available to construct the Children's Health Index for this 1994 Report were collected in 1991.

4. On each of the bar graphs, a path from the baseline to the target is represented by a grey shaded area behind the bars. The grey shaded areas indicate where we should try to push our performance each year if we expect to reach the Goal by the end of the decade. Since progress is seldom perfectly linear, we should expect some ups and downs from year-to-year. What is most important is whether performance is moving in the right direction and whether it is within, or is at least approaching, the grey shaded area.

5. Finally, the graphs themselves should be interpreted with caution. Data are based on representative national surveys, and changes in performance could be attributable to sampling error. The reader should consult the

highlight box next to each graph to determine whether the change is statistically significant and we are confident that real change has occurred. Further information on sampling can be found in the technical notes in Appendix B.

The remainder of this chapter discusses why these core indicators are important to our nation's educational health and economic well-being and where we should be on each of the core indicators if we expect to reach our targets by the year 2000. This chapter also points out some of the actions that will be required of students, teachers, parents, higher education, businesses, communities, and policymakers in order to move our performance in the desired direction.

GOAL 1: READY TO LEARN

School success is partly determined by what happens long before a child ever enters a classroom. In fact, early environmental conditions and characteristics related to later school performance are specifically addressed in the three objectives for Goal 1: children's health and nutrition, family-child activities, and children's preschool experiences. Although we lack a direct measure that can tell us the proportion of the nation's children who are ready to learn at the time of school entry, four indirect indicators tell us a great deal about the "preconditions" related to children's later school success: the Children's Health Index, Immunizations, Family-Child Reading and Storytelling, and Preschool Participation.

Parents play a critical role in achieving the Goals, and parents' behavior (even before birth) can be an important determinant of how well their children will do in school.

Indicator 1. Children's Health Index

• *Reduce the percentage of infants born with 2 or more health and developmental risks.*

• *Eliminate disparities between the proportions of White and minority infants born with 2 or more health and developmental risks.*

Parents play a critical role in achieving the Goals, and parents' behavior (even before birth) can be an important determinant of how well their children will do in school. Six birth characteristics linked to children's later health, behavior, and academic achievement have been combined into a Children's Health Index to monitor the general status of the nation's children.[1] The first four risks listed below can directly affect newborns' physical health, while the last two are more developmental in nature. The at-birth health and developmental risks are:

- Late (third trimester) or no prenatal care

- Low maternal weight gain (less than 21 pounds)

- Mother smoked during pregnancy

- Mother drank alcohol during pregnancy

- Three or more older siblings

- Closely spaced birth (within 18 months of a previous birth)

A mother who receives no prenatal care is three times more likely to deliver a low-birthweight baby than one who has received appropriate prenatal care.

It is important to note that while the Children's Health Index is a very useful population statistic for monitoring the general status of the nation's children, it is not intended to be used as a predictor of any individual child's potential for school success. Absence of the six at-birth health and developmental risks does not necessarily mean that a child will be well-prepared for the challenges of formal schooling. Moreover, children who are born with one or more risks are not necessarily destined for academic failure.

What is of increasing concern, however, is the proportion of children in the U.S. who are born with multiple risk factors, and the cumulative deleterious effects of those risk factors on their school performance. *In and of themselves, these factors do not prescribe particular actions or policies to pursue. However, they do inform such decisions by alerting us, both as parents and policymakers, to some of the earliest links between home and school.*

How are these risks related to coming to school ready to learn? The first three months of pregnancy, or the first trimester, is the most critical period of fetal development. Mothers who receive early and continuous prenatal care are more likely to follow a nutritious diet; gain an adequate amount of weight; abstain from smoking, alcohol, drugs, and other harmful substances; and give birth to a baby who is above the standard for low birthweight (i.e., at or above 5.5 pounds). However, a mother who receives no prenatal care is three times more likely to deliver a low-birthweight baby than one who has received appropriate prenatal care.[2] The percentage of U.S. mothers who began prenatal care during their first trimester of pregnancy increased substantially in the late 1970s, but has leveled off since 1980 at about 75-80% for Asian/Pacific Islander and White women, and about 60% for American Indian/ Alaskan Native, Black, and Hispanic women.

Low birthweight is a condition that may increase a child's risk of developing health, learning, and behavioral problems later in life. In a study of children aged 4-17, children who were born low-birthweight were more likely to be enrolled in special education classes, to repeat a grade, or to fail school than children who were born at a normal birthweight.[3]

Low birthweight is also a condition that disproportionately affects some racial/ethnic groups. Black infants are twice as likely as others to be born low-birthweight. Among Hispanic subgroups, low birthweight is most common among Puerto Rican infants.[4]

Other risks associated with low birthweight include low weight gain during pregnancy, alcohol consumption, illicit drug use, and smoking.[5] According to studies reviewed by the U.S. Department of Health and Human Services, smoking is associated with 20-30% of the low-birthweight births in the United States.[6]

Exhibit 1
Children's Health Index

Percentage[1] of infants born in the U.S.[2] with 2 or more health and developmental risks[3]

The United States was successful in reducing the proportion of infants born with two or more health and developmental risks between 1990 and 1991, from 14% to 13%. This reduction represents a difference of at least 22,500 children who were born with a healthier start in life.

[1] Percentages are based on the number of births used to calculate the risk index, not the actual number of births. Birth records that were missing three or more pieces of information needed to calculate the index were excluded from the calculation. See technical notes in Appendix B.
[2] Five states (California, Indiana, Oklahoma, New York, and South Dakota) did not collect information on all six risks on the state birth certificate in 1990; four states (California, Indiana, New York, and South Dakota) did not collect information on all six risks in 1991. These states and the territories are not included in the U.S. total. New Hampshire is included in the U.S. total, but not in the race/ethnicity totals in the table below because New Hampshire does not collect information on Hispanic origin.
[3] Risks are late (in third trimester) or no prenatal care, low maternal weight gain (less than 21 pounds), mother smoked during pregnancy, mother drank alcohol during pregnancy, three or more older siblings, or closely spaced birth (within 18 months of a previous birth).

* Data for the Children's Health Index will be collected annually through the year 2000.

Source: National Center for Health Statistics and Westat, Inc.

Table 1
Disparities[1] (in percentage points) between White and minority infants born in the U.S. with 2 or more health and developmental risks

The United States was also successful in reducing disparities between White and minority infants born with two or more health and developmental risks.

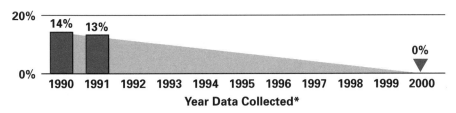

	1990	1991	Change
American Indian/Alaskan Native	16	14	−2
Black	9	8	−1
Hispanic	2	1	−1

[1] Numbers differ slightly from data reported in the *National Data Volume* due to rounding.

The two risks related to children's development are large numbers of siblings and closely spaced births. Infants and toddlers require considerable parental attention and interaction to develop normally. Milestones in children's language development, for example, include imitating sounds, forming words, and eventually combining words into meaningful sentences. Examples of milestones in physical development include holding a spoon, drinking from a cup, and learning to crawl and walk. Parents, older siblings, and other family members help children learn to do these kinds of things by modeling and encouraging their efforts.

However, parents with large numbers of other children have many competing demands for their time and attention. Large numbers of siblings and closely spaced births can be potential developmental risks if parents and other family members do not spend sufficient amounts of time interacting with newborn infants and attending to their developmental needs.

Among industrialized nations, the U.S. ranks 21st out of 28 in the proportion of 1-year-olds immunized against measles.

Promising news is that the U.S. was successful in reducing the proportion of infants born with two or more health and developmental risks between 1990 and 1991, from 14% to 13% (see Exhibit 1). The 1 percentage point reduction represents a difference of at least 22,500 children who were born with a healthier start in life. Further good news is the fact that the U.S. also successfully reduced disparities between White and minority infants born with two or more health and developmental risks between 1990 and 1991 (see Table 1). Gaps declined by 1 percentage point for Black and for Hispanic infants and by 2 percentage points for American Indian/ Alaskan Native infants. Increased efforts by parents and by health and social service agencies will be required to reduce the proportions of at-risk infants still further.

Indicator 2. Immunizations

• *Increase the percentage of 2-year-olds who have been fully immunized against preventable childhood diseases.*

One of the most important preventive actions parents can take to see that their children receive the "health care needed to arrive at school with healthy minds and bodies" specified in the third objective for this Goal, is to make certain that they are fully immunized against nine preventable childhood diseases: diphtheria, tetanus (lockjaw), pertussis (whooping cough), measles, mumps, rubella (German measles), polio, hepatitis B, and influenza (*Haemophilus influenzae type b*). Measles, as the National Center for Health Statistics points out, is an example of a dangerous, yet preventable, disease that should be fairly easy for the United States to control because a vaccination has been available since 1963.[7] Immunizations against measles actually can help protect children against other diseases, malnutrition, and disabling conditions, such as deafness and blindness.[8] Yet despite the availability of a measles vaccine, outbreaks of measles increased sharply at the turn of the decade, from approximately 3,400 cases in 1988 to nearly 28,000 cases in 1990.[9]

The American Academy of Pediatrics recommends a regular series of immunizations and booster shots to protect children completely against preventable diseases, beginning at birth and continuing through young adulthood. The good news is that by age 5 most children in the United States have been immunized, because immunizations are required by nearly all states for school entry. In 1990, child immunization rates at the time of entry into either kindergarten or first grade were 97% for polio and diphtheria-tetanus-pertussis, and 98% for measles, mumps, and rubella.[10]

However, the bad news is that only slightly more than half of younger U.S. children (between the ages of 1.5 and 3) have been fully immunized (see Exhibit 2). Increased efforts must target this age group because most U.S. children have been weaned by this age and are no longer protected by their mothers' antibodies against infectious diseases. At the national level, low-income children and Black children are less likely to be fully immunized than others, but each individual state and locality must determine which populations of children are at

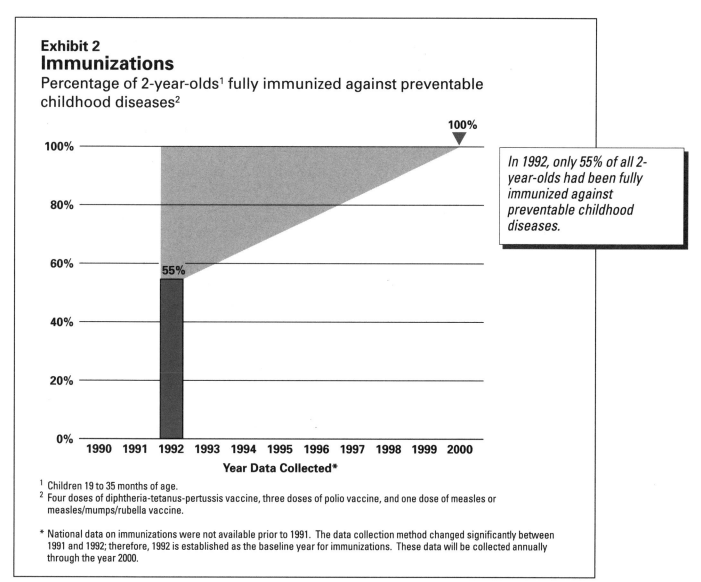

Exhibit 2
Immunizations
Percentage of 2-year-olds[1] fully immunized against preventable childhood diseases[2]

In 1992, only 55% of all 2-year-olds had been fully immunized against preventable childhood diseases.

Year Data Collected*

[1] Children 19 to 35 months of age.
[2] Four doses of diphtheria-tetanus-pertussis vaccine, three doses of polio vaccine, and one dose of measles or measles/mumps/rubella vaccine.

* National data on immunizations were not available prior to 1991. The data collection method changed significantly between 1991 and 1992; therefore, 1992 is established as the baseline year for immunizations. These data will be collected annually through the year 2000.

Source: National Center for Health Statistics and Centers for Disease Control and Prevention

greatest risk in order to target their immunization efforts appropriately.

International comparisons offer additional evidence that the U.S. has far to go before we can claim success in this area. Data collected by UNICEF indicate that the United States compares favorably to nations such as Japan, France, and Australia in the percentage of its 1-year-olds who are immunized against measles, but the U.S. is also at or below the measles immunization levels in a number of developing nations such as Pakistan, Thailand, Panama, Zimbabwe, and Colombia. Among industrialized nations, the U.S. ranks very low — 21st out of 28.[11]

Indicator 3. Family-child reading and storytelling

• *Increase the percentage of 3- to 5-year-olds whose parents read to them or tell them stories regularly.*

Early, regular reading to children is one of the most important activities parents can do with their children to improve their readiness for school, serve as their child's first teacher, and instill a love of books and reading. Reading to children familiarizes them with story components such as characters, plot, action, and sequence ("Once upon a time . . .," ". . . and they lived happily ever after."), and helps them associate oral language with printed text. Most important, reading to children builds their vocabularies and background knowledge about the world. Telling stories is another important way that parents can participate in shared literacy activities with their children. In fact, in some cultures storytelling and oral traditions play a more central role than reading books aloud.[12]

Despite the acknowledged importance of these home activities, only two-thirds of U.S. preschoolers were read to or told stories regularly in 1993 (see Exhibit 3). The same study revealed that only about four out of ten preschoolers participated regularly in other types of beneficial early language and literacy activities with their families, such as visiting a library or talking about their family history or ethnic heritage.

Some reading experts argue that successful achievement of Goal 1 is contingent upon achievement of Goal 2 (increasing the high school completion rate) and Goal 6 (increasing the proportion of adults who are literate). In other words, if we do not simultaneously increase the educational levels and reading skills of parents, we cannot possibly hope to improve the school readiness of children.

A number of recent studies provide strong support for this argument. In 1993, parents who were college graduates reported that they read

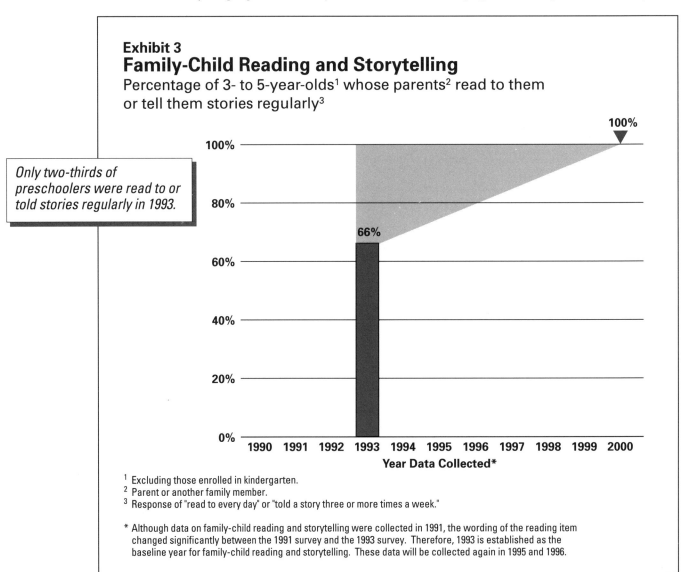

Exhibit 3
Family-Child Reading and Storytelling
Percentage of 3- to 5-year-olds[1] whose parents[2] read to them or tell them stories regularly[3]

Only two-thirds of preschoolers were read to or told stories regularly in 1993.

Year Data Collected*

[1] Excluding those enrolled in kindergarten.
[2] Parent or another family member.
[3] Response of "read to every day" or "told a story three or more times a week."

* Although data on family-child reading and storytelling were collected in 1991, the wording of the reading item changed significantly between the 1991 survey and the 1993 survey. Therefore, 1993 is established as the baseline year for family-child reading and storytelling. These data will be collected again in 1995 and 1996.

Source: National Center for Education Statistics and Westat, Inc.

daily to their preschool-aged children at twice the rate of parents with less than a high school education.[13] National reading achievement results from 1992 found that students in Grades 4, 8, and 12 whose parents had completed higher levels of education consistently outperformed classmates whose parents did not have a high school diploma.[14]

Most revealing is the fact that parents' educational attainment continues to be a strong predictor of reading and writing abilities even after children reach adulthood. On average, adults whose parents had completed high school or beyond scored 1 to 1.5 levels higher on English literacy tasks in 1992 than adults whose parents had never completed high school.[15] If the inter-

generational link between parents' educational attainment and children's literacy skills is as strong as these and other studies suggest, approaches which support the development of both adult and child literacy skills may merit increased attention if we are to achieve Goal 1.

Indicator 4. Preschool participation

• *Eliminate disparities in preschool participation rates between 3- to 5-year-olds from high-income families and those from low-income families.*

Because the first objective for Goal 1 specifies that "all children will have *access* to high-quality and developmentally appropriate

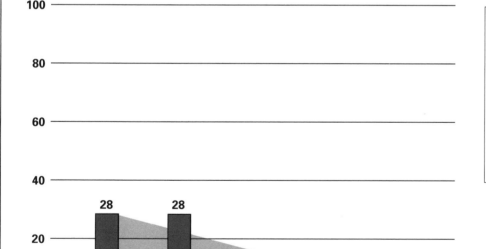

Exhibit 4
Preschool Participation
Disparity (in percentage points) in preschool[1] participation rates between 3- to 5-year-olds[2] from high-income[3] families and 3- to 5-year-olds from low-income[4] families

> In 1991, 45% of 3- to 5-year-olds from low-income families were enrolled in preschool programs, compared to 73% of those from high-income families. The 28 percentage-point difference in participation rates had not improved by 1993.

[1] Includes nursery schools, prekindergarten programs, preschools, daycare centers, and Head Start.
[2] Excluding those enrolled in kindergarten.
[3] High income is defined as the highest 20 percent of all households.
[4] Low income is defined as the lowest 20 percent of all households.

* Data on preschool participation will be collected again in 1995 and 1996.

Source: National Center for Education Statistics and Westat, Inc.

preschool programs that help prepare children for school," it is essential to monitor the extent to which factors such as family income are barriers to preschool participation. Thus, this indicator is framed in terms of equity — the goal is *not* that all 3- to 5-year-olds will attend preschool, because experts agree that the decision to send a child to preschool should be based on informed parental choice. Instead, the goal is to eliminate obstacles to participation for those parents who do want to send their child to preschool. This indicator measures the extent to which the United States has eliminated the gap in preschool participation rates between children from high-income families and those from low-income families.

Exhibit 4 shows that the U.S. is far from achieving this goal. In 1991, only 45% of 3- to 5-year-olds from low-income families (i.e., households in the bottom fifth of the income distribution) were enrolled in preschool programs, compared to 73% of preschoolers from high-income families (i.e., households in the top fifth of the income distribution), a difference of 28 percentage points. Although preschool enrollments have increased over the past twenty years for all children regardless of family income, the gap between rich and poor has actually widened over time. In 1993, the preschool participation gap between 3- to 5-year-olds from low-income families and those from high-income families was still 28 percentage points.

Although preschool enrollments have increased over the past twenty years for all children regardless of family income, the gap between rich and poor has actually widened over time.

Enrolling a child in preschool is no guarantee, of course, that he or she will be better prepared for the challenges of formal schooling unless there is assurance that the preschool program is of high quality. Although we know a great deal about the factors that influence the quality of preschool settings, such as highly trained teachers, low staff turnover, small class size, and low child/staff ratios, we lack a comprehensive, regularly updated, national measure of the quality of preschool care that children are receiving in this country.

More than two-thirds of all states do not require child care center teachers to complete any specialized preservice training, and three-fourths either do not require or do not regulate preservice training for family child care providers.[16] Recent evidence suggests that while the majority of preschool center teachers in the United States did have some child-related training in 1990, only about one-third had teacher training, and only one-fourth held a Child Development Associate credential, as recommended by the National Association for the Education of Young Children.[17] Achieving Goal 1 and ensuring that all children start school ready to learn will require dramatic improvements in both preschool program quality and teacher training.

GOAL 2: SCHOOL COMPLETION

While possession of a high school diploma no longer guarantees easy access to jobs, lack of a high school diploma or its equivalent almost certainly means that an individual will experience difficulty entering the labor market and will be at pronounced educational, social, and economic disadvantages throughout his or her life. In 1992, the unemployment rate among high school dropouts was nearly twice as high as it was for high school graduates who did not enter college. Furthermore, the median income of dropouts who did find full-time employment was only half the income of high school graduates.[18] Between 1979 and 1992, average annual earnings of 20- to 29-year-old men who had dropped out of high school declined by 35% after adjusting for inflation, while real earnings of college graduates remained relatively unchanged.[19]

Failure to complete high school carries social costs as well as personal ones. One-half of the U.S. prison population in 1992 were high school dropouts, compared to about one-quarter of the general population.[20] And in 1991, nearly one-half of all heads of households receiving welfare support from Aid to Families with Dependent Children (AFDC) had never finished high school.[21]

Exhibit 5
High School Completion
Percentage of 19- to 20-year-olds[1] with a high school credential[2]

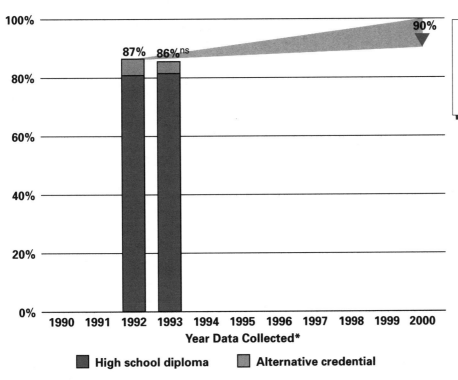

In 1992, 87% of 19- to 20-year-olds had completed a high school credential. By 1993, the overall completion rate had not increased.

■ **High school diploma**　■ **Alternative credential**

[1] Does not include those still enrolled in high school.
[2] Includes traditional high school diploma and alternative credential.
ns Interpret with caution. Change was not statistically significant.

* The wording of the item for high school completion changed substantially between the 1991 survey and the 1992 survey; therefore, 1992 is established as the baseline year for high school completion. These data will be collected annually through the year 2000.

Source: National Center for Education Statistics and Management Planning Research Associates, Inc.

Table 2
Disparities (in percentage points) between White and minority students aged 19-20 who completed a high school diploma or an alternative credential

Disparities in high school completion rates between White and minority students did not improve between 1992 and 1993.

	1992	1993	Change
Black	10	10	0
Hispanic	26	24	−2 ns

ns Interpret with caution. Change was not statistically significant.

Recent findings indicate that parents who have not completed high school are also less likely than others to engage their preschool children in the types of family activities that can help prepare them for school. Parents with less than a high school diploma were only half as likely as parents with college degrees to report that they read to their preschool children daily, took them to visit a library once a month, participated in arts and crafts projects with them regularly, or took them to events sponsored by community or religious groups monthly.[22] Moreover, young children whose mothers had dropped out of high school were nearly four times as likely as children whose mothers held college degrees to watch more than four hours of television every day.[23] Paying urgent attention to Goal 2 may improve the life chances not only of significant numbers of adults, but of significant numbers of children, for one infant is born every 34 seconds in the U.S. to a mother who has not completed high school.[24]

One infant is born every 34 seconds in the U.S. to a mother who has not completed high school.

Indicator 5. High school completion

• *Increase the percentage of 19- and 20-year-olds who have a high school credential to at least 90%.*

• *Eliminate disparities in high school completion rates between White and minority students aged 19-20.*

While the high school completion rate in the U.S. did increase markedly in the early 1980s among 19- and 20-year-olds, it has been relatively stable since that time. In 1992, the high school completion rate was 87% for young adults in this age group, but it has not changed significantly since then (see Exhibit 5).

Although the current high school completion rate indicates that the nation is already very close to achieving the 90% target specified in the Goal, the 1992 completion rates for Black students (81%) and for Hispanic students (65%) were considerably lower than the rate for White students (91%). At that time the high school completion gap was 10 percentage points between Blacks and Whites, and 26 percentage points between Hispanics and Whites (see Table 2). Between 1992 and 1993, the size of the gaps showed no significant change for either group. If we are to achieve Goal 2, the U.S. must not only boost the high school completion rate to at least 90% by the end of the decade, but must make serious efforts to close the persistent gap in completion rates between White and minority students.

GOAL 3: STUDENT ACHIEVEMENT AND CITIZENSHIP

Although all of the National Education Goals are important, increasing student achievement in the core subject areas — English, mathematics, science, foreign languages, civics and government, economics, arts, history, and geography — will be the ultimate test of successful education reform. The third Goal states that upon completion of Grades 4, 8, and 12, *all* students will demonstrate competency in challenging subject matter in these areas. Ensuring that all students rise to this challenge will require fundamental changes in the expectations that parents and teachers set, the standards for teaching and learning that states adopt, the way teachers are trained and certified, and the way subject matter is taught. It will also require changes in the types of courses schools offer, the ways that the school day and school year are structured, the ways in which educational resources are directed and employed, and the incentives that colleges and employers offer for higher student achievement.

How do we determine whether U.S. students have demonstrated competency in challenging subject matter? The National Education Goals Panel has set its performance standard for student achievement at the Proficient or Advanced levels of performance on the National Assessment of Educational Progress (NAEP). NAEP is the only nationally representative and continuing assessment that measures what students know and are able to do in different subject areas. The Goals Panel considers student performance below this standard (i.e., performance at or below the Basic level) as evidence that students have not yet mastered challenging subject matter.

Thus far, student achievement levels have been established by the National Assessment Governing Board in only two of the core subject areas, mathematics and reading. The list of core indicators for Goal 3 will be expanded as new NAEP assessments are developed in other subject areas and achievement levels are established, so that it is possible to determine the proportion of students who meet the Goals Panel's performance standard.

Indicator 6. Mathematics achievement

• *Increase the percentage of students in Grades 4, 8, and 12 who meet the Goals Panel's performance standard in mathematics.*

• *Eliminate disparities between the percentages of White and minority students, and male and female students, who meet the Goals Panel's performance standard.*

At the beginning of the decade when the National Education Goals were first established, NAEP mathematics results revealed that the proportion of U.S. students who could be considered competent in mathematics was disheartening, at best. Exhibit 6 shows that only one out of every five students in Grade 8, and worse still, only one out of every eight students in Grades 4 and 12, were able to meet the Goals Panel's performance standard in mathematics in 1990.

Encouraging news is that between 1990 and 1992, the percentages of students in Grades 4 and 8 who met the Goals Panel's performance standard in mathematics did increase significantly. However, upon closer examination of the results, it is clear that not all students shared equally in these gains. Females performed as well as males in Grades 4 and 8, but had significantly lower scores at Grade 12. Among the different racial/ethnic groups, only White students in Grades 4 and 8 significantly improved

their mathematics performance. The proportion of students who met the Goals Panel's standard in 1992 ranged from a low of 3% for Black students at each grade to a high of 44% for Asians/ Pacific Islanders in Grade 8.

Most disturbing is that the gap in mathematics performance actually widened over the two-year period between Hispanic and White students in Grade 8, and between Black and White students in Grades 4 and 8 (see Table 3). In other words, as White students moved ahead, Black and Hispanic students fell further behind. And while gaps in performance between White and American Indian/Alaskan Native students did not get significantly worse, they also did not improve. Unfortunately, recent studies of changes in students' mathematics proficiency over time indicate that those students who have fallen furthest behind in mathematics by Grade 8 have little hope of catching up to their classmates. In fact, they are the most likely to continue to fall behind two years later.[25]

Although reducing existing disparities in student achievement between White and minority students is critical if we are to achieve Goal 3, it is important to underscore the fact that socioeconomic status is closely intertwined with race/ethnicity in the United States. That is, when socioeconomic variables are held constant, such as parents' income and highest level of education, the effects of race/ethnicity on student achievement diminish.

What factors might help explain these distressing disparities in performance? As one might expect, students are at a distinct disadvantage if they have not been encouraged to study mathematics and have not enrolled in higher-level courses. In addition, students are less likely to achieve at high levels if they happen to attend schools which do not set high expectations that all students will master challenging mathematics content, and which do not

Students are less likely to achieve at high levels if they happen to attend schools which do not set high expectations that all students will master challenging mathematics content, and which do not offer higher-level mathematics courses taught by teachers with advanced mathematics training.

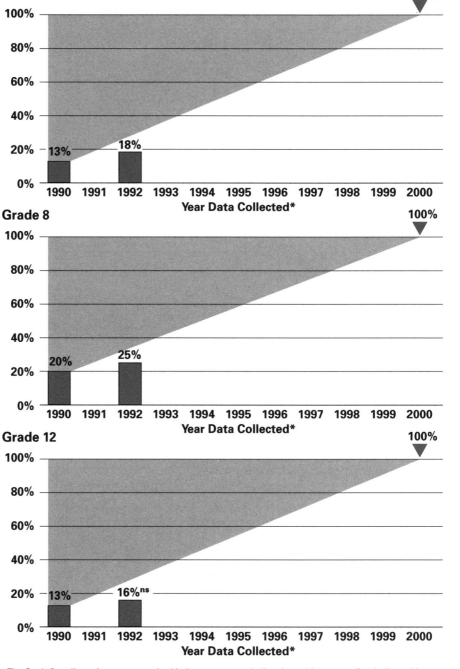

Exhibit 6
Mathematics Achievement
Percentage of students who met the Goals Panel's performance standard[1] in mathematics

> In 1990, only one out of every five students in Grade 8, and only one out of every eight students in Grades 4 and 12, had met the Goals Panel's performance standard in mathematics. Mathematics achievement increased significantly in 1992 among 4th and 8th graders, but not among 12th graders.

Grade 4

13%   18%

1990 1991 1992 1993 1994 1995 1996 1997 1998 1999 2000
Year Data Collected*

Grade 8

20%   25%

1990 1991 1992 1993 1994 1995 1996 1997 1998 1999 2000
Year Data Collected*

Grade 12

13%   16%ns

1990 1991 1992 1993 1994 1995 1996 1997 1998 1999 2000
Year Data Collected*

[1] The Goals Panel's performance standard is "mastery over challenging subject matter" as indicated by performance at the Proficient or Advanced levels on the National Assessment of Educational Progress (NAEP). These levels were established by the National Assessment Governing Board (NAGB) and reported by the National Center for Education Statistics (NCES) in NAEP publications. A more complete description of the performance standard can be found in Appendix B.

ns Interpret with caution. Change was not statistically significant.

* Data on mathematics achievement will be collected again in 1996.

Source: National Center for Education Statistics

Table 3
GRADE 4 – MATHEMATICS
Disparities (in percentage points) between White and minority students who met the Goals Panel's performance standard in mathematics

	1990	1992	Change
American Indian/Alaskan Native	12	13	+1 ns
Black	15	20	+5
Hispanic	12	17	+5 ns

Disparities (in percentage points) between males and females

	1990	1992	Change
Females < males	1	3	+2 ns

GRADE 8 – MATHEMATICS
Disparities (in percentage points) between White and minority students who met the Goals Panel's performance standard in mathematics

	1990	1992	Change
American Indian/Alaskan Native	15	23	+8 ns
Black	18	29	+11
Hispanic	18	24	+6

Disparities (in percentage points) between males and females

	1990	1992	Change
Females < males	3	1	–2 ns

> *Between 1990 and 1992, the gap in mathematics performance widened between Hispanic and White students in Grade 8, and between Black and White students in Grades 4 and 8. In other words, as White students moved ahead, Black and Hispanic students fell further behind.*

GRADE 12 – MATHEMATICS
Disparities (in percentage points) between White and minority students who met the Goals Panel's performance standard in mathematics

	1990	1992	Change
American Indian/Alaskan Native	12	15	+3 ns
Black	14	16	+2 ns
Hispanic	12	13	+1 ns

Disparities (in percentage points) between males and females

	1990	1992	Change
Females < males	6	4	–2 ns

ns Interpret with caution. Change was not statistically significant.

offer higher-level mathematics courses taught by teachers with advanced mathematics training.

Unfortunately, research indicates that these conditions are frequently determined by factors beyond students' control. Analyses of data from a national survey of secondary schools conducted in 1986 revealed that in general, the higher the concentration of White students in a secondary school and the lower the concentration of minority students, the greater the likelihood that the school's mathematics (and science) teachers were certified, held a bachelor's degree, and held a master's degree in their assigned teaching field.[26] The same pattern held true when school locations were compared. Inner-city schools were less likely than suburban or rural schools to employ teachers with advanced mathematics training. A 1992 pilot study by the Council of Chief State School Officers conducted in California, New York, and Ohio also found that the proportion of certified mathematics and science teachers in large cities was lower than the state average in each case.[27]

> Student absenteeism, TV-watching, and daily reading accounted heavily for state differences in mathematics achievement.

Further analyses of the 1986 secondary school data also showed that the higher the concentration of White students in a secondary school and the lower the concentration of minority students, the greater the number of college preparatory science and mathematics classes available, and the fewer the number of general science and mathematics classes.[28] College preparatory science and mathematics classes were also discovered to be increasingly prevalent in schools with greater wealth.

Obviously, schools must offer students high quality instruction and provide the necessary resources for students to achieve higher performance standards. States and localities, in turn, are responsible for supporting the operation of schools in a manner that will allow students to achieve at high levels. But students and their parents must also assume a portion of the responsibility for achieving Goal 3 and attaining higher levels of mathematics proficiency.

Analyses of five factors reflective of family behaviors and characteristics were recently examined to determine their relationship to student achievement on the 1990 NAEP mathematics assessment.[29] These factors were:

- student absenteeism from school;

- amount of TV watched;

- reading more than 10 pages daily for school and homework;

- the presence of at least three types of reading materials in the home; and

- the presence of two parents in the home.

Together, these five factors accounted for 91% of the variation in states' NAEP mathematics scores. While the variety of reading materials in the home and the presence of two parents in the home are tied to family income and are therefore not easily controllable, the researchers argue that the remaining three factors — absence from school, TV watching, and student reading — are fully within the scope of parental control. Engaging greater numbers of parents in partnerships with schools to promote the academic growth of children is, in fact, one of the aims of the new National Education Goal on Parental Participation.

Indicator 7. Reading achievement

- *Increase the percentage of students in Grades 4, 8, and 12 who meet the Goals Panel's performance standard in reading.*

- *Eliminate disparities between the percentages of White and minority students, and male and female students, who meet the Goals Panel's performance standard.*

Although U.S. student performance in reading is still well below the national target established for Goal 3, it is considerably higher than comparable student achievement in mathematics. In 1992, approximately one-fourth of 4th and 8th graders, and more than one-third of

Exhibit 7
Reading Achievement
Percentage of students who met the Goals Panel's performance standard[1] in reading

Grade 4

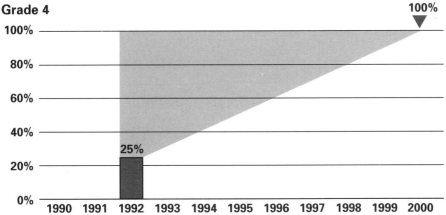

In 1992, approximately one-fourth of 4th and 8th graders and more than one-third of 12th graders met the Goals Panel's performance standard in reading.

Grade 8

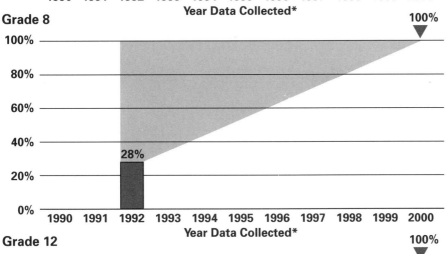

Grade 12

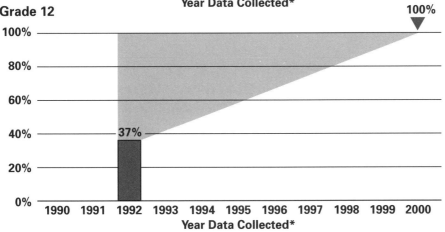

[1] The Goals Panel's performance standard is "mastery over challenging subject matter" as indicated by performance at the Proficient or Advanced levels on the National Assessment of Educational Progress (NAEP). These levels were established by the National Assessment Governing Board (NAGB) and reported by the National Center for Education Statistics (NCES) in NAEP publications. A more complete description of the performance standard can be found in Appendix B.

* Student achievement levels in reading were not established until 1992. Data on reading achievement will be collected again in 1994.

Source: National Center for Education Statistics

Table 4
GRADE 4 – READING
Disparities (in percentage points) between White and minority students who met the Goals Panel's performance standard in reading

	1992
American Indian/Alaskan Native	16
Black	24
Hispanic	18

Disparities (in percentage points) between males and females

	1992
Females > males	6

GRADE 8 – READING
Disparities (in percentage points) between White and minority students who met the Goals Panel's performance standard in reading

	1992
American Indian/Alaskan Native	16
Black	26
Hispanic	21

Disparities (in percentage points) between males and females

	1992
Females > males	11

> In 1992, the proportions of White and minority students who met the Goals Panel's performance standard in reading differed by 16-27 percentage points. Achievement gaps beween White and minority students and between female and male students were increasingly larger in higher grades.

GRADE 12 – READING
Disparities (in percentage points) between White and minority students who met the Goals Panel's performance standard in reading

	1992
American Indian/Alaskan Native	19
Black	27
Hispanic	22

Disparities (in percentage points) between males and females

	1992
Females > males	11

12th graders, scored at the Proficient or Advanced levels on the NAEP reading assessment (see Exhibit 7). Moreover, international assessments of basic literacy skills administered to 9- and 14-year-olds from 32 countries that year showed that the U.S. scored among the highest-ranking countries, outperforming students of similar ages in Canada, Italy, Spain, and West Germany.[30]

However, performance gaps in reading between White and minority students in the U.S. were just as wide, if not wider, than they were in mathematics. The proportion of students who met the Goals Panel's performance standard in reading ranged from a low of 7% for Black 4th graders to a high of 43% for White 12th graders. Furthermore, achievement gaps between White and minority students and between female and male students were increasingly larger in higher grades (see Table 4).

Demographic variables such as parent education and the socioeconomic status of the community are very strong predictors of student achievement in reading, as the 1992 NAEP results attest. Students in Grades 4, 8, and 12 whose parents had completed higher levels of education consistently outperformed classmates whose parents did not have a high school diploma. And at all three grades, students attending school in advantaged urban communities scored significantly higher than those attending school in disadvantaged urban communities.** Approximately half of all advantaged urban students at each grade level met the Goals Panel's performance standard in reading, compared to only 5% of 4th graders, 9% of 8th graders, and 20% of 12th graders attending school in disadvantaged urban settings.

Despite the strong relationship between reading achievement and demographic characteristics that are not easily changed, the NAEP reading results suggest that parents can play a significant role in shaping students' reading abilities by the reading practices and attitudes

that they model at home. Students in all three grades who reported that they regularly read for fun on their own time consistently outperformed students who tended to read only what was required of them for school. And at all three grade levels, students who reported that they regularly discussed their reading with family and friends scored significantly higher in reading than students who reported that they rarely or never did so.

Students who regularly read for fun on their own time outperform students who read only what is required for school.

Moreover, student reading proficiency declined as television viewing at home increased. Average reading performance declined significantly among 4th graders when television viewing exceeded four hours each night, among 8th graders when television viewing exceeded three hours each night, and among 12th graders when students watched as little as one hour of television per night. Least surprising was the finding that students at all three grades who reported watching television six or more hours each night had the lowest reading proficiency of all. Twenty percent of 4th graders, 14% of 8th graders, and 6% of 12th graders reported that they watched this much television nightly.

GOAL 4: TEACHER EDUCATION AND PROFESSIONAL DEVELOPMENT

No core indicators have been selected for this new Goal yet. They will be addressed in future Goals Reports.

GOAL 5: MATHEMATICS AND SCIENCE

This year marks the 25th anniversary of one of the most significant scientific accomplishments in the history of the world, the 1969 Apollo 11 moon landing. No other nation has ever accomplished such a feat. It was achieved because of a national commitment to the space race and to

---

** The National Center for Education Statistics defines these terms as follows:

Advantaged Urban: Students in this group reside in metropolitan statistical areas and attend schools where a high proportion of the students' parents are in professional or managerial positions.

Disadvantaged Urban: Students in this group reside in metropolitan statistical areas and attend schools where a high proportion of the students' parents are on welfare or are not regularly employed.

Exhibit 8
International Mathematics Achievement Comparisons
Number of countries in which 13-year-olds outperformed U.S. students in more than one area of mathematics on an international assessment, 1991*

Mathematics Achievement

Areas	Countries which scored lower than U.S.	Countries in which students' scores were similar to those of the U.S.	Countries which scored higher than U.S.
Numbers and Operations	■		▨ ▨ ▨
Measurement			▨ ▨ ▨
Geometry			▨ ▨ ▨
Data Analysis, Probability, and Statistics		■	▨ ▨ ▨
Algebra and Functions			▨ ▨ ▨

■ France　■ Hungary　▨ Korea　■ Switzerland　▨ Taiwan

> In 1991, American 13-year-olds were outperformed by students in Korea, Switzerland, and Taiwan in all areas tested on an international mathematics assessment, and by students in France and Hungary in four out of the five areas tested.

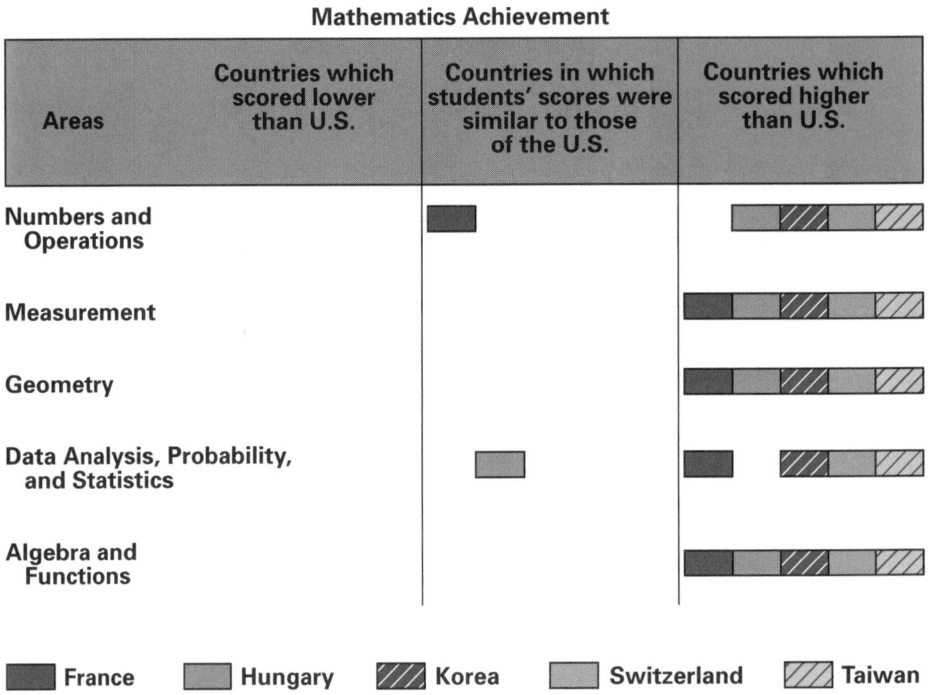

* International mathematics achievement data will be collected again in 1995. Data will be available for approximately 50 countries.

Source: Educational Testing Service

developing the necessary technology and skills of the nation's mathematicians and scientists.

The year 1994 also marks another exceptional achievement, the year that the U.S. high school mathematics team won first place among 69 countries participating in an international mathematics competition held in Hong Kong. The U.S. team was the first in the 35-year history of the annual International Mathematical Olympiad to earn a perfect score on the intense nine-hour examination.

This accomplishment is certainly cause for celebration, particularly because all six team members attended public U.S. schools. Clearly, these students have proven themselves capable of competing with the very best students in the world. However, if the nation is to achieve Goal 5 and ensure a competitive workforce which possesses the necessary scientific and technological skills to fill the jobs of the future and compete in a global economy, we must develop the mathematics and science skills of all of our students, not simply the very best.

Indicator 8. International mathematics achievement comparisons

• *Increase the standing of the United States on international mathematics assessments of 13-year-olds.*

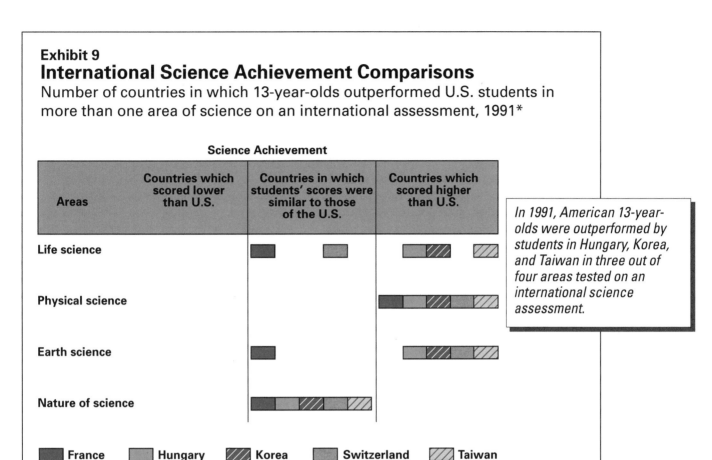

Exhibit 9
International Science Achievement Comparisons
Number of countries in which 13-year-olds outperformed U.S. students in more than one area of science on an international assessment, 1991*

Science Achievement

Areas	Countries which scored lower than U.S.	Countries in which students' scores were similar to those of the U.S.	Countries which scored higher than U.S.
Life science			
Physical science			
Earth science			
Nature of science			

In 1991, American 13-year-olds were outperformed by students in Hungary, Korea, and Taiwan in three out of four areas tested on an international science assessment.

■ France ■ Hungary ▨ Korea ■ Switzerland ▨ Taiwan

* International science achievement data will be collected again in 1995. Data will be available for approximately 50 countries.

Source: Educational Testing Service

Indicator 9. International science achievement comparisons

• *Increase the standing of the United States on international science assessments of 13-year-olds.*

For quite some time, U.S. students have not fared well in international mathematics and science comparisons. During the early 1980s, American 13-year-olds were outperformed by students in Japan and the Netherlands in all mathematics areas tested by the International Education Association.[31] Among the fifteen countries which participated in the assessment, the U.S. outperformed only Luxembourg, Nigeria, and Swaziland in more than half of the mathematics areas.

Toward the end of the decade, the first International Assessment of Educational Progress (IAEP) was administered to reassess international performance and yielded similar results. In 1988, American 13-year-olds scored substantially lower than students from three out of the four other countries tested in science (Korea, Spain, and the United Kingdom). In mathematics the U.S. scored lowest among 13-year-olds from the same three countries, plus Ireland.[32]

When the second International Assessment of Educational Progress was administered in 1991, American students fared no better. American 13-year-olds were outperformed by students in Korea, Switzerland, and Taiwan in all areas tested in mathematics, and by students

39

in France and Hungary in four out of the five areas tested (see Exhibit 8). American 13-year-olds also lagged behind students in Hungary, Korea, and Taiwan in three out of the four areas tested in science (see Exhibit 9).

What factors might account for such consistently poor international showings? The good news from the most recent IAEP assessment was that American 13-year-olds were generally more likely to use computers, to do science experiments, and to have more books in their homes than their counterparts in other countries. However, the bad news was that American students also tended to spend less time doing mathematics and science homework and using calculators in school, and led the other participating nations in the amount of television watched.

Despite the nation's previous shortcomings in mathematics and science achievement, promising new developments are under way to reverse consistently poor patterns of performance.

In addition, teachers surveyed in 1992 indicated that substantial numbers of 8th graders were not receiving the kind of instruction recommended by mathematics education experts, such as developing reasoning and problem-solving abilities and communicating mathematics ideas. Only one in five 8th graders had computers in their classrooms, and only one in twelve worked with mathematics tools such as measuring instruments or geometric solids.[33] In 1991, approximately one-third of high school mathematics teachers did not hold a degree in either mathematics or mathematics education.[34]

Science results were similar. In 1990, most students were not receiving the kinds of instruction needed to apply science ideas outside of the classroom, such as conducting and writing up science experiments, using computers, or producing oral or written science reports. Moreover, many teachers reported that they did not have adequate facilities or supplies to pursue these types of instruction. Nearly one-fourth of high school science teachers did not hold a degree in science or science education.[35]

In addition, school administrators reported during the early 1990s that science and mathematics had not been identified as priorities in substantial numbers of the nation's schools, particularly secondary level science.[36] As students moved into progressively higher grades, they were also less likely to agree that they liked mathematics and science. The gap between the percentages of male and female students who expressed positive attitudes increased substantially from Grade 4 to Grade 12, and was particularly pronounced in science. Whereas the gap between the proportions of male and female students who liked science was only 3 percentage points in Grade 4, it had grown to 17 percentage points by Grade 12.[37]

Despite the nation's previous shortcomings in mathematics and science achievement, promising new developments are under way to reverse consistently poor patterns of performance. In 1989, the National Council of Teachers of Mathematics (NCTM) became the first group of education experts in the U.S. to develop new voluntary nationwide standards which challenge conventional wisdom about what is taught in mathematics and how it is taught.[38] The NCTM standards call for far more rigorous content so that all students will achieve at higher levels in mathematics. They also place heavy emphasis on developing problem-solving, communication, and reasoning skills in mathematics so that students become confident in their own mathematical abilities. The standards encourage teachers to create classroom settings where students work on a variety of interesting, real-world problems requiring the application of mathematics and the integration of knowledge and skills from other disciplines.

Similar efforts to develop challenging standards in other subject areas are currently under way at the national level, as well as in a number of states. National arts standards were released earlier this year, and standards in geography, history, civics, science, and foreign languages are expected to follow soon. The original mathematics standards are already being revised by the National Council of Teachers of Mathematics to reflect new thinking about mathematics teaching and learning and to incorporate lessons learned from other fields. The fruits of these labors will be seen in 1995, when the U.S.

is scheduled to participate once again in international mathematics and science assessments.

GOAL 6: ADULT LITERACY AND LIFELONG LEARNING

Escalating concerns about the low literacy skills of America's workers mirror the increasing amount of attention that literacy is receiving worldwide. As the Organization for Economic Cooperation and Development (OECD) recently observed, what was previously considered to be an education problem of developing nations is increasingly seen as an issue of economic survival for industrialized ones.[39] Not only must industrialized nations ensure a steady stream of highly trained young adults to replace retiring workers, but they must also swiftly upgrade the literacy and technological skills of their present workforces to keep pace with rapidly changing job demands and fierce global competition.

According to OECD, low levels of literacy were previously assumed to be characteristic of only a select minority of U.S. adults, notably the unemployed or young high school dropouts. Findings from the National Adult Literacy Survey (NALS), conducted in the United States two years ago, defy those widely held assumptions.[40] While it was undeniably true that, on average, Americans who were not in the workforce or who had not completed high school tended to perform poorly on the assessment, literacy performance was also unacceptably low for many other segments of the population.

Perhaps most disturbing was the finding that the majority of Americans saw little need to upgrade their current level of skills. Despite the fact that nearly half of all American adults scored at the two lowest of five levels of proficiency, nearly all American adults believed that they could read and write English well. Similarly, an international study conducted at the beginning of the decade found that U.S. workers were far more likely than Belgian, German, or Japanese workers to predict that their present job skills would be very useful in five years.[41] U.S. satisfaction contrasted most sharply with Japan, where fewer than one in five workers predicted that their skills would be sufficient to meet job demands in the future.

The degree to which America remains economically competitive depends not only on the ability of our nation's schools and teachers to prepare students to meet higher expectations, but the degree to which business, labor, higher education, and adults themselves are willing to accept shared responsibility for increasing the skills and training of the nation's current labor force.

Indicator 10: Adult literacy

• *Increase the percentage of adults aged 16 and older who score at or above Level 3 in prose literacy on the National Adult Literacy Survey (NALS).*

Although literacy assessments of adults in the labor force and young adults had been conducted in the United States prior to 1992, the National Adult Literacy Survey was the first nationally representative assessment of the literacy skills of the entire adult population. NALS assessed proficiency on three scales (prose, document, and quantitative), and grouped scores into five levels (with Level 5 being most proficient and Level 1 being least proficient). Prose literacy tasks required readers to understand and use information contained in texts such as newspapers and pamphlets. Document literacy tasks required readers to locate and use information contained in materials such as tables, charts, and maps. Quantitative literacy tasks required readers to perform arithmetic computations using numbers found in printed materials. Because performance was fairly similar across the three scales, only one scale (prose literacy) is used to illustrate performance for this indicator.

Despite the fact that nearly half of all American adults scored at the two lowest of five levels of proficiency, nearly all American adults believed that they could read and write English well.

NALS results revealed that nearly half of all American adults read and write at the two lowest levels of English literacy. Only 52% scored at Level 3 or higher (see Exhibit 10). While adults who score below Level 3 do have some

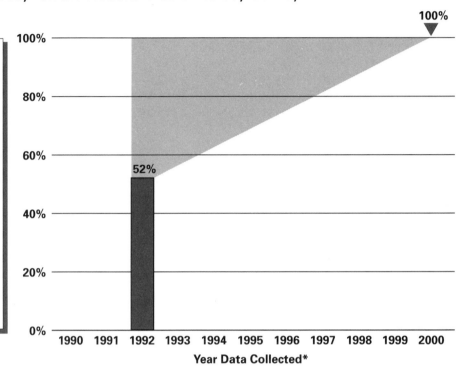

Exhibit 10

Adult Literacy

Percentage of adults aged 16 and older who scored at or above Level 3[1] in prose literacy[2] on the National Adult Literacy Survey

Nearly half of all American adults read and write at the two lowest of five levels of English proficiency; 52% scored at or above Level 3. Although adults who score below Level 3 do have some limited literacy skills, they are not likely to be able to perform the range of complex literacy tasks that the National Education Goals Panel considers important for competing successfully in a global economy and exercising fully the rights and responsibilities of citizenship.

Year Data Collected*

[1] Test results are reported on scales of 0 to 500 points. Scores are grouped into five levels, with Level 5 being most proficient and Level 1 being least proficient. Complete descriptions of each level can be found in Appendix B.

[2] Prose literacy tasks require readers to understand and use information contained in texts such as newspapers and pamphlets. Quantitative and document literacy tasks were also assessed.

* National data on adult literacy were not available prior to 1992. There are no current plans to collect these data again before the year 2000.

Source: National Center for Education Statistics

limited literacy skills, they are not likely to be able to perform the range of complex literacy tasks that the National Education Goals Panel considers important for competing successfully in a global economy or exercising the rights and responsibilities of citizenship.

The Goals Panel strongly supports increasing the literacy skills of every adult, because even adults with college degrees and those working in managerial, professional, or technical occupations scored, on average, no higher than Level 3. However, improving the skills of those at the two lowest levels is the most urgent priority because the proportion of adults at Levels 1 and 2 is so large and because the relationship between poverty and low levels of literacy is so

strong. For example, nearly three-fourths of adults receiving AFDC scored at the two lowest literacy levels.[42]

What do low levels of literacy mean in terms of costs to individuals and to the nation? When compared to adults who scored at the highest level (Level 5):

• Adults at Level 1 were less than half as likely to be employed.

• They worked, on average, less than half as many weeks during the previous year.

• Their median weekly wages were less than half of what adults at Level 5 earned.

- They were ten times as likely to live in poverty.

- They were seventeen times as likely to receive food stamps.

NALS results also suggest that adults with low levels of literacy are not likely to possess the skills and knowledge required of an informed electorate who can "exercise fully the rights and responsibilities of citizenship." Adults at Level 1 were twenty times as likely as those at Level 5 to report that they never read the newspaper. And while nearly 90% of adults at Level 5 had voted in a national or state election during the previous five years, only slightly more than half of those at Level 1 had done so.

At present, an international study involving 11 countries is under way to measure similar types of literacy skills of adults in other countries. Participants include some of the United States' chief economic competitors, such as Germany and Canada. The National Center for Education Statistics is exploring ways to link this new international study to the NALS results, which would enable us to benchmark the literacy skills of American adults against the rest of the world for the very first time.

Indicator 11. Participation in adult education

• *Eliminate disparities in adult education participation between adults aged 17 years and older (a) who have a high school diploma or less, and (b) who have completed a college degree or some post-secondary education or technical training.*

Exhibit 11
Participation in Adult Education
Disparity (in percentage points) between adults[1] aged 17 and older who have a high school diploma or less, and those who have additional post-secondary education or technical training

In 1991, the gap in adult education participation rates between adults who had a high school diploma or less and those with additional post-secondary education or technical training was 27 percentage points.

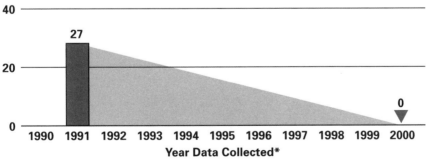

Year Data Collected*

[1] Excluding those participating in full-time educational programs exclusively.

* Data on participation in adult education will be collected again in 1995.

Source: National Center for Education Statistics and Westat, Inc.

Although lifelong learning is an admirable goal for all adults, those with a high school diploma or less are specifically targeted for this indicator, since analyses of labor and education data indicate that adults with the highest levels of education and skills are the ones most likely to receive additional training. (While this indicator focuses on disparities in formal training provided through adult education courses, it does not discount the importance of informal, on-the-job training, which accounts for the majority of job training that many workers receive.)

Data collected by the American Society for Training and Development show that roughly two-thirds of the funds invested annually by businesses in worker training are spent to train workers who already have college degrees. According to the National Center on Education and the Economy, these workers receive a highly disproportionate share of training dollars, since they fill only 30% of the nation's jobs.[43] Additional data from the Department of Labor support this argument. Between 1983 and 1991, the percentage of U.S. workers who took training to improve their current job skills rose from 35% to 41%. Yet white collar workers and college graduates were nearly twice as likely to participate in training as blue collar workers or those with a high school education or less.[44]

Adults with the highest levels of education and skills are the ones most likely to receive additional training.

Approximately four out of ten employed adults took adult education courses during 1990-91. Approximately three out of ten reported that they received some type of support from their employers so that they could participate, such as time off from work or payment toward fees or tuition.[45] However, those with four-year college degrees were nearly twice as likely as those with high school degrees, and six times as likely as those without a high school diploma, to report that they received some type of employer support. In 1991, the gap in adult education participation rates between adults with a high school diploma or less, and those with additional post-secondary education or technical training was 27 percentage points (see Exhibit 11).

In general, the data suggest that those who may need additional training the most to upgrade their current levels of skills and qualify for better jobs (i.e., those with a high school diploma or less) tend to be those least likely to participate. Increased efforts should be targeted toward this population of adults if the nation expects to achieve this Goal.

Indicator 12. Participation in higher education

• *Eliminate disparities in college entrance rates between White and minority high school graduates who enroll in two- or four-year colleges immediately after graduation.*

• *Eliminate disparities in college completion rates between White and minority students aged 25-29.*

Although enrolling in college immediately after high school is not necessarily the optimal choice for all students, there is widespread agreement that no qualified student who chooses to go to college should be denied access. Thus, this indicator is framed in terms of equity — that the gap in college enrollment and completion rates will be eliminated between White and minority students.

About six out of ten 1990 high school graduates enrolled in either two- or four-year colleges immediately after graduation. While 63% of White high school graduates went on to post-secondary education, only 49% of Black graduates and 52% of Hispanic graduates immediately did so, resulting in a 14-percentage-point disparity between Blacks and Whites, and an 11-point disparity between Hispanics and Whites (see Exhibit 12). Since that time the differences have fluctuated slightly (and most noticeably for Hispanics), but changes have not been large enough to reduce disparities significantly for either Black or Hispanic students.

Exhibit 12
Participation in Higher Education

College Enrollment

Disparities (in percentage points[1]) in college entrance rates between White and minority high school graduates who enroll in two- or four-year colleges[2] immediately after graduation

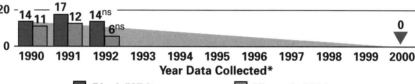

In 1990, disparities in college enrollment rates were 14 percentage points between White and Black students and 11 percentage points between White and Hispanic students. Gaps had not decreased significantly for either group by 1992.

■ Black/White gap   ■ Hispanic/White gap

[1] Based on three-year averages (1989-91 for 1990; 1990-92 for 1991; and 1991-93 for 1992).
[2] Includes junior colleges, community colleges, and universities.
[ns] Interpret with caution. Change from the baseline was not statistically significant.

* Data on college enrollment will be collected annually through the year 2000.

Source: Bureau of Census and National Center for Education Statistics

College Completion

Disparities[1] (in percentage points) in college completion rates[2] between White and minority high school graduates aged 25-29

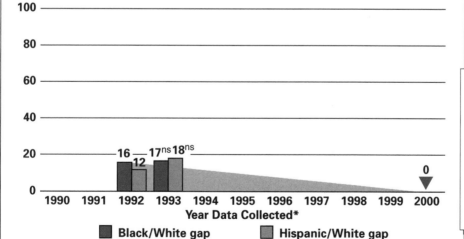

In 1992, disparities in college completion rates were 16 percentage points between White and Black students and 12 percentage points between White and Hispanic students. Gaps showed no significant change for either group the following year.

■ Black/White gap   ■ Hispanic/White gap

[1] Numbers differ slightly from data reported in the *National Data Volume* due to rounding.
[2] Includes Associate's degree, Bachelor's degree, and graduate/professional degree.
[ns] Interpret with caution. Change from the baseline was not statistically significant.

* The wording of the item for college completion changed substantially between the 1991 survey and the 1992 survey; therefore, 1992 is established as the baseline year for college completion. These data will be collected annually through the year 2000.

Source: Bureau of Census, National Center for Education Statistics, and Pinkerton Computer Consultants

Even if the United States does manage to reduce the gap in college enrollment between White and minority students, we will be only partially successful if we do not also reduce the gap in college completion. Newly released analyses of 1992 Census data conducted by University of Michigan researchers underscore the effect that college completion has on earnings.[46] On average, salaries of women with bachelor's degrees were 16% higher than the salaries of women with high school diplomas; for men, the difference was 21%. Even more important was the finding that it was college completion, not merely college enrollment, that had the greatest effect. Men who had completed a college degree earned $110-$139 more per week, on average, than those who had completed an equivalent number of college courses without actually earning a credential.

Therefore, in addition to reducing disparities in college enrollment rates, it is crucial to eliminate disparities in college completion rates, since Black and Hispanic students also complete college at lower rates than do Whites. In 1992, slightly more than one-third of all U.S. high school graduates aged 25-29 possessed a college degree. Figures ranged from 37% for Whites to 21% for Blacks and 25% for Hispanics, resulting in a 16-percentage-point Black/White college completion gap and a 12-percentage-point Hispanic/White gap (see Exhibit 12). Neither gap had changed significantly by the following year.

According to the latest Gallup poll, Americans consider school violence and discipline to be the worst problems facing today's public schools.

The Southern Regional Education Board proposes that in order to move this indicator in the desired direction, colleges need to consider how they are providing support and remedial services to students whom they admit, and how they can develop effective policies to smooth transitions from 2-year to 4-year colleges.[47] Equally important, elementary and secondary school systems and students themselves must assume responsibility for meeting higher achievement standards, so that students are fully prepared for the academic demands of a high-quality college education.

GOAL 7: SAFE, DISCIPLINED, AND ALCOHOL- AND DRUG-FREE SCHOOLS

In the 1994 Phi Delta Kappa/Gallup poll on education, the American public was asked to identify the single worst problem confronting today's public schools. Two problems tied for first place, each cited by 18% of the respondents: "fighting, violence, and gangs," and "lack of discipline." "Drug abuse," which was cited by 11% of respondents, came in third in the 1994 poll, indicating that this problem also continues to be a chief concern.[48]

Lowell Rose, Phi Delta Kappa's Executive Director, points out that public perception of the frequency of violent acts may be exaggerated somewhat by intense media attention when incidents of school violence do occur, and that most of the nation's schools really are safe places to be. Nevertheless, this year's Gallup poll results suggest that even isolated incidents of school violence and disciplinary problems will not be tolerated by parents and taxpayers.

Statistics compiled from a number of recent studies on school violence and presented by *U.S. News & World Report* in a special report last November suggest that the public has a right to be concerned:[49]

• The number of crimes committed at or near the 85,000 U.S. public schools was estimated at more than 3 million annually.

• Nearly 6,000 violent incidents occurred in New York City schools alone in 1992, an increase of 16% from the previous year.

• Surveys of principals from more than 1,200 school systems conducted by researchers from Xavier University in Cincinnati revealed that violence is not solely a problem of urban schools: 64%, 54%, and 43% of principals in urban, suburban, and rural areas, respectively, reported that violence had increased in their schools during the previous five years.

• One in five suburban high school students surveyed by Tulane University researchers

Exhibit 13
Overall Student Drug and Alcohol Use

Drugs
Percentage of 10th graders who reported using any illicit drug[1] during the previous year

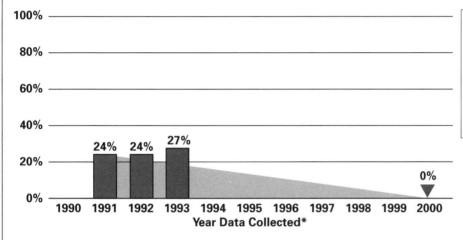

Between 1991 and 1993, the percentage of 10th graders who reported that they had used an illicit drug during the previous year increased significantly, from 24% to 27%.

[1] See Appendix B for complete description.

* Data on overall drug use by 10th graders will be collected annually through the year 2000.

Source: University of Michigan

Alcohol
Percentage of 10th graders who reported using alcohol during the previous year

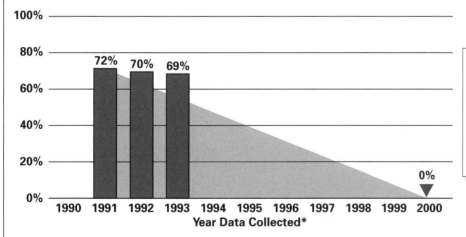

Between 1991 and 1993, the percentage of 10th graders who reported that they had used alcohol during the previous year decreased significantly, from 72% to 69%.

* Data on overall alcohol use by 10th graders will be collected annually through the year 2000.

Source: University of Michigan

approved of shooting someone "who has stolen something from you," and one in twelve approved of shooting someone "who has done something to offend or insult you."

If the nation's schools cannot guarantee a safe haven free from violence, drugs and alcohol, and other disciplinary problems that interfere with teaching and learning, it is unlikely that any other attempts at education reform will lead to the higher levels of student performance that are addressed in the other Goals. Obviously, schools alone cannot be expected to solve these problems, which reflect increasing amounts of violence in the larger community and, at least among some students, increasing tolerance toward acts of retaliation. Securing long-term commitments from parents and communities to work in partnership with schools will be critical in order to achieve Goal 7.

Indicator 13. Overall student drug and alcohol use

• *Reduce the percentages of 10th graders reporting that they used illicit drugs or alcohol during the previous year.*

Student drug use is the only core indicator for which U.S. performance has gotten significantly worse since the National Education Goals were adopted.

National progress toward reducing student drug and alcohol use provides some of the best news, as well as some of the worst news, this year. Between 1991 and 1993, the percentage of 10th graders who reported using alcohol during the previous year declined significantly, from 72% to 69% (see Exhibit 13). Individual state data, reported in the accompanying *1994 State Data Volume*, also show that some states saw a sharp decline in extreme episodes of alcohol consumption among public high school students (i.e., the proportion who reported having five or more drinks in a row during the previous month).[50]

Although this improvement is certainly heartening, student alcohol use is likely to require far greater, long-term efforts to reduce it substantially, because it is still extremely widespread. Alcohol is by far the most commonly used drug, according to student reports, and is used by more than half of all 8th graders, seven out of ten 10th graders, and more than three-fourths of all 12th graders.[51] Although the Goals Panel acknowledges that schools cannot be held solely accountable for student behavior that takes place away from school or school-sponsored events, drug and alcohol use at any time can have detrimental effects on student learning. Therefore, reducing overall student drug and alcohol use (rather than simply reducing at-school use) has been selected as the core indicator, and will require the close cooperation of parents and communities with schools to see that it is achieved. Tenth graders were chosen as illustrative for each of the Goal 7 core indicators, although we expect improvements to occur across all grades.

In contrast to the decline in the proportion of students consuming alcohol, overall student drug use has actually increased (see Exhibit 13). Between 1991 and 1993, the percentage of 10th graders who reported using any illicit drug during the previous year increased from 24% to 27%, reversing previous trends which showed that overall student drug use had been declining since 1980. Data reported in this year's *National Data Volume* reveal significant two-year increases in the proportion of 8th and 10th graders who reported using marijuana, as well as the proportion of 8th graders who reported using cocaine.[52] Student drug use is the only core indicator for which U.S. performance has gotten significantly worse since the National Education Goals were adopted.

Indicator 14: Sale of drugs at school

• *Reduce the percentage of 10th graders reporting that someone offered to sell or give them an illegal drug at school during the previous year.*

In addition to reducing overall student drug and alcohol use, the Goals Panel considers reducing the sale of drugs at school to be a core indicator of progress toward Goal 7. Even though schools cannot be held solely accountable for student behavior that occurs off the school campus, they do bear primary responsi-

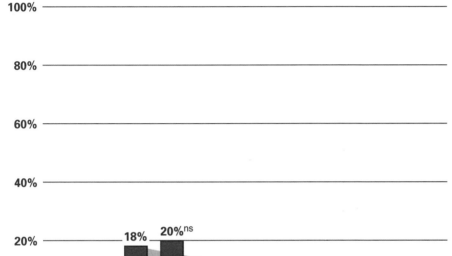

Exhibit 14
Sale of Drugs at School
Percentage of 10th graders who reported that someone offered to sell or give them an illegal drug at school[1] during the previous year

About one in five 10th graders reported in 1992 that someone had offered to sell or give them an illegal drug at school during the previous year. No significant reduction in attempted drug sales at school had been made by the following year.

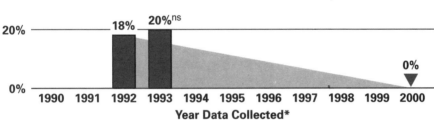

[1] Or someone had actually sold or given them an illegal drug at school.
ns Interpret with caution. Change was not statistically significant.

* Information on the sale of drugs at school was not asked of 10th graders prior to 1992. These data will be collected annually through the year 2000.

Source: University of Michigan

bility for eliminating the sale of drugs at school, and they should be able to exert considerable control in this area.

Students report that they rarely use alcohol, marijuana, and other illicit drugs at school during the day, and the vast majority report never being under the influence of alcohol or other drugs while at school.[53] Nevertheless, data reported in this year's *National Data Volume* indicate that the percentages of 8th and 10th graders who reported using marijuana or other illicit drugs at school during the day increased significantly between 1991 and 1993. The proportion of 8th graders who reported drinking alcohol at school during the day also increased significantly over the same two-year period.[54]

Last year nearly three out of ten students (and four out of ten high school students) reported that it was easy to obtain alcohol and marijuana at school or on school grounds.[55] Thirteen percent of 8th graders, 20% of 10th graders, and 25% of 12th graders reported that they had been approached at school by someone trying to sell or give them drugs during the previous year.[56] Exhibit 14 indicates that we have made no discernible progress in reducing attempted drug sales at school between 1992 and 1993.

Indicator 15. Student and teacher victimization

• *Reduce the percentages of 10th grade students and public school teachers reporting that they were threatened or injured at school during the previous year.*

According to reports from 8th, 10th, and 12th graders, substantial numbers of students

Exhibit 15
Student and Teacher Victimization

Students
Percentage of 10th graders who reported that they were threatened or injured[1] at school during the previous year

> *In 1991, four out of ten 10th graders reported that they had been threatened or injured at school during the previous year. By 1993, the percentage had been significantly reduced.*

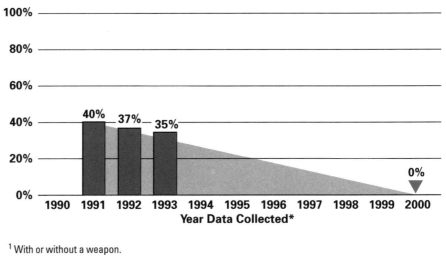

[1] With or without a weapon.

* Data on student victimization will be collected annually through the year 2000.

Source: University of Michigan

Teachers
Percentage of public school teachers who reported that they were threatened with physical injury or physically attacked by a student from their school during the previous 12 months

> *One out of every ten public school teachers reported in 1991 that they had been threatened or physically attacked by a student from their school during the previous year.*

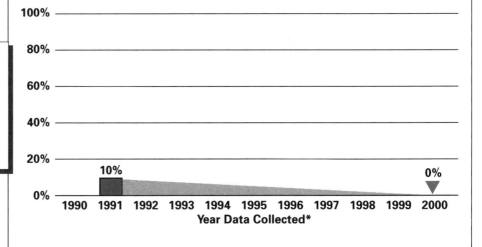

* Data on teacher victimization will be collected again in 1994 and 1998.

Source: National Center for Education Statistics and Westat, Inc.

continue to be victims of violent acts, theft, and vandalism at school. According to student reports, threats and injuries are generally higher among younger students than among students in upper grades, and Black and Hispanic students are more likely than White students to be victims of violent acts at school involving weapons.[57] Last year over one-third of all students reported that other students at their school belonged to gangs.[58]

Encouraging news is that the percentage of 10th graders who reported that they were threatened or injured at school during the previous year declined significantly between 1991 and 1993 (see Exhibit 15). The bad news is that this percentage is still unacceptably high, at 35%. Moreover, state data presented for the first time in this year's *State Data Volume* indicate that in 1993, substantial numbers of students reported staying home from school at least once during the previous month because of concerns for their physical safety.[59] Surveys of public school teachers in 1991 indicate that one in ten had been threatened with physical injury or physically attacked by a student from their school during the previous year (see Exhibit 15).

Evidence suggests that continually moving this indicator in the desired direction is not likely to be easy. Weapons are becoming more prevalent in schools, increasing the likelihood that students will resort to violence to resolve conflicts. Last year, 11% of 8th graders, 10% of 10th graders, and 8% of 12th graders admitted that they had brought a weapon to school at least once during the previous month, such as a gun, knife, or club. Percentages increased significantly from the previous year for both 8th and 12th graders, and 3-4% of the students at each grade reported that they habitually carried a weapon to school ten or more days in the previous month.[60] Newly released data from state surveys conducted the same year show that in 20 of the 24 participating states and territories, at least 10% of public high school students reported carrying a weapon on school property at least once during the previous month (see *State Data Volume*).[61]

Indicator 16. Disruptions in class by students

• *Reduce the percentages of 10th grade students and high school teachers reporting that disruptions often interfere with teaching and learning.*

In addition to eliminating drugs, alcohol, and violence from schools, Goal 7 aims to increase the proportion of the nation's schools which offer a disciplined environment conducive to learning. Reducing classroom disruptions that interfere with teaching and learning has been chosen as the final core indicator of progress toward the Goals. Minimizing classroom disruptions should be considered a necessary, though not sufficient, condition to ensure that learning takes place.

Last year the majority of students in Grades 8, 10, and 12 reported that student disruptions were fairly common occurrences in their classes. About half of the students estimated that misbehavior by other students interfered with their own learning only occasionally (five times a week or less), but 16% of 8th graders and 11% of 10th graders reported that teachers interrupted class twenty times a week or more to deal with student misbehavior.[62]

Weapons are becoming more prevalent in schools, increasing the likelihood that students will resort to violence to resolve conflicts.

According to student reports thus far, we have made no real improvement in reducing classroom misbehavior (see Exhibit 16). By next year we should be able to report whether the percentage of high school teachers who feel that student misbehavior interferes with their teaching has been significantly reduced from the 33% baseline reported in 1991.

GOAL 8: PARENTAL PARTICIPATION

No core indicators have been selected for this new Goal yet. They will be addressed in future Goals Reports.

Exhibit 16
Disruptions in Class by Students

Student Reports
Percentage of 10th graders who reported that during an average week misbehavior by other students often[1] interferes with their own learning

In 1992, 17% of 10th graders reported that other students interfered with their own learning at least six times a week. No significant reduction in class disruptions was seen the following year.

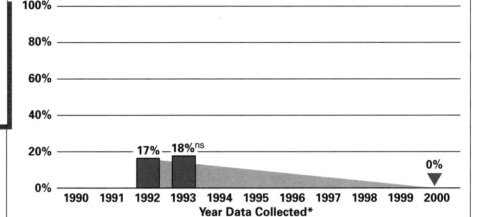

[1] Often=6 times a week or more.
[ns] Interpret with caution. Change was not statistically significant.

* Information on disruptions in class was not asked of 10th graders prior to 1992. These data will be collected annually through the year 2000.

Source: University of Michigan

Teacher Reports
Percentage of all high school teachers who reported[1] that student misbehavior interferes with their teaching

In 1991, one-third of all high school teachers felt that student misbehavior interfered with their teaching.

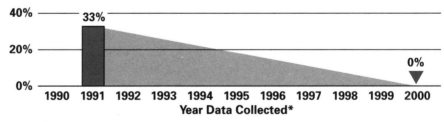

[1] Responses of "agree" and "strongly agree" combined.

* Teacher reports on disruptions in class will be collected again in 1994 and 1998.

Source: National Center for Education Statistics

Conclusion

The findings reported in this chapter indicate that our current rate of progress is nowhere near the levels that will be required in order to achieve the National Education Goals within the next six years. Although we have made significant improvements on four of the core indicators of progress, much greater concerted effort will be required to accelerate our pace and move the others in the desired direction.

While policymakers will be instrumental in building a national consensus for the education reforms that will be necessary to achieve the National Education Goals, it is clear that the Goals will not be achieved within the nation's capital, at the state capitals, or in downtown city halls. In fact, they will not be achieved by any single level of government. Only by involving students, parents, educators, schools, higher education, and local business and community leaders as active partners will we be able to mobilize sufficient grass-roots community effort to achieve the Goals.

This does not mean, however, that government has no role to play in achieving the Goals. In fact, one of the new charges Congress has given to the National Education Goals Panel is to identify actions that federal, state, and local governments should take to enhance progress toward achieving the Goals. This charge is addressed in the following chapter.

ENDNOTES

[1] Prince, C., Nord, C.W., & Zill, N. (1993, April). *Social indicators predictive of school success: Linking health and social information available at birth to measures of children's health, behavior, and academic status.* Paper presented at the annual meetings of the American Educational Research Association, Atlanta, GA.

Nord, C.W., Zill, N., Prince, C., Clarke, S., & Ventura, S. (1993, October). *Developing an index of educational risk from health and social characteristics known at birth.* Paper presented at the meetings of the Southern Demographic Association, New Orleans, LA.

[2] U.S. Department of Health and Human Services, National Center for Health Statistics. (1990). *Healthy people 2000: National health promotion and disease prevention objectives.* DHHS Publication No. (PHS) 91-50212. Washington, DC: U.S. Government Printing Office.

[3] McCormick, M., Gortmaker, S.L., & Sobol, A.M. (1990). Very low birthweight children: Behavior problems and school failure in a national sample. *Journal of Pediatrics,* 117(5), 687-693.

[4] U.S. Department of Health and Human Services, National Center for Health Statistics. (1992). *Health, United States, 1991, and prevention profile.* DHHS Publication No. (PHS) 92-1232. Washington, DC: U.S. Government Printing Office.

[5] Kleinman, J.C., & Kessel, S.S. (1987). Racial differences in low birthweight: Trends and risk factors. *New England Journal of Medicine* 317:749-753.

[6] Kleinman, J.C., & Madans, J.H. (1985). The effects of maternal smoking, physical stature, and education attainment on the incidence of low birthweight. *American Journal of Epidemiology* 121(6):843-855.

[7] U.S. Department of Health and Human Services, National Center for Health Statistics. (1991). *Healthy people 2000: National health promotion and disease prevention objectives.* DHHS Publication No. (PHS) 91-50212. Washington, DC: U.S. Government Printing Office.

[8] United Nations Children's Fund (UNICEF). (1993). *The progress of nations.* New York: author.

[9] U.S. Department of Health and Human Services, National Center for Health Statistics. (1992). *Health, United States, 1991, and prevention profile.* DHHS Publication No. (PHS) 92-1232. Washington, DC: U.S. Government Printing Office.

[10] *Ibid.*

[11] United Nations Children's Fund (UNICEF). (1993). *The progress of nations.* New York: author.

[12] Heath, S.B. (1983). *Ways with words.* Cambridge: Cambridge University Press.

[13] U.S. Department of Education, National Center for Education Statistics. (1993). *National Household Education Survey (NHES): 1993 school readiness interview*, unpublished tabulations prepared by Westat, Inc.

[14] Mullis, I., Campbell, J.R., & Farstrup, A.E. (1993). *NAEP 1992 reading report card for the nation and the states*. Report prepared by Educational Testing Service under contract with the National Center for Education Statistics, U.S. Department of Education. Washington, DC: U.S. Government Printing Office.

[15] Kirsch, I.S., Jungeblut, A., Jenkins, L., & Kolstad, A. (1993). *Adult literacy in America: A first look at the results of the National Adult Literacy Survey*. Report prepared by Educational Testing Service under contract with the National Center for Education Statistics, U.S. Department of Education. Washington, DC: U.S. Government Printing Office.

[16] Morgan, G., et al. (1993). *Making a career of it*. Boston: Wheelock College, Center for Career Development in Early Education. (as reported in Children's Defense Fund. (1994). *The state of America's children: 1994 yearbook*. Washington, DC: author.)

[17] Kisker, E.E., Hofferth, S.L., & Phillips, D.A. (1991). *Profile of child care settings study: Early education and care in 1990*. Report submitted to the U.S. Department of Education, Office of Planning, Budget and Evaluation. Princeton, NJ: Mathematica Policy Research, Inc.

[18] Center for the Study of Social Policy (1994). *Kids Count data book: State profiles of child well-being*. Washington, DC: author.

[19] U.S. Department of Commerce, Bureau of the Census. *Current Population Survey*. Calculations by the Center for Labor Market Studies, Northwestern University. (as reported in Children's Defense Fund. (1994). *The state of America's children: 1994 yearbook*. Washington, DC: author.)

[20] Kirsch, I.S., Jungeblut, A., Jenkins, L., & Kolstad, A. (1993). *Adult literacy in America: A first look at the results of the National Adult Literacy Survey*. Report prepared by Educational Testing Service under contract with the National Center for Education Statistics, U.S. Department of Education. Washington, DC: U.S. Government Printing Office.

[21] U.S. Congress, House Committee on Ways and Means. (1993). *Overview of entitlement programs*. 103rd Congress, 2nd session. Washington, DC: U.S. Government Printing Office.

[22] U.S. Department of Education, National Center for Education Statistics. (1993). *National Household Education Survey (NHES): 1993 school readiness interview*, unpublished tabulations prepared by Westat, Inc.

[23] U.S. Department of Education, National Center for Education Statistics. (1991). *National Household Education Survey*. Data appearing in *ETS Policy Notes* 4(2):9. Princeton, NJ: Educational Testing Service.

[24] Children's Defense Fund. (1994). *The state of America's children: 1994 yearbook*. Washington, DC: author.

[25] Rock, D., Owings, J., & Lee, R. (1994, January). Changes in math proficiency between 8th and 10th grades. *Statistics in Brief*, NCES Report No. 93-455. Washington, DC: U.S. Department of Education, National Center for Education Statistics.

[26] Oakes, J. (1990). *Multiplying inequalities: The effects of race, social class, and tracking on opportunities to learn mathematics and science*. Santa Monica, CA: Rand Corporation.

Council of Chief State School Officers. (1993). State Education Assessment Center, Washington, DC.

[27] State Departments of Education, Data on Public Schools, Fall 1991; California, Fall 1990.

Council of Chief State School Officers. (1993). State Education Assessment Center, Washington, DC.

[28] *Ibid.*

[29] Educational Testing Service. (1993, Summer). State assessments: Home and school differences. *ETS Policy Notes* 5(3):6-8. Princeton, NJ: author.

[30] Elley, W.B. (1992). *How in the world do students read?* Hamburg: The International Association for the Evaluation of Educational Achievement.

[31] International Association for the Evaluation of Educational Achievement. (1989). Data from Robitaille, D. & Garden, R., (Eds.), *The IEA study of mathematics II: Contexts and outcomes of school mathematics*, (pp.105-119). Oxford: Pergamon Press.

U.S. Department of Education, National Center for Education Statistics. (1991). *Digest of education statistics, 1990*, (p. 383). Washington, DC: U.S. Government Printing Office.

[32] Lapointe, A.E., Mead, N.A., & Phillips, G.W. (1989). *A world of differences: An international assessment of mathematics and science.* Princeton, NJ: Educational Testing Service, Center for the Assessment of Educational Progress.

[33] U.S. Department of Education, National Center for Education Statistics. (1993). *Data compendium for the NAEP 1992 mathematics assessment of the nation and the states.* Washington, DC: U.S. Government Printing Office.

[34] U.S. Department of Education, National Center for Education Statistics. (1992). Teacher survey of the *Schools and Staffing Survey (SASS)*, unpublished tabulations.

[35] *Ibid.*

[36] Jones, L.R., Mullis, I., Raizen, S.A., Weiss, J.R., & Weston, E.A. (1992). *The 1990 science report card: NAEP's assessment of fourth, eighth, and twelfth graders.* Washington, DC: U.S. Government Printing Office.

U.S. Department of Education, National Center for Education Statistics. (1993). *Data compendium for the NAEP 1992 mathematics assessment of the nation and the states.* Washington, DC: U.S. Government Printing Office.

[37] *Ibid.*

[38] National Council of Teachers of Mathematics. (1989, March). *Curriculum and evaluation standards for school mathematics.* Reston, VA: author.

[39] Centre for Educational Research and Innovation. (1992). *Adult illiteracy and economic performance.* Paris: Organization for Economic Cooperation and Development.

[40] Kirsch, I., Jungeblut, A., Jenkins, L., & Kolstad, A. (1993). *Adult literacy in America: A first look at the results of the National Adult Literacy Survey.* Report prepared by Educational Testing Service, under contract with the National Center for Education Statistics, U.S. Department of Education. Washington, DC: U.S. Government Printing Office.

[41] Ruiz Quintanilla, S.A. (1992). *Work-related attitudes among workers in Flanders (Belgium), F.R. Germany, Japan, and the U.S.A.* Report prepared for the National Education Goals Panel. Ithaca, NY: Cornell University.

[42] Martinson, K. (1994). *Emerging evidence on the literacy performance of welfare recipients.* Commissioned paper prepared under contract to the National Education Goals Panel.

[43] National Center on Education and the Economy. (1990). *America's choice: High skills or low wages!* Rochester, NY: author.

[44] Amirault, T. (1992). *Job qualifying and skill improvement training: 1991.* Washington, DC: U.S. Department of Labor, Bureau of Labor Statistics.

[45] U.S. Department of Education, National Center for Education Statistics. (1991, August). *National Household Education Survey: 1991 adult education component*, unpublished tabulations prepared by Westat, Inc.

[46] University of Michigan Population Studies Center. (1994). *Degrees matter: New evidence on sheepskin effects in the returns to education.* Ann Arbor, MI: University of Michigan.

[47] Creech, J.D. (1994). *Educational benchmarks 1994.* Atlanta, GA: Southern Regional Education Board.

[48] Schools should do better, and they can, Americans say. (1994, August 31). *Report on Education Research*, Special Supplement, 25(17), 1-4. Alexandria, VA: Capitol Publications, Inc.

[49] Toch, T., with Gest, T., & Guttman, M. (1993, November 8). Violence in schools. *U.S. News & World Report*, 31-32, 34-36.

[50] U.S. Department of Health and Human Services, Centers for Disease Control and Prevention. (1991). *Current tobacco, alcohol, marijuana, and cocaine use among high school students — United States, 1990.* Atlanta, GA: author.

U.S. Department of Health and Human Services, Centers for Disease Control and Prevention. (1992). *Current tobacco, alcohol, marijuana, and cocaine use among high school students — United States, 1991.* Atlanta, GA: author.

U.S. Department of Health and Human Services, Centers for Disease Control and Prevention. (1994). *Current tobacco, alcohol, marijuana, and cocaine use among high school students — United States, 1993.* Atlanta, GA: author.

[51] Johnston, L.D., O'Malley, P.M., & Bachman, J.G. (1994, July). *Selected 1993 outcome measures from the Monitoring the Future Study for Goal 7 of the National Education Goals: A special report for the National Education Goals Panel.* Ann Arbor, MI: University of Michigan, Institute for Social Research.

[52] *Ibid.*

[53] *Ibid.*

[54] *Ibid.*

[55] U.S. Department of Education, National Center for Education Statistics. (1993, August). *National Household Education Survey: 1993 school safety and discipline component.* Unpublished tabulations prepared by Westat, Inc.

[56] Johnston, L.D., O'Malley, P.M., & Bachman, J.G. (1994, July). *Selected 1993 outcome measures from the Monitoring the Future Study for Goal 7 of the National Education Goals: A special report for the National Education Goals Panel.* Ann Arbor, MI: University of Michigan, Institute for Social Research.

[57] *Ibid.*

[58] U.S. Department of Education, National Center for Education Statistics. (1993, August). *National Household Education Survey: 1993 school safety and discipline component.* Unpublished tabulations prepared by Westat, Inc.

[59] U.S. Department of Health and Human Services, Centers for Disease Control and Prevention. (1994). *Current tobacco, alcohol, marijuana, and cocaine use among high school students — United States, 1993.* Atlanta, GA: author.

[60] Johnston, L.D., O'Malley, P.M., & Bachman, J.G. (1994, July). *Selected 1993 outcome measures from the Monitoring the Future Study for Goal 7 of the National Education Goals: A special report for the National Education Goals Panel.* Ann Arbor, MI: University of Michigan, Institute for Social Research.

[61] U.S. Department of Health and Human Services, Centers for Disease Control and Prevention. (1994). *Current tobacco, alcohol, marijuana, and cocaine use among high school students — United States, 1993.* Atlanta, GA: author.

[62] Johnston, L.D., O'Malley, P.M., & Bachman, J.G. (1994, July). *Selected 1993 outcome measures from the Monitoring the Future Study for Goal 7 of the National Education Goals: A special report for the National Education Goals Panel.* Ann Arbor, MI: University of Michigan, Institute for Social Research.

Chapter 3:
The Federal – State – Local Partnership

Collaborative efforts to achieve the National Education Goals, reinforced by major legislative initiatives passed by Congress in 1994, usher in a new era of federal, state, and local partnerships. In the past, education policies focused primarily on regulations, categorical programs, and simply allocating resources for education, rather than focusing on the results that parents, educators, and policymakers really want to achieve, namely:

- higher levels of student performance;

- better qualified teachers;

- safer schools;

- young children who are healthier and better prepared for school and learning;

- stronger links between home and school, and between school and work;

- higher rates of high school graduation;

- a well-informed citizenry; and

- an internationally competitive and highly trained workforce.

Setting National Education Goals has changed the environment for education policy-making substantially, to one in which desired results drive policy decisions. The *Goals 2000: Educate America Act* recognizes that while education reform will remain a state and local responsibility, education reform must also be a national priority. More than ever before, federal, state, and local leadership must work collaboratively to make decisions that will rebuild the education system from the bottom up.

One of the new charges that Congress has given to the National Education Goals Panel is "to identify actions that federal, state, and local governments should take to enhance progress toward achieving the Goals." Now and in the coming years the Goals Panel hopes to stimulate discussion and action at all levels of governance regarding the shared responsibilities that this new charge entails.

> *One of the new charges that Congress has given to the National Education Goals Panel is "to identify actions that federal, state, and local governments should take to enhance progress toward achieving the Goals."*

A number of actions have already been taken by the federal government this year to enhance progress toward the Goals through legislative initiatives such as *Goals 2000* and the *Safe Schools Act*,[1] the *School-to-Work Opportunities Act*,[2] the *Student Loan Reform Act*,[3] and the redesign of the *Elementary and Secondary Education Act.* Actions include:

- increasing investments in early childhood programs such as child nutrition, immunization, and Head Start to improve the chance that children will arrive at school ready to learn;

- improving the federal student loan program to ensure continued access to higher education;

- providing support and financial resources through *Goals 2000* to help states, communities, and schools develop and implement comprehensive, long-term education improvement plans targeted to achievement of the National Education Goals;

- making regulatory flexibility a key priority by granting authority to the Secretary of Education to waive certain federal requirements that impede the implementation of state and local education reform efforts; and

- funding research to identify and make available information about promising and effective actions to achieve the National Education Goals.

The National Education Goals call for all students to demonstrate competency in challenging subject matter and to do so at internationally competitive levels of achievement.

The Goals Panel believes that these initiatives enable states and local communities to take further steps to achieve the Goals. This year we focus on two actions that deserve the immediate attention of federal, state, and local policymakers because they are central to the Goals Process: supporting the development of challenging academic standards, and filling data gaps that impede our ability to measure our progress. The Goals Panel believes that:

1. clear, measurable academic standards of student performance should serve as the centerpiece of education reform; and

2. if we are to meet the Goals by the end of the decade, an immediate priority is to improve the capacity of all levels of governance to collect and analyze essential data that will drive education improvement.

Setting High Academic Standards

The National Education Goals call for all students to demonstrate competency in challenging subject matter and to do so at internationally competitive levels of achievement. Rather than just comparing students against each other or setting a minimum criterion for student performance, the National Education Goals call for performance against world-class standards that set targets for:

- what all students should know and be able to do (content standards); and

- the level of performance we expect students to reach (performance standards).

Standards define what it takes to know or do something well, and are oriented to quality, excellence, and proficiency. The process of redesigning public education around academic standards is aimed at ensuring that all students leave school with the knowledge and skills they will need to be successful adults. High, clear, and consistent academic standards for all students will raise our expectations for schools and help us focus on achieving tangible results.

The Goals Panel believes that academic standards reflecting broad public consensus and adapted to the needs and priorities of local communities should be the anchor for other reform efforts. Locally developed standards are a chance to involve community members, parents, and educators in discussions about what is important for students to know and be able to do, and to define the community's expectations for student achievement. Professional development, instructional materials, curricula, and assessments should be aligned with the standards so that the entire school system is focused on helping students meet these expectations.

The Goals Panel has encouraged the development of world-class, academic standards in key subject areas to inspire greater effort, encourage higher levels of achievement, and measure progress. During the past three years significant steps have been taken by the federal government, as well as a number of states, to support their development.

In June of 1991, upon recommendation of the Goals Panel, Congress established a bipartisan National Council on Education Standards and Testing to advise them on the desirability and feasibility of developing national standards and a system of assessments. In January 1992, the Council issued its report, *Raising Standards for American Education*,[4] which endorsed both the desirability and feasibility of establishing national education standards, as long as they were voluntary, and recommended that such standards should:

- reflect high expectations, not minimal competency;

- provide focus and direction, not become a national curriculum;

- be national in scope, but not federally mandated; and

- be dynamic, not static, in order to keep pace with the development of knowledge.

Following the release of the Council's report, the U.S. Department of Education, other federal agencies, and private foundations awarded grants to private professional organizations to begin a multi-year effort to develop voluntary national standards in key subject areas. These efforts followed the pattern established three years earlier by the National Council of Teachers of Mathematics, who were the first to create standards in their academic discipline.[5]

The Goals Panel convened a task force of advisors to suggest specific review criteria and processes that might be used to review and certify proposed standards submitted voluntarily by these national professional organizations or by states. The advisors' report, *Promises to Keep: Creating High Standards for American Students*,[6] was submitted to the Goals Panel last November. The Goals Panel took that occasion to reiterate its support for local, state, and voluntary national standards by adopting the following statement:

Statement adopted November 15, 1993 by the National Education Goals Panel

The National Education Goals Panel strongly supports the development of clear, rigorous content standards by States and local communities, and it believes that voluntary national standards are essen-tial to this effort. The following principles will serve as the foundation for continuing Goals Panel involvement in establishment of these standards:

Voluntary

The Panel will participate only in the establishment of voluntary national content standards that may serve as models and resources for State and local school reform efforts.

The Panel would oppose any federal effort to require States and local schools to use such national standards.

Academic

The Panel believes that voluntary national content standards should address only core academic areas, such as those stated in the National Education Goals.

> The Goals Panel has encouraged the development of world-class, academic education standards in key subject areas to inspire greater effort, encourage higher levels of achievement, and measure progress.

Voluntary national content standards should not address non-academic areas such as student values, beliefs, attitudes, and behaviors.

World-Class

The Panel will endorse only those national content standards which, though uniquely American, are at least as challenging and rigorous as the academic expectations for students in other countries of the world.

Voluntary national content standards must not be compromised or watered down for any reason. The Panel believes that our focus should be on helping each student reach higher levels of academic achievement.

Bottom-Up Development

National and State content standards must be developed through a consensus-building process that involves educators, parents and community leaders from schools and neighborhoods across the country.

For these voluntary national education standards to be useful, they must be relevant to each community using them. The Panel has no intention of developing content standards on its own and would oppose any standards that were not developed through a broad-based, participatory process.

Useful and Adaptable

National voluntary content standards must allow local educators the flexibility to design their own curriculum plans within the broad outlines of the standards. Standards should focus upon a limited set of the most important and lasting knowledge and skills, so they are useful for teachers, parents and students, and represent the most important knowledge, skills and understandings we expect students to learn.

Voluntary national content standards will not be a "national curriculum" but, rather, provide a broad outline of the kind of knowledge and skills necessary "for responsible citizenship, further learning, and productive employment in our modern economy." (Goal 3)

Federal legislation to help coordinate the emerging standards was passed into law in March 1994 in the *Goals 2000: Educate America Act. Goals 2000* created a National Education Standards and Improvement Council (NESIC) to review and certify standards that are submitted voluntarily by professional organizations and by states. NESIC and the Goals Panel will work cooperatively to ensure that standards are of the highest quality.

The Goals Panel believes that standards need to be broadly discussed and adapted by states and localities to express their own priorities. *Goals 2000* makes provision for awards of federal dollars to states and communities to engage in a broad-based process of setting goals and standards sensitive to state and local priorities and aligning other education policies to them. Standards developed by national organizations and then approved by NESIC and the Goals Panel may prove invaluable resources to states and communities, but it is the standards and

efforts of the states and communities themselves that will be decisive in improving the entire system of education.

Gathering and Using Data for Education Improvement

Gathering and using data to make informed decisions that will lead to education improvement is a central tenet of the Goals Process, and collecting appropriate, complete, and reliable data should be a priority at all levels of governance. Federal, state, and local officials have a responsibility to monitor their progress, to share what they have done, and to use the data they collect to hold their policies and public systems accountable. At the 1994 annual meeting of the National Governors' Association, Governors affirmed their commitment to the "invention of a new education system" and to the constitutional responsibility of the states, not the federal government, to make that happen. Nevertheless, the Governors want the federal level to identify "areas where appropriate data to measure progress on achieving the Goals are not available and initiate data collection in such areas."

The Goals Panel finds that serious gaps still exist in our ability to measure educational progress at the national and state levels in comparable ways. The gaps are starkly evident in charts which portray the current data collection schedules for the Goals Panel's sixteen core indicators (see Tables 5 and 6), and in the state pages which appear in Appendix A.

At the national level the most glaring needs for information are in the nine academic subjects listed in Goal 3 in which students are expected to demonstrate competency in challenging subject matter. There are no current plans to collect student achievement data in civics, economics, or foreign languages through the National Assessment of Educational Progress (NAEP) before the year 2000, and there are no current plans to collect data more than once in history, geography, and the arts. While funding is proposed in the U.S. Department of Education's

> Gathering and using data to make informed decisions that will lead to education improvement is a central tenet of the Goals Process, and collecting appropriate, complete, and reliable data should be a priority at all levels of governance.

budget to administer national-level NAEP assessments in 1998 and 2000, no decision about which subjects will be assessed has been made. Additional national updates will also be needed before the end of the decade for family-child reading and storytelling, preschool participation, international mathematics and science comparisons, adult education participation, and particularly for adult literacy, since no further data collection is planned beyond the 1992 baseline.

At the state level, the picture is even bleaker. Though many states do collect and report data annually to monitor their own progress toward the Goals, what we primarily lack are *comparable* measures of state performance which use uniform definitions, sampling procedures, and methods of collection. At present, comparable state data will be collected regularly for only a few of the Goals Panel's sixteen core indicators. Promising news is that states have been working cooperatively with the U.S. Department of Education for the past several years to develop annual, comparable measures of high school dropout and completion rates. These data will be included in annual Goals Reports when they become available.

For the other core indicators, comparable state data will be almost nonexistent. In fact, fewer state-level achievement data were collected in 1994 than in 1992. As is the case with national-level NAEP assessments, funding is proposed in the U.S. Department of Education's budget to administer state-level NAEP assessments in 1998 and 2000, but the subjects to be assessed have not been determined. States that are calibrating their own assessment programs to NAEP need a predictable schedule of which subjects will be assessed in NAEP and when.

But simply collecting more data will not produce better results. Instead, we must ensure that the efforts and expense invested in collecting data are appropriate, are directed toward filling the most critical gaps in our knowledge about our educational progress, and yield comparable, reliable information that truly becomes a useful tool for policymakers. The Goals Panel will formally organize a task force to work with federal, state, and local data providers and data users to address these ongoing needs.

The following questions are those we need to ask in order to remedy the extensive gaps and build a solid information system that will enable us to gauge our progress:

- *Do we have what we need?* All presumptions about what are necessary data should be reviewed to ensure that what is being collected will actually answer the most important questions to be addressed. Moreover, consideration must be given to whether the data are collected and reported frequently enough to enable policymakers to monitor progress and answer those questions. On a national level, data must not only be comparable among states (e.g., by using uniform definitions to measure dropout rates), but must also be commonly collected by all states or by the federal government for all of the states.

- *Is it integrated?* An integrated data collection plan would ensure both horizontal and vertical alignment of resources and coordination of effort. That is, individual agencies (e.g., departments of education, labor, health and human services) across different levels of government (e.g., federal, state, and local) would coordinate their data needs and cooperate in the collection and analysis of the data.

- *Does it make good use of education information technology?* Taking advantage of advanced technologies to design and carry out data collection systems can make them more accurate and timely. Quality education technology information systems should be comprehensive, easy to use, locally accessible, and connected to other systems. Effective and full use of technology can also reduce costs.

- *Does it protect privacy?* While new technologies can greatly improve data collection, they also must be thoughtfully employed, especially in ways that avoid invasion of privacy regarding children and their families.

> Though many states do collect and report data annually to monitor their own progress toward the Goals, what we primarily lack are comparable measures of state performance.

Table 5
Data Collection Schedule for Core Indicators at the National Level

Indicator	1990	'91	'92	'93	'94	'95	'96	'97	'98	'99	2000
Children's Health Index	X	X	X	X	X	X	X	X	X	X	X
Immunizations			X	X	X	X	X	X	X	X	X
Family-Child Reading and Storytelling				X		X	X				
Preschool Participation		X		X		X	X				
High School Completion			X	X	X	X	X	X	X	X	X
Student Achievement[1] (Grades 4, 8, and 12)											
Reading[2]	X		X		X						
Writing[3]	X		X								
Mathematics	X		X				X				
Science[4]	X						X				
Foreign Languages											
Civics and Government											
Economics											
Arts							X				
History					X						
Geography					X						
International Mathematics Achievement Comparisons											
IAEP[5]		X									
TIMSS[6]						X					
International Science Achievement Comparisons											
IAEP[5]		X									
TIMSS[6]						X					
Adult Literacy			X								
Participation in Adult Education		X				X					
Participation in Higher Education											
College Enrollment	X	X	X	X	X	X	X	X	X	X	X
College Completion			X	X	X	X	X	X	X	X	X
Overall Student Drug and Alcohol Use		X	X	X	X	X	X	X	X	X	X
Sale of Drugs at School			X	X	X	X	X	X	X	X	X
Student and Teacher Victimization		S,T	S	S	S,T	S	S	S	S,T	S	S
Disruptions in Class by Students (student, teacher reports)		T	S	S	S,T	S	S	S	S,T	S	S

[1] Funding has been proposed in the U.S. Department of Education's budget to administer both national- and state-level NAEP assessments in 1998 and 2000, but no decision has been made about which subjects will be assessed.

[2] In 1990, average reading scores were reported; student achievement levels were not established until 1992.

[3] In 1990 and 1992, average writing scores were reported; student achievement levels were not established.

[4] In 1990, average science scores were reported; student achievement levels were not established.

[5] IAEP is the International Assessment of Educational Progress.

[6] TIMSS is the Third International Mathematics and Science Study.

Table 6
Data Collection Schedule for Core Indicators at the State Level

Indicator	1990	'91	'92	'93	'94	'95	'96	'97	'98	'99	2000
Children's Health Index	X	X	X	X	X	X	X	X	X	X	X
Immunizations					X	X	X	X			
Family-Child Reading and Storytelling											
Preschool Participation											
High School Completion	X										X
Student Achievement[1]											
Reading											
Grade 4			X		X						
Grade 8											
Grade 12											
Writing											
Mathematics											
Grade 4			X				X				
Grade 8	X		X				X				
Grade 12							X				
Science											
Grade 4							X				
Grade 8							X				
Grade 12							X				
Foreign Languages											
Civics and Government											
Economics											
Arts											
History											
Geography											
International Mathematics Achievement Comparisons			X								
International Science Achievement Comparisons											
Adult Literacy			X								
Participation in Adult Education											
Participation in Higher Education											
Overall Student Drug and Alcohol Use	X	X		X		X		X		X	
Sale of Drugs at School				X		X		X		X	
Student and Teacher Victimization				S		S		S		S	
Disruptions in Class by Students											

[1] Funding has been proposed in the U.S. Department of Education's budget to administer both national- and state-level NAEP assessments in 1998 and 2000, but no decision has been made about which subjects will be assessed.

- *Is it cost-efficient?* Eliminating duplication of effort is one way to make data collection more cost-efficient, but the value and importance of data must also be considered in relation to their cost. Some important information which is currently unavailable will require new investments to collect and analyze it. However, other information that is being gathered may no longer be needed, which could offset the costs of new data collections.

- *Is it timely?* Policymaking needs are moving too rapidly to rely on traditional data collections that often provide essential information too late to be useful. A lag of even a year on major data items — considered a rapid turnover in the past — can skew policymaking and make decisions more costly.

- *Does it allow disaggregation?* Collecting general categories of data provides general pictures. Issues related to race and gender, for example, are obscured when data collection systems do not take them into account and the real dimensions of a problem cannot be analyzed. For example, the likelihood of dropping out of school varies greatly by the age, gender, and race of students. Disaggregation of data allows policymakers to target dropout prevention efforts to those at greatest risk of leaving school early.

The Goals Panel proposes that one of the most important and immediate actions that should be taken at all levels to help achieve the National Education Goals is to improve current data collection plans.

Federal Responsibilities

The Goals Panel proposes that one of the most important and immediate actions that should be taken at the federal level to help achieve the National Education Goals is to address improvements in current data collection plans. The Panel recommends that the Administration and Congress:

- Coordinate the collection of data necessary to measure progress toward the National Education Goals across and within agencies.

- Ensure more timely collection and dissemination of data by employing new technology, interim census reports, and fast-collection strategies developed by the National Center for Education Statistics.

- Allocate sufficient funding to allow the continued assessment of the academic knowledge and skills of U.S. students on NAEP and on international assessments in order to support the Goals Panel's mandate to benchmark U.S. educational performance against world-class standards.

- Continue to provide technical assistance and seed money for states to improve and coordinate their data-gathering efforts, including employing new technology, to ensure uniform data collection, sampling, and reporting methods which yield comparable state data.

State Responsibilities

States, too, need sound data. As pointed out in the National Governors' Association's 1994 statement, the National Education Goals are performance oriented "with a commitment to achieving results, rather than to maintaining existing procedures, practices, or institutions." In order to know whether improvement is taking place, states need sophisticated, comprehensive data-gathering systems.

Therefore, the Goals Panel recommends that states:

- Work with other states and with federal agencies such as the National Center for Education Statistics to make data-gathering systems related to the National Education Goals compatible.

- Design long-term evaluations of educational performance.

- Assume leadership for engaging the public in discussions about what is important for all students to know and be able to do, and how best to measure the results.

- Ensure that data systems collect adequate information to allow disaggregation of results for different student subpopulations to make certain that education reforms address the needs of all students.

Local Responsibilities

Finally, the Goals Panel recommends that in order to develop an exemplary data system nationwide, local communities will need to:

- Determine the specific indicators of progress that will tell the community what it needs to know about the success of local education initiatives. The Goals Panel's new Community Action Toolkit includes a *Local Goals Reporting Handbook* to help communities do this.

- Design data collection systems that will allow school-level data to be reported so that parents can determine whether their own child's school is performing to expectations.

- Consider the needs of the "consumers" of education, such as parents, employers, and institutions of higher education, when measuring and reporting educational progress. For example, high school graduation rates are only a partial evaluation of a school's effectiveness. Additional data that would be of particular interest to local employers, colleges, and universities might be the proportion of the school's graduates who possess the types of skills that local employers say they want, the proportion who meet the admissions requirements established by the local college or university, or the proportion of the school's graduates entering college who require remedial work.

Conclusion

This 1994 *National Education Goals Report* represents a significant departure from previous Goals Panel reports. In the past, the Report's primary focus was to measure where the nation and states stood in relation to the National Education Goals. This year, the charge of the Goals Panel has been broadened to identify not simply where we are, but where we *should* be, and the level of effort it will require from all citizens to move national and state performance in the right direction. In response to this broader charge, this year's Report focuses greater attention on the interpretation of data, analysis of trends, and recommended strategies that will accelerate our progress toward the Goals.

This Report also emphasizes that now more than ever, successful education reform will require policymakers to align federal, state, and local education policies and work collaboratively to achieve the Goals. Strengthening partnerships between federal, state, and local participants in the education system will allow greater flexibility in decisionmaking and will support innovative state and local reforms. Two priorities that the Panel believes should be immediately addressed by federal, state, and local levels of governance are supporting the development of clear, challenging academic education standards, and improving our capacity to collect and analyze information needed to make well-informed decisions that will benefit children and schools.

But governmental efforts will not bring about the long-term, nationwide education reforms that the United States needs unless parents, students, teachers, higher education, business, and community leaders are actively involved, too. The Goals Panel encourages all states and local communities to implement the Goals Process: adopt the National Education Goals, set high expectations for students and schools, create accountability systems to measure progress, and regularly monitor and report results. The National Education Goals should be considered only the starting points for local decisionmaking. State and local participation is necessary to make the Goals relevant to local conditions and reachable through local actions.

ENDNOTES

[1] P.L. 103-227.

[2] P.L. 103-239.

[3] P.L. 103-66.

[4] National Council on Education Standards and Testing. (1992, January 24). *Raising standards for American education*. Washington, DC: U.S. Government Printing Office.

[5] National Council of Teachers of Mathematics. (1989, March). *Curriculum and evaluation standards for school mathematics*. Reston, VA: author.

[6] Goals 3 and 4 Technical Planning Group. (1993, November 15). *Promises to keep: Creating high standards for American students*. (Technical Report No. 94-01). Washington, DC: National Education Goals Panel.

Appendices

2000

1994

Appendix A: State Progress on Core Indicators

The Goals Panel is charged with monitoring and reporting national and state progress toward the National Education Goals. National progress on a set of core indicators was discussed in Chapter 2. In this Appendix, state progress on the same set of core indicators is presented.[1]

The core indicators were selected with the assistance of members of the Goals Panel's Resource and Technical Planning Groups, who were asked to recommend a small set of indicators for the core that were, to the extent possible:[2]

- comprehensive across the Goals;
- most critical in determining whether the Goals are actually achieved;
- policy-actionable, so that policymakers and the public will have a better understanding of what they can do to improve education performance; and
- updated at frequent intervals, so that the Panel can provide regular progress reports.

It is important to understand that the indicators selected for the core are not necessarily the ideal measures of progress, nor are they all policy-actionable. They do represent, however, the best currently available measures at the national level. Unfortunately, at the state level comparable data are limited. At this time, comparable data are available for only nine of the sixteen core indicators. Not all states have data for all of these indicators.[3,4]

In future Reports,

- state data will be available for the second core indicator, immunizations;

- the list of core indicators will be expanded as other central measures become available for the original six Goals (e.g., new state-level information on science achievement) and for the two new Goals on Teacher Education and Professional Development, and Parental Participation;[5] and

- state data on high school dropout and completion rates will be available from the National Center for Education Statistics (NCES) and the states, who have been working to develop comparable measures.

The Goals Panel will formally organize a task force to work with federal, state, and local data providers and data users to develop strategies to fill the most critical data gaps.

Notes

[1] The data for the core indicators for overall student drug and alcohol use, sale of drugs at school, and student victimization are from different sources at the state and national levels. There are two differences in the core indicators: (1) at the national level, information is presented for 10th graders, while at the state level, information is presented for public high school students; and (2) overall student drug and alcohol use during the previous year is reported at the national level, but overall use during the previous month is reported at the state level.

[2] The importance of each of the core indicators is discussed in Chapter 2.

[3] Table 6 in Chapter 3 points out that few comparable state data are available.

[4] States choose whether to participate in national data collections that have a state representative component, such as NCES' National Assessment of Educational Progress, NCES' National Adult Literacy Survey, and the Centers for Disease Control and Prevention's Youth Risk Behavior Survey (YRBS). States must pay to participate in the NCES data collections; participation in the YRBS is at no cost to the states.

[5] A more comprehensive set of indicators for each Goal can be found in the 1994 National and State Data Volumes.

Guide to Reading the National and State Pages

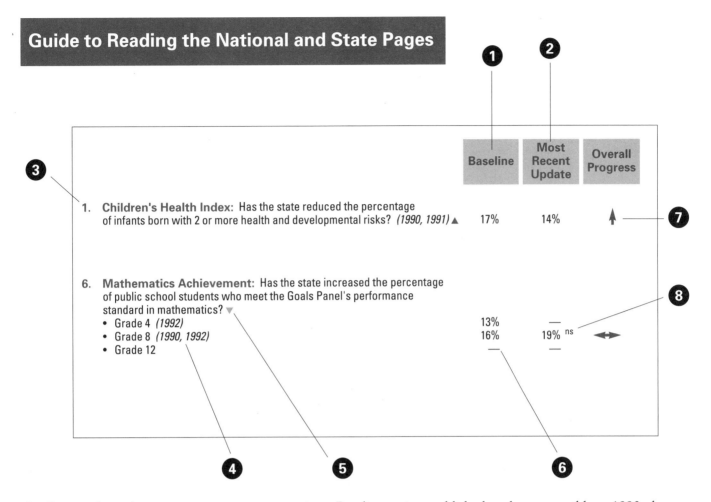

1. Children's Health Index: Has the state reduced the percentage of infants born with 2 or more health and developmental risks? *(1990, 1991)* ▲ Baseline 17% Most Recent Update 14% Overall Progress ↑

6. Mathematics Achievement: Has the state increased the percentage of public school students who meet the Goals Panel's performance standard in mathematics? ▼
- Grade 4 *(1992)* 13% —
- Grade 8 *(1990, 1992)* 16% 19% ns ↔
- Grade 12 — —

1 Data in this column represent our starting points. Baselines were established as close as possible to 1990, the year that the National Education Goals were adopted.

2 Data in this column represent our current level of performance and are the most recent data available.

3 The source of the data for each core indicator is referenced by this number in Appendix B.

4 The date or dates in parentheses indicates the year(s) in which data were collected for the core indicator. If there are two dates, the first indicates the baseline year and the second indicates the most recent year in which data were collected.

5 Triangles and squares indicate a technical note; see bottom of the page for the location of the note.

6 — means data not available.

7 Overall progress is shown by an arrow. Arrows which point upward indicate that we have made significant progress. Arrows which point downward indicate that we have fallen further behind. Horizontal arrows indicate that performance has not changed or that the change was not statistically significant.

8 **ns** means that a change from the baseline year to the most recent year was not statistically significant.

	Baseline	Most Recent Update	Overall Progress
1. Children's Health Index: Has the U.S. reduced the percentage of infants born with 2 or more health and developmental risks? *(1990, 1991)* ▲	14%	13%	↑
2. Immunizations: Has the U.S. increased the percentage of 2-year-olds who have been fully immunized against preventable childhood diseases? *(1992)*	55%	—	
3. Family-Child Reading and Storytelling: Has the U.S. increased the percentage of 3- to 5-year-olds whose parents read to them or tell them stories regularly? *(1993)*	66%	—	
4. Preschool Participation: Has the U.S. reduced the gap in preschool participation between 3- to 5-year-olds from high- and low-income families? *(1991, 1993)*	28 points	28 points	↔
5. High School Completion: Has the U.S. increased the percentage of 19- to 20-year-olds who have a high school credential? *(1992, 1993)*	87%	86% ns	↔
6. Mathematics Achievement: Has the U.S. increased the percentage of students who meet the Goals Panel's performance standard in mathematics? ▼ • Grade 4 *(1990, 1992)* • Grade 8 *(1990, 1992)* • Grade 12 *(1990, 1992)*	 13% 20% 13%	 18% 25% 16% ns	 ↑ ↑ ↔
7. Reading Achievement: Has the U.S. increased the percentage of students who meet the Goals Panel's performance standard in reading? ▼ • Grade 4 *(1992)* • Grade 8 *(1992)* • Grade 12 *(1992)*	 25% 28% 37%	 — — —	
8. International Mathematics Achievement: Has the U.S. improved its standing on international mathematics assessments of 13-year-olds? *(1991)* ●	U.S. below 5 out of 5 countries	—	
9. International Science Achievement: Has the U.S. improved its standing on international science assessments of 13-year-olds? *(1991)* ●	U.S. below 3 out of 5 countries	—	
10. Adult Literacy: Has the U.S. increased the percentage of adults who score at or above Level 3 in prose literacy? *(1992)* ■	52%	—	
11. Participation in Adult Education: Has the U.S. reduced the gap in adult education participation between adults who have a high school diploma or less, and those who have additional post-secondary education or technical training? *(1991)*	27 points	—	
12. Participation in Higher Education: Has the U.S. reduced the gap between White and Black high school graduates who: • enroll in college? *(1990, 1992)* • complete a college degree? *(1992, 1993)* Has the U.S. reduced the gap between White and Hispanic high school graduates who: • enroll in college? *(1990, 1992)* • complete a college degree? *(1992, 1993)*	 14 points 16 points 11 points 12 points	 14 points 17 points ns 6 points ns 18 points ns	 ↔ ↔ ↔ ↔
13. Overall Student Drug and Alcohol Use: Has the U.S. reduced the percentage of 10th graders reporting doing the following during the previous year: • using any illicit drug? *(1991, 1993)* ■ • using alcohol? *(1991, 1993)*	 24% 72%	 27% 69%	 ↓ ↑
14. Sale of Drugs at School: Has the U.S. reduced the percentage of 10th graders reporting that someone offered to sell or give them an illegal drug at school during the previous year? *(1992, 1993)*	18%	20% ns	↔
15. Student and Teacher Victimization: Has the U.S. reduced the percentage of students and teachers reporting that they were threatened or injured at school during the previous year? • 10th graders *(1991, 1993)* • public school teachers *(1991)*	 40% 10%	 35% —	 ↑
16. Disruptions in Class by Students: Has the U.S. reduced the percentage of students and teachers reporting that disruptions often interfere with teaching and learning? • 10th grade students *(1992, 1993)* • high school teachers *(1991)*	 17% 33%	 18% ns —	 ↔

— Data not available.
ns Interpret with caution. Change was not statistically significant.

▲ See technical note on page 133.
▼ See technical note on pages 134-135.
● See technical note on pages 135-136.

■ See technical note on page 136.
■ See technical note on page 137.

ALABAMA

	Baseline	Most Recent Update	Overall Progress
1. Children's Health Index: Has the state reduced the percentage of infants born with 2 or more health and developmental risks? *(1990, 1991)* ▲	14%	12%	↑
2. Immunizations: Has the state increased the percentage of 2-year-olds who have been fully immunized against preventable childhood diseases?	—	—	
3. Family-Child Reading and Storytelling: Has the state increased the percentage of 3- to 5-year-olds whose parents read to them or tell them stories regularly?	—	—	
4. Preschool Participation: Has the state reduced the gap in preschool participation between 3- to 5-year-olds from high- and low-income families?	—	—	
5. High School Completion: Has the state increased the percentage of 19- to 20-year-olds who have a high school credential? *(1990)*	82%	—	
6. Mathematics Achievement: Has the state increased the percentage of public school students who meet the Goals Panel's performance standard in mathematics? ▼			
• Grade 4 *(1992)*	10%	—	
• Grade 8 *(1990, 1992)*	12%	12%	↔
• Grade 12	—	—	
7. Reading Achievement: Has the state increased the percentage of public school students who meet the Goals Panel's performance standard in reading? ▼			
• Grade 4 *(1992)*	17%	—	
• Grade 8	—	—	
• Grade 12	—	—	
8. International Mathematics Achievement: Has the state reduced the gap between the percentage of public school 8th graders and the percentage of 13-year-olds in the highest-scoring country who meet the Goals Panel's performance standard in mathematics? *(1991 and 1992)*	29 percentage points	—	
9. International Science Achievement: Has the state reduced the gap between the percentage of public school 8th graders and the percentage of 13-year-olds in the highest-scoring country who meet the Goals Panel's performance standard in science?	—	—	
10. Adult Literacy: Has the state increased the percentage of adults who score at or above Level 3 in prose literacy? *(1992)* ■	—	—	
11. Participation in Adult Education: Has the state reduced the gap in adult education participation between adults who have a high school diploma or less, and those who have additional post-secondary education or technical training?	—	—	
12. Participation in Higher Education: Has the state reduced the gap between White and minority high school graduates who:			
• enroll in college?	—	—	
• complete a college degree?	—	—	
13. Overall Student Drug and Alcohol Use: Has the state reduced the percentage of public high school students reporting doing the following during the past 30 days: ■			
• using marijuana at least once? *(1990, 1993)*	7%	10% ns	↔
• having 5 or more drinks in a row? *(1990, 1993)*	35%	25%	↑
14. Sale of Drugs at School: Has the state reduced the percentage of public high school students reporting that someone offered, sold, or gave them an illegal drug on school property during the past 12 months? *(1993)* ■	18%	—	
15. Student and Teacher Victimization: Has the state reduced the percentage of students and teachers reporting that they were threatened or injured on school property during the past 12 months?			
• public high school students *(1993)* ■	—	—	
• public school teachers	—	—	
16. Disruptions in Class by Students: Has the state reduced the percentage of students and teachers reporting that disruptions often interfere with teaching and learning?			
• high school students	—	—	
• high school teachers	—	—	

— Data not available.
ns Interpret with caution. Change was not statistically significant.

▲ See technical note on page 133.
▼ See technical note on pages 134-135.

■ See technical note on page 136.
■ See technical note on page 137.

ALASKA

	Baseline	Most Recent Update	Overall Progress

1. **Children's Health Index:** Has the state reduced the percentage of infants born with 2 or more health and developmental risks? *(1990, 1991)* ▲ — 18% — 19% — ↓

2. **Immunizations:** Has the state increased the percentage of 2-year-olds who have been fully immunized against preventable childhood diseases? — —

3. **Family-Child Reading and Storytelling:** Has the state increased the percentage of 3- to 5-year-olds whose parents read to them or tell them stories regularly? — —

4. **Preschool Participation:** Has the state reduced the gap in preschool participation between 3- to 5-year-olds from high- and low-income families? — —

5. **High School Completion:** Has the state increased the percentage of 19- to 20-year-olds who have a high school credential? *(1990)* — 85% — —

6. **Mathematics Achievement:** Has the state increased the percentage of public school students who meet the Goals Panel's performance standard in mathematics? ▼
   - Grade 4 *(1992)* — —
   - Grade 8 *(1990, 1992)* — —
   - Grade 12 — —

7. **Reading Achievement:** Has the state increased the percentage of public school students who meet the Goals Panel's performance standard in reading? ▼
   - Grade 4 *(1992)* — —
   - Grade 8 — —
   - Grade 12 — —

8. **International Mathematics Achievement:** Has the state reduced the gap between the percentage of public school 8th graders and the percentage of 13-year-olds in the highest-scoring country who meet the Goals Panel's performance standard in mathematics? *(1991 and 1992)* — —

9. **International Science Achievement:** Has the state reduced the gap between the percentage of public school 8th graders and the percentage of 13-year-olds in the highest-scoring country who meet the Goals Panel's performance standard in science? — —

10. **Adult Literacy:** Has the state increased the percentage of adults who score at or above Level 3 in prose literacy? *(1992)* ■ — —

11. **Participation in Adult Education:** Has the state reduced the gap in adult education participation between adults who have a high school diploma or less, and those who have additional post-secondary education or technical training? — —

12. **Participation in Higher Education:** Has the state reduced the gap between White and minority high school graduates who:
    - enroll in college? — —
    - complete a college degree? — —

13. **Overall Student Drug and Alcohol Use:** Has the state reduced the percentage of public high school students reporting doing the following during the past 30 days: ■
    - using marijuana at least once? *(1990, 1993)* — —
    - having 5 or more drinks in a row? *(1990, 1993)* — —

14. **Sale of Drugs at School:** Has the state reduced the percentage of public high school students reporting that someone offered, sold, or gave them an illegal drug on school property during the past 12 months? *(1993)* ■ — —

15. **Student and Teacher Victimization:** Has the state reduced the percentage of students and teachers reporting that they were threatened or injured on school property during the past 12 months?
    - public high school students *(1993)* ■ — —
    - public school teachers — —

16. **Disruptions in Class by Students:** Has the state reduced the percentage of students and teachers reporting that disruptions often interfere with teaching and learning?
    - high school students — —
    - high school teachers — —

— Data not available.
ns Interpret with caution. Change was not statistically significant.

▲ See technical note on page 133.
▼ See technical note on pages 134-135.

■ See technical note on page 136.
■ See technical note on page 137.

ARIZONA

	Baseline	Most Recent Update	Overall Progress

1. **Children's Health Index:** Has the state reduced the percentage of infants born with 2 or more health and developmental risks? *(1990, 1991)* ▲ — 17% — 14% — ↑

2. **Immunizations:** Has the state increased the percentage of 2-year-olds who have been fully immunized against preventable childhood diseases? — —

3. **Family-Child Reading and Storytelling:** Has the state increased the percentage of 3- to 5-year-olds whose parents read to them or tell them stories regularly? — —

4. **Preschool Participation:** Has the state reduced the gap in preschool participation between 3- to 5-year-olds from high- and low-income families? — —

5. **High School Completion:** Has the state increased the percentage of 19- to 20-year-olds who have a high school credential? *(1990)* — 80% — —

6. **Mathematics Achievement:** Has the state increased the percentage of public school students who meet the Goals Panel's performance standard in mathematics? ▼
   - Grade 4 *(1992)* — 13% — —
   - Grade 8 *(1990, 1992)* — 16% — 19% ns — ↔
   - Grade 12 — —

7. **Reading Achievement:** Has the state increased the percentage of public school students who meet the Goals Panel's performance standard in reading? ▼
   - Grade 4 *(1992)* — 18% — —
   - Grade 8 — —
   - Grade 12 — —

8. **International Mathematics Achievement:** Has the state reduced the gap between the percentage of public school 8th graders and the percentage of 13-year-olds in the highest-scoring country who meet the Goals Panel's performance standard in mathematics? *(1991 and 1992)* — 22 percentage points — —

9. **International Science Achievement:** Has the state reduced the gap between the percentage of public school 8th graders and the percentage of 13-year-olds in the highest-scoring country who meet the Goals Panel's performance standard in science? — —

10. **Adult Literacy:** Has the state increased the percentage of adults who score at or above Level 3 in prose literacy? *(1992)* ■ — —

11. **Participation in Adult Education:** Has the state reduced the gap in adult education participation between adults who have a high school diploma or less, and those who have additional post-secondary education or technical training? — —

12. **Participation in Higher Education:** Has the state reduced the gap between White and minority high school graduates who:
    - enroll in college? — —
    - complete a college degree? — —

13. **Overall Student Drug and Alcohol Use:** Has the state reduced the percentage of public high school students reporting doing the following during the past 30 days: ■
    - using marijuana at least once? *(1990, 1993)* — —
    - having 5 or more drinks in a row? *(1990, 1993)* — —

14. **Sale of Drugs at School:** Has the state reduced the percentage of public high school students reporting that someone offered, sold, or gave them an illegal drug on school property during the past 12 months? *(1993)* ■ — —

15. **Student and Teacher Victimization:** Has the state reduced the percentage of students and teachers reporting that they were threatened or injured on school property during the past 12 months?
    - public high school students *(1993)* ■ — —
    - public school teachers — —

16. **Disruptions in Class by Students:** Has the state reduced the percentage of students and teachers reporting that disruptions often interfere with teaching and learning?
    - high school students — —
    - high school teachers — —

— Data not available.
ns Interpret with caution. Change was not statistically significant.

▲ See technical note on page 133.
▼ See technical note on pages 134-135.

■ See technical note on page 136.
■ See technical note on page 137.

ARKANSAS

	Baseline	Most Recent Update	Overall Progress
1. **Children's Health Index:** Has the state reduced the percentage of infants born with 2 or more health and developmental risks? *(1990, 1991)* ▲	16%	15%	↑
2. **Immunizations:** Has the state increased the percentage of 2-year-olds who have been fully immunized against preventable childhood diseases?	—	—	
3. **Family-Child Reading and Storytelling:** Has the state increased the percentage of 3- to 5-year-olds whose parents read to them or tell them stories regularly?	—	—	
4. **Preschool Participation:** Has the state reduced the gap in preschool participation between 3- to 5-year-olds from high- and low-income families?	—	—	
5. **High School Completion:** Has the state increased the percentage of 19- to 20-year-olds who have a high school credential? *(1990)*	83%	—	
6. **Mathematics Achievement:** Has the state increased the percentage of public school students who meet the Goals Panel's performance standard in mathematics? ▼			
• Grade 4 *(1992)*	10%	—	
• Grade 8 *(1990, 1992)*	12%	13% ns	↔
• Grade 12	—		
7. **Reading Achievement:** Has the state increased the percentage of public school students who meet the Goals Panel's performance standard in reading? ▼			
• Grade 4 *(1992)*	20%	—	
• Grade 8	—	—	
• Grade 12	—	—	
8. **International Mathematics Achievement:** Has the state reduced the gap between the percentage of public school 8th graders and the percentage of 13-year-olds in the highest-scoring country who meet the Goals Panel's performance standard in mathematics? *(1991 and 1992)*	28 percentage points	—	
9. **International Science Achievement:** Has the state reduced the gap between the percentage of public school 8th graders and the percentage of 13-year-olds in the highest-scoring country who meet the Goals Panel's performance standard in science?	—	—	
10. **Adult Literacy:** Has the state increased the percentage of adults who score at or above Level 3 in prose literacy? *(1992)* ■	—	—	
11. **Participation in Adult Education:** Has the state reduced the gap in adult education participation between adults who have a high school diploma or less, and those who have additional post-secondary education or technical training?	—	—	
12. **Participation in Higher Education:** Has the state reduced the gap between White and minority high school graduates who:			
• enroll in college?	—	—	
• complete a college degree?	—	—	
13. **Overall Student Drug and Alcohol Use:** Has the state reduced the percentage of public high school students reporting doing the following during the past 30 days: ■			
• using marijuana at least once? *(1990, 1993)*	—	—	
• having 5 or more drinks in a row? *(1990, 1993)*	—	—	
14. **Sale of Drugs at School:** Has the state reduced the percentage of public high school students reporting that someone offered, sold, or gave them an illegal drug on school property during the past 12 months? *(1993)* ■	—	—	
15. **Student and Teacher Victimization:** Has the state reduced the percentage of students and teachers reporting that they were threatened or injured on school property during the past 12 months?			
• public high school students *(1993)* ■	—	—	
• public school teachers	—	—	
16. **Disruptions in Class by Students:** Has the state reduced the percentage of students and teachers reporting that disruptions often interfere with teaching and learning?			
• high school students	—	—	
• high school teachers	—	—	

— Data not available.
ns Interpret with caution. Change was not statistically significant.

▲ See technical note on page 133.
▼ See technical note on pages 134-135.

■ See technical note on page 136.
■ See technical note on page 137.

CALIFORNIA

	Baseline	Most Recent Update	Overall Progress
1. Children's Health Index: Has the state reduced the percentage of infants born with 2 or more health and developmental risks? *(1990, 1991)* ▲	—	—	
2. Immunizations: Has the state increased the percentage of 2-year-olds who have been fully immunized against preventable childhood diseases?	—	—	
3. Family-Child Reading and Storytelling: Has the state increased the percentage of 3- to 5-year-olds whose parents read to them or tell them stories regularly?	—	—	
4. Preschool Participation: Has the state reduced the gap in preschool participation between 3- to 5-year-olds from high- and low-income families?	—	—	
5. High School Completion: Has the state increased the percentage of 19- to 20-year-olds who have a high school credential? *(1990)*	77%	—	
6. Mathematics Achievement: Has the state increased the percentage of public school students who meet the Goals Panel's performance standard in mathematics? ▼			
• Grade 4 *(1992)*	13%	—	
• Grade 8 *(1990, 1992)*	16%	20% ns	←→
• Grade 12	—		
7. Reading Achievement: Has the state increased the percentage of public school students who meet the Goals Panel's performance standard in reading? ▼			
• Grade 4 *(1992)*	17%	—	
• Grade 8	—	—	
• Grade 12	—	—	
8. International Mathematics Achievement: Has the state reduced the gap between the percentage of public school 8th graders and the percentage of 13-year-olds in the highest-scoring country who meet the Goals Panel's performance standard in mathematics? *(1991 and 1992)*	21 percentage points	—	
9. International Science Achievement: Has the state reduced the gap between the percentage of public school 8th graders and the percentage of 13-year-olds in the highest-scoring country who meet the Goals Panel's performance standard in science?	—	—	
10. Adult Literacy: Has the state increased the percentage of adults who score at or above Level 3 in prose literacy? *(1992)* ■	—	—	
11. Participation in Adult Education: Has the state reduced the gap in adult education participation between adults who have a high school diploma or less, and those who have additional post-secondary education or technical training?	—	—	
12. Participation in Higher Education: Has the state reduced the gap between White and minority high school graduates who:			
• enroll in college?	—	—	
• complete a college degree?	—	—	
13. Overall Student Drug and Alcohol Use: Has the state reduced the percentage of public high school students reporting doing the following during the past 30 days: ■			
• using marijuana at least once? *(1990, 1993)*	—	—	
• having 5 or more drinks in a row? *(1990, 1993)*	—	—	
14. Sale of Drugs at School: Has the state reduced the percentage of public high school students reporting that someone offered, sold, or gave them an illegal drug on school property during the past 12 months? *(1993)* ■	—	—	
15. Student and Teacher Victimization: Has the state reduced the percentage of students and teachers reporting that they were threatened or injured on school property during the past 12 months?			
• public high school students *(1993)* ■	—	—	
• public school teachers	—	—	
16. Disruptions in Class by Students: Has the state reduced the percentage of students and teachers reporting that disruptions often interfere with teaching and learning?			
• high school students	—	—	
• high school teachers	—	—	

— Data not available.
ns Interpret with caution. Change was not statistically significant.

▲ See technical note on page 133.
▼ See technical note on pages 134-135.

■ See technical note on page 136.
■ See technical note on page 137.

COLORADO

	Baseline	Most Recent Update	Overall Progress
1. Children's Health Index: Has the state reduced the percentage of infants born with 2 or more health and developmental risks? *(1990, 1991)* ▲	13%	12%	↑
2. Immunizations: Has the state increased the percentage of 2-year-olds who have been fully immunized against preventable childhood diseases?	—	—	
3. Family-Child Reading and Storytelling: Has the state increased the percentage of 3- to 5-year-olds whose parents read to them or tell them stories regularly?	—	—	
4. Preschool Participation: Has the state reduced the gap in preschool participation between 3- to 5-year-olds from high- and low-income families?	—	—	
5. High School Completion: Has the state increased the percentage of 19- to 20-year-olds who have a high school credential? *(1990)*	87%	—	
6. Mathematics Achievement: Has the state increased the percentage of public school students who meet the Goals Panel's performance standard in mathematics? ▼			
• Grade 4 *(1992)*	18%	—	
• Grade 8 *(1990, 1992)*	22%	26%	↑
• Grade 12	—		
7. Reading Achievement: Has the state increased the percentage of public school students who meet the Goals Panel's performance standard in reading? ▼			
• Grade 4 *(1992)*	22%	—	
• Grade 8	—	—	
• Grade 12	—	—	
8. International Mathematics Achievement: Has the state reduced the gap between the percentage of public school 8th graders and the percentage of 13-year-olds in the highest-scoring country who meet the Goals Panel's performance standard in mathematics? *(1991 and 1992)*	15 percentage points	—	
9. International Science Achievement: Has the state reduced the gap between the percentage of public school 8th graders and the percentage of 13-year-olds in the highest-scoring country who meet the Goals Panel's performance standard in science?	—	—	
10. Adult Literacy: Has the state increased the percentage of adults who score at or above Level 3 in prose literacy? *(1992)* ■	—	—	
11. Participation in Adult Education: Has the state reduced the gap in adult education participation between adults who have a high school diploma or less, and those who have additional post-secondary education or technical training?	—	—	
12. Participation in Higher Education: Has the state reduced the gap between White and minority high school graduates who:			
• enroll in college?	—	—	
• complete a college degree?	—	—	
13. Overall Student Drug and Alcohol Use: Has the state reduced the percentage of public high school students reporting doing the following during the past 30 days: ■			
• using marijuana at least once? *(1990, 1993)*	16%	—	
• having 5 or more drinks in a row? *(1990, 1993)*	38%	—	
14. Sale of Drugs at School: Has the state reduced the percentage of public high school students reporting that someone offered, sold, or gave them an illegal drug on school property during the past 12 months? *(1993)* ■	—	—	
15. Student and Teacher Victimization: Has the state reduced the percentage of students and teachers reporting that they were threatened or injured on school property during the past 12 months?			
• public high school students *(1993)* ■	—	—	
• public school teachers	—	—	
16. Disruptions in Class by Students: Has the state reduced the percentage of students and teachers reporting that disruptions often interfere with teaching and learning?			
• high school students	—	—	
• high school teachers	—	—	

— Data not available.
ns Interpret with caution. Change was not statistically significant.

▲ See technical note on page 133.
▼ See technical note on pages 134-135.

■ See technical note on page 136.
■ See technical note on page 137.

CONNECTICUT

	Baseline	Most Recent Update	Overall Progress

1. **Children's Health Index:** Has the state reduced the percentage of infants born with 2 or more health and developmental risks? *(1990, 1991)* ▲ — 8% — 9% — ↓

2. **Immunizations:** Has the state increased the percentage of 2-year-olds who have been fully immunized against preventable childhood diseases? — —

3. **Family-Child Reading and Storytelling:** Has the state increased the percentage of 3- to 5-year-olds whose parents read to them or tell them stories regularly? — —

4. **Preschool Participation:** Has the state reduced the gap in preschool participation between 3- to 5-year-olds from high- and low-income families? — —

5. **High School Completion:** Has the state increased the percentage of 19- to 20-year-olds who have a high school credential? *(1990)* — 88% — —

6. **Mathematics Achievement:** Has the state increased the percentage of public school students who meet the Goals Panel's performance standard in mathematics? ▼
   - Grade 4 *(1992)* — 25% — —
   - Grade 8 *(1990, 1992)* — 26% — 30% — ↑
   - Grade 12 — —

7. **Reading Achievement:** Has the state increased the percentage of public school students who meet the Goals Panel's performance standard in reading? ▼
   - Grade 4 *(1992)* — 30% — —
   - Grade 8 — —
   - Grade 12 — —

8. **International Mathematics Achievement:** Has the state reduced the gap between the percentage of public school 8th graders and the percentage of 13-year-olds in the highest-scoring country who meet the Goals Panel's performance standard in mathematics? *(1991 and 1992)* — 11 percentage points — —

9. **International Science Achievement:** Has the state reduced the gap between the percentage of public school 8th graders and the percentage of 13-year-olds in the highest-scoring country who meet the Goals Panel's performance standard in science? — —

10. **Adult Literacy:** Has the state increased the percentage of adults who score at or above Level 3 in prose literacy? *(1992)* ■ — —

11. **Participation in Adult Education:** Has the state reduced the gap in adult education participation between adults who have a high school diploma or less, and those who have additional post-secondary education or technical training? — —

12. **Participation in Higher Education:** Has the state reduced the gap between White and minority high school graduates who:
    - enroll in college? — —
    - complete a college degree? — —

13. **Overall Student Drug and Alcohol Use:** Has the state reduced the percentage of public high school students reporting doing the following during the past 30 days: ■
    - using marijuana at least once? *(1990, 1993)* — —
    - having 5 or more drinks in a row? *(1990, 1993)* — —

14. **Sale of Drugs at School:** Has the state reduced the percentage of public high school students reporting that someone offered, sold, or gave them an illegal drug on school property during the past 12 months? *(1993)* ■ — —

15. **Student and Teacher Victimization:** Has the state reduced the percentage of students and teachers reporting that they were threatened or injured on school property during the past 12 months?
    - public high school students *(1993)* ■ — —
    - public school teachers — —

16. **Disruptions in Class by Students:** Has the state reduced the percentage of students and teachers reporting that disruptions often interfere with teaching and learning?
    - high school students — —
    - high school teachers — —

— Data not available.
ns Interpret with caution. Change was not statistically significant.

▲ See technical note on page 133.
▼ See technical note on pages 134-135.

■ See technical note on page 136.
■ See technical note on page 137.

81

DELAWARE

	Baseline	Most Recent Update	Overall Progress

1. **Children's Health Index:** Has the state reduced the percentage of infants born with 2 or more health and developmental risks? *(1990, 1991)* ▲

	15%	15%	↔

2. **Immunizations:** Has the state increased the percentage of 2-year-olds who have been fully immunized against preventable childhood diseases?

| | — | — | |

3. **Family-Child Reading and Storytelling:** Has the state increased the percentage of 3- to 5-year-olds whose parents read to them or tell them stories regularly?

| | — | — | |

4. **Preschool Participation:** Has the state reduced the gap in preschool participation between 3- to 5-year-olds from high- and low-income families?

| | — | — | |

5. **High School Completion:** Has the state increased the percentage of 19- to 20-year-olds who have a high school credential? *(1990)*

| | 88% | — | |

6. **Mathematics Achievement:** Has the state increased the percentage of public school students who meet the Goals Panel's performance standard in mathematics? ▼
   - Grade 4 *(1992)*
   - Grade 8 *(1990, 1992)*
   - Grade 12

	Baseline	Most Recent Update	Overall Progress
Grade 4	17%	—	
Grade 8	19%	18% ns	↔
Grade 12	—	—	

7. **Reading Achievement:** Has the state increased the percentage of public school students who meet the Goals Panel's performance standard in reading? ▼
   - Grade 4 *(1992)*
   - Grade 8
   - Grade 12

	Baseline	Most Recent Update	
Grade 4	21%	—	
Grade 8	—	—	
Grade 12	—	—	

8. **International Mathematics Achievement:** Has the state reduced the gap between the percentage of public school 8th graders and the percentage of 13-year-olds in the highest-scoring country who meet the Goals Panel's performance standard in mathematics? *(1991 and 1992)*

| | 23 percentage points | — | |

9. **International Science Achievement:** Has the state reduced the gap between the percentage of public school 8th graders and the percentage of 13-year-olds in the highest-scoring country who meet the Goals Panel's performance standard in science?

| | — | — | |

10. **Adult Literacy:** Has the state increased the percentage of adults who score at or above Level 3 in prose literacy? *(1992)* ■

| | — | — | |

11. **Participation in Adult Education:** Has the state reduced the gap in adult education participation between adults who have a high school diploma or less, and those who have additional post-secondary education or technical training?

| | — | — | |

12. **Participation in Higher Education:** Has the state reduced the gap between White and minority high school graduates who:
   - enroll in college?
   - complete a college degree?

	—	—	
enroll in college	—	—	
complete a college degree	—	—	

13. **Overall Student Drug and Alcohol Use:** Has the state reduced the percentage of public high school students reporting doing the following during the past 30 days: ■
   - using marijuana at least once? *(1990, 1993)*
   - having 5 or more drinks in a row? *(1990, 1993)*

| | — | — | |
| — | — | |

14. **Sale of Drugs at School:** Has the state reduced the percentage of public high school students reporting that someone offered, sold, or gave them an illegal drug on school property during the past 12 months? *(1993)* ■

| | — | — | |

15. **Student and Teacher Victimization:** Has the state reduced the percentage of students and teachers reporting that they were threatened or injured on school property during the past 12 months?
   - public high school students *(1993)* ■
   - public school teachers

| | — | — | |
| — | — | |

16. **Disruptions in Class by Students:** Has the state reduced the percentage of students and teachers reporting that disruptions often interfere with teaching and learning?
   - high school students
   - high school teachers

| | — | — | |
| — | — | |

— Data not available.
ns Interpret with caution. Change was not statistically significant.

▲ See technical note on page 133.
▼ See technical note on pages 134-135.

■ See technical note on page 136.
■ See technical note on page 137.

	Baseline	Most Recent Update	Overall Progress
1. **Children's Health Index:** Has the District reduced the percentage of infants born with 2 or more health and developmental risks? *(1990, 1991)*▲	23%	22%	↑
2. **Immunizations:** Has the District increased the percentage of 2-year-olds who have been fully immunized against preventable childhood diseases?	—	—	
3. **Family-Child Reading and Storytelling:** Has the District increased the percentage of 3- to 5-year-olds whose parents read to them or tell them stories regularly?	—	—	
4. **Preschool Participation:** Has the District reduced the gap in preschool participation between 3- to 5-year-olds from high- and low-income families?	—	—	
5. **High School Completion:** Has the District increased the percentage of 19- to 20-year-olds who have a high school credential? *(1990)*	83%	—	
6. **Mathematics Achievement:** Has the District increased the percentage of public school students who meet the Goals Panel's performance standard in mathematics? ▼			
• Grade 4 *(1992)*	6%	—	
• Grade 8 *(1990, 1992)*	4%	6% ns	↔
• Grade 12	—	—	
7. **Reading Achievement:** Has the District increased the percentage of public school students who meet the Goals Panel's performance standard in reading? ▼			
• Grade 4 *(1992)*	8%	—	
• Grade 8	—	—	
• Grade 12	—	—	
8. **International Mathematics Achievement:** Has the District reduced the gap between the percentage of public school 8th graders and the percentage of 13-year-olds in the highest-scoring country who meet the Goals Panel's performance standard in mathematics? *(1991 and 1992)*	35 percentage points	—	
9. **International Science Achievement:** Has the District reduced the gap between the percentage of public school 8th graders and the percentage of 13-year-olds in the highest-scoring country who meet the Goals Panel's performance standard in science?	—	—	
10. **Adult Literacy:** Has the District increased the percentage of adults who score at or above Level 3 in prose literacy? *(1992)*■	—	—	
11. **Participation in Adult Education:** Has the District reduced the gap in adult education participation between adults who have a high school diploma or less, and those who have additional post-secondary education or technical training?	—	—	
12. **Participation in Higher Education:** Has the District reduced the gap between White and minority high school graduates who:			
• enroll in college?	—	—	
• complete a college degree?	—	—	
13. **Overall Student Drug and Alcohol Use:** Has the District reduced the percentage of public high school students reporting doing the following during the past 30 days: ■			
• using marijuana at least once? *(1993)*	18%	—	
• having 5 or more drinks in a row? *(1990, 1993)*	17%	16% ns	↔
14. **Sale of Drugs at School:** Has the District reduced the percentage of public high school students reporting that someone offered, sold, or gave them an illegal drug on school property during the past 12 months? *(1993)*■	16%	—	
15. **Student and Teacher Victimization:** Has the District reduced the percentage of students and teachers reporting that they were threatened or injured on school property during the past 12 months?			
• public high school students *(1993)*■	11%	—	
• public school teachers	—	—	
16. **Disruptions in Class by Students:** Has the District reduced the percentage of students and teachers reporting that disruptions often interfere with teaching and learning?			
• high school students	—	—	
• high school teachers	—	—	

— Data not available.
ns Interpret with caution. Change was not statistically significant.

▲ See technical note on page 133.
▼ See technical note on pages 134-135.

■ See technical note on page 136.
■ See technical note on page 137.

FLORIDA

	Baseline	Most Recent Update	Overall Progress
1. **Children's Health Index:** Has the state reduced the percentage of infants born with 2 or more health and developmental risks? *(1990, 1991)* ▲	15%	13%	↑
2. **Immunizations:** Has the state increased the percentage of 2-year-olds who have been fully immunized against preventable childhood diseases?	—	—	
3. **Family-Child Reading and Storytelling:** Has the state increased the percentage of 3- to 5-year-olds whose parents read to them or tell them stories regularly?	—	—	
4. **Preschool Participation:** Has the state reduced the gap in preschool participation between 3- to 5-year-olds from high- and low-income families?	—	—	
5. **High School Completion:** Has the state increased the percentage of 19- to 20-year-olds who have a high school credential? *(1990)*	79%	—	
6. **Mathematics Achievement:** Has the state increased the percentage of public school students who meet the Goals Panel's performance standard in mathematics? ▼ • Grade 4 *(1992)* • Grade 8 *(1990, 1992)* • Grade 12	 14% 15% —	 — 18% ns —	 ↔
7. **Reading Achievement:** Has the state increased the percentage of public school students who meet the Goals Panel's performance standard in reading? ▼ • Grade 4 *(1992)* • Grade 8 • Grade 12	 18% — —	 — — —	
8. **International Mathematics Achievement:** Has the state reduced the gap between the percentage of public school 8th graders and the percentage of 13-year-olds in the highest-scoring country who meet the Goals Panel's performance standard in mathematics? *(1991 and 1992)*	23 percentage points	—	
9. **International Science Achievement:** Has the state reduced the gap between the percentage of public school 8th graders and the percentage of 13-year-olds in the highest-scoring country who meet the Goals Panel's performance standard in science?	—	—	
10. **Adult Literacy:** Has the state increased the percentage of adults who score at or above Level 3 in prose literacy? *(1992)* ■	51%	—	
11. **Participation in Adult Education:** Has the state reduced the gap in adult education participation between adults who have a high school diploma or less, and those who have additional post-secondary education or technical training?	—	—	
12. **Participation in Higher Education:** Has the state reduced the gap between White and minority high school graduates who: • enroll in college? • complete a college degree?	 — —	 — —	
13. **Overall Student Drug and Alcohol Use:** Has the state reduced the percentage of public high school students reporting doing the following during the past 30 days: ■ • using marijuana at least once? *(1990, 1993)* • having 5 or more drinks in a row? *(1990, 1993)*	 — —	 — —	
14. **Sale of Drugs at School:** Has the state reduced the percentage of public high school students reporting that someone offered, sold, or gave them an illegal drug on school property during the past 12 months? *(1993)* ■	—	—	
15. **Student and Teacher Victimization:** Has the state reduced the percentage of students and teachers reporting that they were threatened or injured on school property during the past 12 months? • public high school students *(1993)* ■ • public school teachers	 — —	 — —	
16. **Disruptions in Class by Students:** Has the state reduced the percentage of students and teachers reporting that disruptions often interfere with teaching and learning? • high school students • high school teachers	 — —	 — —	

— Data not available.
ns Interpret with caution. Change was not statistically significant.

▲ See technical note on page 133.
▼ See technical note on pages 134-135.

■ See technical note on page 136.
■ See technical note on page 137.

	Baseline	Most Recent Update	Overall Progress
1. Children's Health Index: Has the state reduced the percentage of infants born with 2 or more health and developmental risks? *(1990, 1991)* ▲	14%	12%	↑
2. Immunizations: Has the state increased the percentage of 2-year-olds who have been fully immunized against preventable childhood diseases?	—	—	
3. Family-Child Reading and Storytelling: Has the state increased the percentage of 3- to 5-year-olds whose parents read to them or tell them stories regularly?	—	—	
4. Preschool Participation: Has the state reduced the gap in preschool participation between 3- to 5-year-olds from high- and low-income families?	—	—	
5. High School Completion: Has the state increased the percentage of 19- to 20-year-olds who have a high school credential? *(1990)*	80%	—	
6. Mathematics Achievement: Has the state increased the percentage of public school students who meet the Goals Panel's performance standard in mathematics? ▼			
• Grade 4 *(1992)*	16%	—	
• Grade 8 *(1990, 1992)*	17%	16% ns	↔
• Grade 12	—	—	
7. Reading Achievement: Has the state increased the percentage of public school students who meet the Goals Panel's performance standard in reading? ▼			
• Grade 4 *(1992)*	22%	—	
• Grade 8	—	—	
• Grade 12	—	—	
8. International Mathematics Achievement: Has the state reduced the gap between the percentage of public school 8th graders and the percentage of 13-year-olds in the highest-scoring country who meet the Goals Panel's performance standard in mathematics? *(1991 and 1992)*	25 percentage points	—	
9. International Science Achievement: Has the state reduced the gap between the percentage of public school 8th graders and the percentage of 13-year-olds in the highest-scoring country who meet the Goals Panel's performance standard in science?	—	—	
10. Adult Literacy: Has the state increased the percentage of adults who score at or above Level 3 in prose literacy? *(1992)* ■	—	—	
11. Participation in Adult Education: Has the state reduced the gap in adult education participation between adults who have a high school diploma or less, and those who have additional post-secondary education or technical training?	—	—	
12. Participation in Higher Education: Has the state reduced the gap between White and minority high school graduates who:			
• enroll in college?	—	—	
• complete a college degree?	—	—	
13. Overall Student Drug and Alcohol Use: Has the state reduced the percentage of public high school students reporting doing the following during the past 30 days: ■			
• using marijuana at least once? *(1990, 1993)*	9%	14%	↓
• having 5 or more drinks in a row? *(1990, 1993)*	31%	25% ns	↔
14. Sale of Drugs at School: Has the state reduced the percentage of public high school students reporting that someone offered, sold, or gave them an illegal drug on school property during the past 12 months? *(1993)* ■	21%	—	
15. Student and Teacher Victimization: Has the state reduced the percentage of students and teachers reporting that they were threatened or injured on school property during the past 12 months?			
• public high school students *(1993)* ■	9%	—	
• public school teachers	—	—	
16. Disruptions in Class by Students: Has the state reduced the percentage of students and teachers reporting that disruptions often interfere with teaching and learning?			
• high school students	—	—	
• high school teachers	—	—	

— Data not available.
ns Interpret with caution. Change was not statistically significant.

▲ See technical note on page 133.
▼ See technical note on pages 134-135.

■ See technical note on page 136.
■ See technical note on page 137.

HAWAII

	Baseline	Most Recent Update	Overall Progress
1. **Children's Health Index:** Has the state reduced the percentage of infants born with 2 or more health and developmental risks? *(1990, 1991)* ▲	11%	12%	↓
2. **Immunizations:** Has the state increased the percentage of 2-year-olds who have been fully immunized against preventable childhood diseases?	—	—	
3. **Family-Child Reading and Storytelling:** Has the state increased the percentage of 3- to 5-year-olds whose parents read to them or tell them stories regularly?	—	—	
4. **Preschool Participation:** Has the state reduced the gap in preschool participation between 3- to 5-year-olds from high- and low-income families?	—	—	
5. **High School Completion:** Has the state increased the percentage of 19- to 20-year-olds who have a high school credential? *(1990)*	91%	—	
6. **Mathematics Achievement:** Has the state increased the percentage of public school students who meet the Goals Panel's performance standard in mathematics? ▼ • Grade 4 *(1992)* • Grade 8 *(1990, 1992)* • Grade 12	15% 14%	— 16% ns	↔
7. **Reading Achievement:** Has the state increased the percentage of public school students who meet the Goals Panel's performance standard in reading? ▼ • Grade 4 *(1992)* • Grade 8 • Grade 12	15% — —	— — —	
8. **International Mathematics Achievement:** Has the state reduced the gap between the percentage of public school 8th graders and the percentage of 13-year-olds in the highest-scoring country who meet the Goals Panel's performance standard in mathematics? *(1991 and 1992)*	25 percentage points	—	
9. **International Science Achievement:** Has the state reduced the gap between the percentage of public school 8th graders and the percentage of 13-year-olds in the highest-scoring country who meet the Goals Panel's performance standard in science?	—	—	
10. **Adult Literacy:** Has the state increased the percentage of adults who score at or above Level 3 in prose literacy? *(1992)* ■	—	—	
11. **Participation in Adult Education:** Has the state reduced the gap in adult education participation between adults who have a high school diploma or less, and those who have additional post-secondary education or technical training?	—	—	
12. **Participation in Higher Education:** Has the state reduced the gap between White and minority high school graduates who: • enroll in college? • complete a college degree?	— —	— —	
13. **Overall Student Drug and Alcohol Use:** Has the state reduced the percentage of public high school students reporting doing the following during the past 30 days: ■ • using marijuana at least once? *(1993)* • having 5 or more drinks in a row? *(1993)*	17% 23%	— —	
14. **Sale of Drugs at School:** Has the state reduced the percentage of public high school students reporting that someone offered, sold, or gave them an illegal drug on school property during the past 12 months? *(1993)* ■	26%	—	
15. **Student and Teacher Victimization:** Has the state reduced the percentage of students and teachers reporting that they were threatened or injured on school property during the past 12 months? • public high school students *(1993)* ■ • public school teachers	7% —	— —	
16. **Disruptions in Class by Students:** Has the state reduced the percentage of students and teachers reporting that disruptions often interfere with teaching and learning? • high school students • high school teachers	— —	— —	

— Data not available.
ns Interpret with caution. Change was not statistically significant.

▲ See technical note on page 133.
▼ See technical note on pages 134-135.

■ See technical note on page 136.
■ See technical note on page 137.

IDAHO

	Baseline	Most Recent Update	Overall Progress
1. **Children's Health Index:** Has the state reduced the percentage of infants born with 2 or more health and developmental risks? *(1990, 1991)* ▲	16%	15%	↑
2. **Immunizations:** Has the state increased the percentage of 2-year-olds who have been fully immunized against preventable childhood diseases?	—	—	
3. **Family-Child Reading and Storytelling:** Has the state increased the percentage of 3- to 5-year-olds whose parents read to them or tell them stories regularly?	—	—	
4. **Preschool Participation:** Has the state reduced the gap in preschool participation between 3- to 5-year-olds from high- and low-income families?	—	—	
5. **High School Completion:** Has the state increased the percentage of 19- to 20-year-olds who have a high school credential? *(1990)*	86%	—	
6. **Mathematics Achievement:** Has the state increased the percentage of public school students who meet the Goals Panel's performance standard in mathematics? ▼ • Grade 4 *(1992)* • Grade 8 *(1990, 1992)* • Grade 12	16% 23% —	— 27% ns —	↔
7. **Reading Achievement:** Has the state increased the percentage of public school students who meet the Goals Panel's performance standard in reading? ▼ • Grade 4 *(1992)* • Grade 8 • Grade 12	24% — —	— — —	
8. **International Mathematics Achievement:** Has the state reduced the gap between the percentage of public school 8th graders and the percentage of 13-year-olds in the highest-scoring country who meet the Goals Panel's performance standard in mathematics? *(1991 and 1992)*	14 percentage points	—	
9. **International Science Achievement:** Has the state reduced the gap between the percentage of public school 8th graders and the percentage of 13-year-olds in the highest-scoring country who meet the Goals Panel's performance standard in science?	—	—	
10. **Adult Literacy:** Has the state increased the percentage of adults who score at or above Level 3 in prose literacy? *(1992)* ■	—	—	
11. **Participation in Adult Education:** Has the state reduced the gap in adult education participation between adults who have a high school diploma or less, and those who have additional post-secondary education or technical training?	—	—	
12. **Participation in Higher Education:** Has the state reduced the gap between White and minority high school graduates who: • enroll in college? • complete a college degree?	— —	— —	
13. **Overall Student Drug and Alcohol Use:** Has the state reduced the percentage of public high school students reporting doing the following during the past 30 days: ■ • using marijuana at least once? *(1991, 1993)* • having 5 or more drinks in a row? *(1991, 1993)*	10% 30%	13% ns 31% ns	↔ ↔
14. **Sale of Drugs at School:** Has the state reduced the percentage of public high school students reporting that someone offered, sold, or gave them an illegal drug on school property during the past 12 months? *(1993)* ■	24%	—	
15. **Student and Teacher Victimization:** Has the state reduced the percentage of students and teachers reporting that they were threatened or injured on school property during the past 12 months? • public high school students *(1993)* ■ • public school teachers	8% —	— —	
16. **Disruptions in Class by Students:** Has the state reduced the percentage of students and teachers reporting that disruptions often interfere with teaching and learning? • high school students • high school teachers	— —	— —	

— Data not available.
ns Interpret with caution. Change was not statistically significant.

▲ See technical note on page 133.
▼ See technical note on pages 134-135.

■ See technical note on page 136.
■ See technical note on page 137.

ILLINOIS

	Baseline	Most Recent Update	Overall Progress
1. Children's Health Index: Has the state reduced the percentage of infants born with 2 or more health and developmental risks? *(1990, 1991)* ▲	14%	13%	↑
2. Immunizations: Has the state increased the percentage of 2-year-olds who have been fully immunized against preventable childhood diseases?	—	—	
3. Family-Child Reading and Storytelling: Has the state increased the percentage of 3- to 5-year-olds whose parents read to them or tell them stories regularly?	—	—	
4. Preschool Participation: Has the state reduced the gap in preschool participation between 3- to 5-year-olds from high- and low-income families?	—	—	
5. High School Completion: Has the state increased the percentage of 19- to 20-year-olds who have a high school credential? *(1990)*	86%	—	
6. Mathematics Achievement: Has the state increased the percentage of public school students who meet the Goals Panel's performance standard in mathematics? ▼			
• Grade 4 *(1992)*	—	—	
• Grade 8 *(1990, 1992)*	—	—	
• Grade 12	—	—	
7. Reading Achievement: Has the state increased the percentage of public school students who meet the Goals Panel's performance standard in reading? ▼			
• Grade 4 *(1992)*	—	—	
• Grade 8	—	—	
• Grade 12	—	—	
8. International Mathematics Achievement: Has the state reduced the gap between the percentage of public school 8th graders and the percentage of 13-year-olds in the highest-scoring country who meet the Goals Panel's performance standard in mathematics? *(1991 and 1992)*	—	—	
9. International Science Achievement: Has the state reduced the gap between the percentage of public school 8th graders and the percentage of 13-year-olds in the highest-scoring country who meet the Goals Panel's performance standard in science?	—	—	
10. Adult Literacy: Has the state increased the percentage of adults who score at or above Level 3 in prose literacy? *(1992)* ■	52%	—	
11. Participation in Adult Education: Has the state reduced the gap in adult education participation between adults who have a high school diploma or less, and those who have additional post-secondary education or technical training?	—	—	
12. Participation in Higher Education: Has the state reduced the gap between White and minority high school graduates who:			
• enroll in college?	—	—	
• complete a college degree?	—	—	
13. Overall Student Drug and Alcohol Use: Has the state reduced the percentage of public high school students reporting doing the following during the past 30 days: ■			
• using marijuana at least once? *(1993)*	14%	—	
• having 5 or more drinks in a row? *(1993)*	28%	—	
14. Sale of Drugs at School: Has the state reduced the percentage of public high school students reporting that someone offered, sold, or gave them an illegal drug on school property during the past 12 months? *(1993)* ■	19%	—	
15. Student and Teacher Victimization: Has the state reduced the percentage of students and teachers reporting that they were threatened or injured on school property during the past 12 months?			
• public high school students *(1993)* ■	8%	—	
• public school teachers	—	—	
16. Disruptions in Class by Students: Has the state reduced the percentage of students and teachers reporting that disruptions often interfere with teaching and learning?			
• high school students	—	—	
• high school teachers	—	—	

— Data not available.
ns Interpret with caution. Change was not statistically significant.

▲ See technical note on page 133.
▼ See technical note on pages 134-135.

■ See technical note on page 136.
■ See technical note on page 137.

INDIANA

	Baseline	Most Recent Update	Overall Progress

1. **Children's Health Index:** Has the state reduced the percentage of infants born with 2 or more health and developmental risks? *(1990, 1991)* ▲ — —

2. **Immunizations:** Has the state increased the percentage of 2-year-olds who have been fully immunized against preventable childhood diseases? — —

3. **Family-Child Reading and Storytelling:** Has the state increased the percentage of 3- to 5-year-olds whose parents read to them or tell them stories regularly? — —

4. **Preschool Participation:** Has the state reduced the gap in preschool participation between 3- to 5-year-olds from high- and low-income families? — —

5. **High School Completion:** Has the state increased the percentage of 19- to 20-year-olds who have a high school credential? *(1990)*   86%   —

6. **Mathematics Achievement:** Has the state increased the percentage of public school students who meet the Goals Panel's performance standard in mathematics? ▼
   - Grade 4 *(1992)*   16%   —
   - Grade 8 *(1990, 1992)*   21%   24% ns   ◄►
   - Grade 12   — —

7. **Reading Achievement:** Has the state increased the percentage of public school students who meet the Goals Panel's performance standard in reading? ▼
   - Grade 4 *(1992)*   27%   —
   - Grade 8   — —
   - Grade 12   — —

8. **International Mathematics Achievement:** Has the state reduced the gap between the percentage of public school 8th graders and the percentage of 13-year-olds in the highest-scoring country who meet the Goals Panel's performance standard in mathematics? *(1991 and 1992)*   17 percentage points   —

9. **International Science Achievement:** Has the state reduced the gap between the percentage of public school 8th graders and the percentage of 13-year-olds in the highest-scoring country who meet the Goals Panel's performance standard in science? — —

10. **Adult Literacy:** Has the state increased the percentage of adults who score at or above Level 3 in prose literacy? *(1992)* ■   58%   —

11. **Participation in Adult Education:** Has the state reduced the gap in adult education participation between adults who have a high school diploma or less, and those who have additional post-secondary education or technical training? — —

12. **Participation in Higher Education:** Has the state reduced the gap between White and minority high school graduates who:
    - enroll in college?   — —
    - complete a college degree?   — —

13. **Overall Student Drug and Alcohol Use:** Has the state reduced the percentage of public high school students reporting doing the following during the past 30 days: ■
    - using marijuana at least once? *(1990, 1993)*   — —
    - having 5 or more drinks in a row? *(1990, 1993)*   — —

14. **Sale of Drugs at School:** Has the state reduced the percentage of public high school students reporting that someone offered, sold, or gave them an illegal drug on school property during the past 12 months? *(1993)* ■   — —

15. **Student and Teacher Victimization:** Has the state reduced the percentage of students and teachers reporting that they were threatened or injured on school property during the past 12 months?
    - public high school students *(1993)* ■   — —
    - public school teachers   — —

16. **Disruptions in Class by Students:** Has the state reduced the percentage of students and teachers reporting that disruptions often interfere with teaching and learning?
    - high school students   — —
    - high school teachers   — —

— Data not available.
ns Interpret with caution. Change was not statistically significant.

▲ See technical note on page 133.
▼ See technical note on pages 134-135.

■ See technical note on page 136.
■ See technical note on page 137.

IOWA

	Baseline	Most Recent Update	Overall Progress
1. Children's Health Index: Has the state reduced the percentage of infants born with 2 or more health and developmental risks? *(1990, 1991)* ▲	15%	14%	↑
2. Immunizations: Has the state increased the percentage of 2-year-olds who have been fully immunized against preventable childhood diseases?	—	—	
3. Family-Child Reading and Storytelling: Has the state increased the percentage of 3- to 5-year-olds whose parents read to them or tell them stories regularly?	—	—	
4. Preschool Participation: Has the state reduced the gap in preschool participation between 3- to 5-year-olds from high- and low-income families?	—	—	
5. High School Completion: Has the state increased the percentage of 19- to 20-year-olds who have a high school credential? *(1990)*	93%	—	
6. Mathematics Achievement: Has the state increased the percentage of public school students who meet the Goals Panel's performance standard in mathematics? ▼ • Grade 4 *(1992)* • Grade 8 *(1990, 1992)* • Grade 12	 27% 30% —	 — 37% —	 ↑
7. Reading Achievement: Has the state increased the percentage of public school students who meet the Goals Panel's performance standard in reading? ▼ • Grade 4 *(1992)* • Grade 8 • Grade 12	 32% — —	 — — —	
8. International Mathematics Achievement: Has the state reduced the gap between the percentage of public school 8th graders and the percentage of 13-year-olds in the highest-scoring country who meet the Goals Panel's performance standard in mathematics? *(1991 and 1992)*	4 percentage points	—	
9. International Science Achievement: Has the state reduced the gap between the percentage of public school 8th graders and the percentage of 13-year-olds in the highest-scoring country who meet the Goals Panel's performance standard in science?	—	—	
10. Adult Literacy: Has the state increased the percentage of adults who score at or above Level 3 in prose literacy? *(1992)* ■	61%	—	
11. Participation in Adult Education: Has the state reduced the gap in adult education participation between adults who have a high school diploma or less, and those who have additional post-secondary education or technical training?	—	—	
12. Participation in Higher Education: Has the state reduced the gap between White and minority high school graduates who: • enroll in college? • complete a college degree?	 — —	 — —	
13. Overall Student Drug and Alcohol Use: Has the state reduced the percentage of public high school students reporting doing the following during the past 30 days: ■ • using marijuana at least once? *(1990, 1993)* • having 5 or more drinks in a row? *(1990, 1993)*	 — —	 — —	
14. Sale of Drugs at School: Has the state reduced the percentage of public high school students reporting that someone offered, sold, or gave them an illegal drug on school property during the past 12 months? *(1993)* ■	—	—	
15. Student and Teacher Victimization: Has the state reduced the percentage of students and teachers reporting that they were threatened or injured on school property during the past 12 months? • public high school students *(1993)* ■ • public school teachers	 — —	 — —	
16. Disruptions in Class by Students: Has the state reduced the percentage of students and teachers reporting that disruptions often interfere with teaching and learning? • high school students • high school teachers	 — —	 — —	

— Data not available.
ns Interpret with caution. Change was not statistically significant.

▲ See technical note on page 133.
▼ See technical note on pages 134-135.

■ See technical note on page 136.
■ See technical note on page 137.

KANSAS

	Baseline	Most Recent Update	Overall Progress

1. **Children's Health Index:** Has the state reduced the percentage of infants born with 2 or more health and developmental risks? *(1990, 1991)* ▲ — 12% | 11% | ↑

2. **Immunizations:** Has the state increased the percentage of 2-year-olds who have been fully immunized against preventable childhood diseases? — | —

3. **Family-Child Reading and Storytelling:** Has the state increased the percentage of 3- to 5-year-olds whose parents read to them or tell them stories regularly? — | —

4. **Preschool Participation:** Has the state reduced the gap in preschool participation between 3- to 5-year-olds from high- and low-income families? — | —

5. **High School Completion:** Has the state increased the percentage of 19- to 20-year-olds who have a high school credential? *(1990)* — 89% | —

6. **Mathematics Achievement:** Has the state increased the percentage of public school students who meet the Goals Panel's performance standard in mathematics? ▼
   • Grade 4 *(1992)* — | —
   • Grade 8 *(1990, 1992)* — | —
   • Grade 12 — | —

7. **Reading Achievement:** Has the state increased the percentage of public school students who meet the Goals Panel's performance standard in reading? ▼
   • Grade 4 *(1992)* — | —
   • Grade 8 — | —
   • Grade 12 — | —

8. **International Mathematics Achievement:** Has the state reduced the gap between the percentage of public school 8th graders and the percentage of 13-year-olds in the highest-scoring country who meet the Goals Panel's performance standard in mathematics? *(1991 and 1992)* — | —

9. **International Science Achievement:** Has the state reduced the gap between the percentage of public school 8th graders and the percentage of 13-year-olds in the highest-scoring country who meet the Goals Panel's performance standard in science? — | —

10. **Adult Literacy:** Has the state increased the percentage of adults who score at or above Level 3 in prose literacy? *(1992)* ■ — | —

11. **Participation in Adult Education:** Has the state reduced the gap in adult education participation between adults who have a high school diploma or less, and those who have additional post-secondary education or technical training? — | —

12. **Participation in Higher Education:** Has the state reduced the gap between White and minority high school graduates who:
    • enroll in college? — | —
    • complete a college degree? — | —

13. **Overall Student Drug and Alcohol Use:** Has the state reduced the percentage of public high school students reporting doing the following during the past 30 days: ■
    • using marijuana at least once? *(1990, 1993)* — | —
    • having 5 or more drinks in a row? *(1990, 1993)* — | —

14. **Sale of Drugs at School:** Has the state reduced the percentage of public high school students reporting that someone offered, sold, or gave them an illegal drug on school property during the past 12 months? *(1993)* ■ — | —

15. **Student and Teacher Victimization:** Has the state reduced the percentage of students and teachers reporting that they were threatened or injured on school property during the past 12 months?
    • public high school students *(1993)* ■ — | —
    • public school teachers — | —

16. **Disruptions in Class by Students:** Has the state reduced the percentage of students and teachers reporting that disruptions often interfere with teaching and learning?
    • high school students — | —
    • high school teachers — | —

— Data not available.
ns Interpret with caution. Change was not statistically significant.

▲ See technical note on page 133.
▼ See technical note on pages 134-135.

■ See technical note on page 136.
■ See technical note on page 137.

KENTUCKY

	Baseline	Most Recent Update	Overall Progress
1. Children's Health Index: Has the state reduced the percentage of infants born with 2 or more health and developmental risks? *(1990, 1991)* ▲	17%	16%	↑
2. Immunizations: Has the state increased the percentage of 2-year-olds who have been fully immunized against preventable childhood diseases?	—	—	
3. Family-Child Reading and Storytelling: Has the state increased the percentage of 3- to 5-year-olds whose parents read to them or tell them stories regularly?	—	—	
4. Preschool Participation: Has the state reduced the gap in preschool participation between 3- to 5-year-olds from high- and low-income families?	—	—	
5. High School Completion: Has the state increased the percentage of 19- to 20-year-olds who have a high school credential? *(1990)*	82%	—	
6. Mathematics Achievement: Has the state increased the percentage of public school students who meet the Goals Panel's performance standard in mathematics? ▼			
• Grade 4 *(1992)*	13%	—	
• Grade 8 *(1990, 1992)*	14%	17% ns	↔
• Grade 12	—	—	
7. Reading Achievement: Has the state increased the percentage of public school students who meet the Goals Panel's performance standard in reading? ▼			
• Grade 4 *(1992)*	19%	—	
• Grade 8	—	—	
• Grade 12	—	—	
8. International Mathematics Achievement: Has the state reduced the gap between the percentage of public school 8th graders and the percentage of 13-year-olds in the highest-scoring country who meet the Goals Panel's performance standard in mathematics? *(1991 and 1992)*	24 percentage points	—	
9. International Science Achievement: Has the state reduced the gap between the percentage of public school 8th graders and the percentage of 13-year-olds in the highest-scoring country who meet the Goals Panel's performance standard in science?	—	—	
10. Adult Literacy: Has the state increased the percentage of adults who score at or above Level 3 in prose literacy? *(1992)* ■	—	—	
11. Participation in Adult Education: Has the state reduced the gap in adult education participation between adults who have a high school diploma or less, and those who have additional post-secondary education or technical training?	—	—	
12. Participation in Higher Education: Has the state reduced the gap between White and minority high school graduates who:			
• enroll in college?	—	—	
• complete a college degree?	—	—	
13. Overall Student Drug and Alcohol Use: Has the state reduced the percentage of public high school students reporting doing the following during the past 30 days: ■			
• using marijuana at least once? *(1990, 1993)*	—	—	
• having 5 or more drinks in a row? *(1990, 1993)*	—	—	
14. Sale of Drugs at School: Has the state reduced the percentage of public high school students reporting that someone offered, sold, or gave them an illegal drug on school property during the past 12 months? *(1993)* ■	—	—	
15. Student and Teacher Victimization: Has the state reduced the percentage of students and teachers reporting that they were threatened or injured on school property during the past 12 months?			
• public high school students *(1993)* ■	—	—	
• public school teachers	—	—	
16. Disruptions in Class by Students: Has the state reduced the percentage of students and teachers reporting that disruptions often interfere with teaching and learning?			
• high school students	—	—	
• high school teachers	—	—	

— Data not available.
ns Interpret with caution. Change was not statistically significant.

▲ See technical note on page 133.
▼ See technical note on pages 134-135.

■ See technical note on page 136.
■ See technical note on page 137.

LOUISIANA

	Baseline	Most Recent Update	Overall Progress
1. Children's Health Index: Has the state reduced the percentage of infants born with 2 or more health and developmental risks? *(1990, 1991)* ▲	16%	15%	↑
2. Immunizations: Has the state increased the percentage of 2-year-olds who have been fully immunized against preventable childhood diseases?	—	—	
3. Family-Child Reading and Storytelling: Has the state increased the percentage of 3- to 5-year-olds whose parents read to them or tell them stories regularly?	—	—	
4. Preschool Participation: Has the state reduced the gap in preschool participation between 3- to 5-year-olds from high- and low-income families?	—	—	
5. High School Completion: Has the state increased the percentage of 19- to 20-year-olds who have a high school credential? *(1990)*	81%	—	
6. Mathematics Achievement: Has the state increased the percentage of public school students who meet the Goals Panel's performance standard in mathematics? ▼			
• Grade 4 *(1992)*	8%	—	
• Grade 8 *(1990, 1992)*	8%	10% ns	↔
• Grade 12	—	—	
7. Reading Achievement: Has the state increased the percentage of public school students who meet the Goals Panel's performance standard in reading? ▼			
• Grade 4 *(1992)*	13%	—	
• Grade 8	—	—	
• Grade 12	—	—	
8. International Mathematics Achievement: Has the state reduced the gap between the percentage of public school 8th graders and the percentage of 13-year-olds in the highest-scoring country who meet the Goals Panel's performance standard in mathematics? *(1991 and 1992)*	31 percentage points	—	
9. International Science Achievement: Has the state reduced the gap between the percentage of public school 8th graders and the percentage of 13-year-olds in the highest-scoring country who meet the Goals Panel's performance standard in science?	—	—	
10. Adult Literacy: Has the state increased the percentage of adults who score at or above Level 3 in prose literacy? *(1992)* ■	46%	—	
11. Participation in Adult Education: Has the state reduced the gap in adult education participation between adults who have a high school diploma or less, and those who have additional post-secondary education or technical training?	—	—	
12. Participation in Higher Education: Has the state reduced the gap between White and minority high school graduates who:			
• enroll in college?	—	—	
• complete a college degree?	—	—	
13. Overall Student Drug and Alcohol Use: Has the state reduced the percentage of public high school students reporting doing the following during the past 30 days: ■			
• using marijuana at least once? *(1993)*	14%	—	
• having 5 or more drinks in a row? *(1993)*	32%	—	
14. Sale of Drugs at School: Has the state reduced the percentage of public high school students reporting that someone offered, sold, or gave them an illegal drug on school property during the past 12 months? *(1993)* ■	22%	—	
15. Student and Teacher Victimization: Has the state reduced the percentage of students and teachers reporting that they were threatened or injured on school property during the past 12 months?			
• public high school students *(1993)* ■	10%	—	
• public school teachers	—	—	
16. Disruptions in Class by Students: Has the state reduced the percentage of students and teachers reporting that disruptions often interfere with teaching and learning?			
• high school students	—	—	
• high school teachers	—	—	

— Data not available.
ns Interpret with caution. Change was not statistically significant.

▲ See technical note on page 133.
▼ See technical note on pages 134-135.

■ See technical note on page 136.
■ See technical note on page 137.

MAINE

	Baseline	Most Recent Update	Overall Progress
1. Children's Health Index: Has the state reduced the percentage of infants born with 2 or more health and developmental risks? *(1990, 1991)*▲	12%	11%	↑
2. Immunizations: Has the state increased the percentage of 2-year-olds who have been fully immunized against preventable childhood diseases?	—	—	
3. Family-Child Reading and Storytelling: Has the state increased the percentage of 3- to 5-year-olds whose parents read to them or tell them stories regularly?	—	—	
4. Preschool Participation: Has the state reduced the gap in preschool participation between 3- to 5-year-olds from high- and low-income families?	—	—	
5. High School Completion: Has the state increased the percentage of 19- to 20-year-olds who have a high school credential? *(1990)*	90%	—	
6. Mathematics Achievement: Has the state increased the percentage of public school students who meet the Goals Panel's performance standard in mathematics? ▼			
• Grade 4 *(1992)*	28%	—	
• Grade 8 *(1992)*	31%	—	
• Grade 12	—	—	
7. Reading Achievement: Has the state increased the percentage of public school students who meet the Goals Panel's performance standard in reading? ▼			
• Grade 4 *(1992)*	31%	—	
• Grade 8	—	—	
• Grade 12	—	—	
8. International Mathematics Achievement: Has the state reduced the gap between the percentage of public school 8th graders and the percentage of 13-year-olds in the highest-scoring country who meet the Goals Panel's performance standard in mathematics? *(1991 and 1992)*	10 percentage points	—	
9. International Science Achievement: Has the state reduced the gap between the percentage of public school 8th graders and the percentage of 13-year-olds in the highest-scoring country who meet the Goals Panel's performance standard in science?	—	—	
10. Adult Literacy: Has the state increased the percentage of adults who score at or above Level 3 in prose literacy? *(1992)*■	—	—	
11. Participation in Adult Education: Has the state reduced the gap in adult education participation between adults who have a high school diploma or less, and those who have additional post-secondary education or technical training?	—	—	
12. Participation in Higher Education: Has the state reduced the gap between White and minority high school graduates who:			
• enroll in college?	—	—	
• complete a college degree?	—	—	
13. Overall Student Drug and Alcohol Use: Has the state reduced the percentage of public high school students reporting doing the following during the past 30 days: ■			
• using marijuana at least once? *(1990, 1993)*	—	—	
• having 5 or more drinks in a row? *(1990, 1993)*	—	—	
14. Sale of Drugs at School: Has the state reduced the percentage of public high school students reporting that someone offered, sold, or gave them an illegal drug on school property during the past 12 months? *(1993)*■	—	—	
15. Student and Teacher Victimization: Has the state reduced the percentage of students and teachers reporting that they were threatened or injured on school property during the past 12 months?			
• public high school students *(1993)*■	—	—	
• public school teachers	—	—	
16. Disruptions in Class by Students: Has the state reduced the percentage of students and teachers reporting that disruptions often interfere with teaching and learning?			
• high school students	—	—	
• high school teachers	—	—	

— Data not available.
ns Interpret with caution. Change was not statistically significant.

▲ See technical note on page 133.
▼ See technical note on pages 134-135.

■ See technical note on page 136.
■ See technical note on page 137.

MARYLAND

	Baseline	Most Recent Update	Overall Progress
1. Children's Health Index: Has the state reduced the percentage of infants born with 2 or more health and developmental risks? *(1990, 1991)* ▲	11%	12%	↓
2. Immunizations: Has the state increased the percentage of 2-year-olds who have been fully immunized against preventable childhood diseases?	—	—	
3. Family-Child Reading and Storytelling: Has the state increased the percentage of 3- to 5-year-olds whose parents read to them or tell them stories regularly?	—	—	
4. Preschool Participation: Has the state reduced the gap in preschool participation between 3- to 5-year-olds from high- and low-income families?	—	—	
5. High School Completion: Has the state increased the percentage of 19- to 20-year-olds who have a high school credential? *(1990)*	86%	—	
6. Mathematics Achievement: Has the state increased the percentage of public school students who meet the Goals Panel's performance standard in mathematics? ▼			
• Grade 4 *(1992)*	19%	—	
• Grade 8 *(1990, 1992)*	20%	24% ns	↔
• Grade 12	—	—	
7. Reading Achievement: Has the state increased the percentage of public school students who meet the Goals Panel's performance standard in reading? ▼			
• Grade 4 *(1992)*	21%		
• Grade 8	—	—	
• Grade 12	—	—	
8. International Mathematics Achievement: Has the state reduced the gap between the percentage of public school 8th graders and the percentage of 13-year-olds in the highest-scoring country who meet the Goals Panel's performance standard in mathematics? *(1991 and 1992)*	17 percentage points	—	
9. International Science Achievement: Has the state reduced the gap between the percentage of public school 8th graders and the percentage of 13-year-olds in the highest-scoring country who meet the Goals Panel's performance standard in science?	—	—	
10. Adult Literacy: Has the state increased the percentage of adults who score at or above Level 3 in prose literacy? *(1992)* ■	—	—	
11. Participation in Adult Education: Has the state reduced the gap in adult education participation between adults who have a high school diploma or less, and those who have additional post-secondary education or technical training?	—	—	
12. Participation in Higher Education: Has the state reduced the gap between White and minority high school graduates who:			
• enroll in college?	—	—	
• complete a college degree?	—	—	
13. Overall Student Drug and Alcohol Use: Has the state reduced the percentage of public high school students reporting doing the following during the past 30 days: ■			
• using marijuana at least once? *(1990, 1993)*	—	—	
• having 5 or more drinks in a row? *(1990, 1993)*	—	—	
14. Sale of Drugs at School: Has the state reduced the percentage of public high school students reporting that someone offered, sold, or gave them an illegal drug on school property during the past 12 months? *(1993)* ■	—	—	
15. Student and Teacher Victimization: Has the state reduced the percentage of students and teachers reporting that they were threatened or injured on school property during the past 12 months?			
• public high school students *(1993)* ■	—	—	
• public school teachers	—	—	
16. Disruptions in Class by Students: Has the state reduced the percentage of students and teachers reporting that disruptions often interfere with teaching and learning?			
• high school students	—	—	
• high school teachers	—	—	

— Data not available.
ns Interpret with caution. Change was not statistically significant.

▲ See technical note on page 133.
▼ See technical note on pages 134-135.

■ See technical note on page 136.
■ See technical note on page 137.

MASSACHUSETTS

	Baseline	Most Recent Update	Overall Progress
1. Children's Health Index: Has the state reduced the percentage of infants born with 2 or more health and developmental risks? *(1990, 1991)* ▲	20%	19%	↑
2. Immunizations: Has the state increased the percentage of 2-year-olds who have been fully immunized against preventable childhood diseases?	—	—	
3. Family-Child Reading and Storytelling: Has the state increased the percentage of 3- to 5-year-olds whose parents read to them or tell them stories regularly?	—	—	
4. Preschool Participation: Has the state reduced the gap in preschool participation between 3- to 5-year-olds from high- and low-income families?	—	—	
5. High School Completion: Has the state increased the percentage of 19- to 20-year-olds who have a high school credential? *(1990)*	90%	—	
6. Mathematics Achievement: Has the state increased the percentage of public school students who meet the Goals Panel's performance standard in mathematics? ▼			
• Grade 4 *(1992)*	24%	—	
• Grade 8 *(1992)*	28%	—	
• Grade 12	—	—	
7. Reading Achievement: Has the state increased the percentage of public school students who meet the Goals Panel's performance standard in reading? ▼			
• Grade 4 *(1992)*	32%	—	
• Grade 8	—	—	
• Grade 12	—	—	
8. International Mathematics Achievement: Has the state reduced the gap between the percentage of public school 8th graders and the percentage of 13-year-olds in the highest-scoring country who meet the Goals Panel's performance standard in mathematics? *(1991 and 1992)*	13 percentage points	—	
9. International Science Achievement: Has the state reduced the gap between the percentage of public school 8th graders and the percentage of 13-year-olds in the highest-scoring country who meet the Goals Panel's performance standard in science?	—	—	
10. Adult Literacy: Has the state increased the percentage of adults who score at or above Level 3 in prose literacy? *(1992)* ■	—	—	
11. Participation in Adult Education: Has the state reduced the gap in adult education participation between adults who have a high school diploma or less, and those who have additional post-secondary education or technical training?	—	—	
12. Participation in Higher Education: Has the state reduced the gap between White and minority high school graduates who:			
• enroll in college?	—	—	
• complete a college degree?	—	—	
13. Overall Student Drug and Alcohol Use: Has the state reduced the percentage of public high school students reporting doing the following during the past 30 days: ■			
• using marijuana at least once? *(1990, 1993)*	17%	20% ns	↔
• having 5 or more drinks in a row? *(1990, 1993)*	38%	28%	↑
14. Sale of Drugs at School: Has the state reduced the percentage of public high school students reporting that someone offered, sold, or gave them an illegal drug on school property during the past 12 months? *(1993)* ■	31%	—	
15. Student and Teacher Victimization: Has the state reduced the percentage of students and teachers reporting that they were threatened or injured on school property during the past 12 months?			
• public high school students *(1993)* ■	9%	—	
• public school teachers	—	—	
16. Disruptions in Class by Students: Has the state reduced the percentage of students and teachers reporting that disruptions often interfere with teaching and learning?			
• high school students	—	—	
• high school teachers	—	—	

— Data not available.
ns Interpret with caution. Change was not statistically significant.

▲ See technical note on page 133.
▼ See technical note on pages 134-135.

■ See technical note on page 136.
■ See technical note on page 137.

MICHIGAN

	Baseline	Most Recent Update	Overall Progress
1. **Children's Health Index:** Has the state reduced the percentage of infants born with 2 or more health and developmental risks? *(1990, 1991)* ▲	15%	16% ns	⬌
2. **Immunizations:** Has the state increased the percentage of 2-year-olds who have been fully immunized against preventable childhood diseases?	—	—	
3. **Family-Child Reading and Storytelling:** Has the state increased the percentage of 3- to 5-year-olds whose parents read to them or tell them stories regularly?	—	—	
4. **Preschool Participation:** Has the state reduced the gap in preschool participation between 3- to 5-year-olds from high- and low-income families?	—	—	
5. **High School Completion:** Has the state increased the percentage of 19- to 20-year-olds who have a high school credential? *(1990)*	86%	—	
6. **Mathematics Achievement:** Has the state increased the percentage of public school students who meet the Goals Panel's performance standard in mathematics? ▼			
• Grade 4 *(1992)*	19%	—	
• Grade 8 *(1990, 1992)*	20%	23% ns	⬌
• Grade 12	—	—	
7. **Reading Achievement:** Has the state increased the percentage of public school students who meet the Goals Panel's performance standard in reading? ▼			
• Grade 4 *(1992)*	23%	—	
• Grade 8	—	—	
• Grade 12	—	—	
8. **International Mathematics Achievement:** Has the state reduced the gap between the percentage of public school 8th graders and the percentage of 13-year-olds in the highest-scoring country who meet the Goals Panel's performance standard in mathematics? *(1991 and 1992)*	18 percentage points	—	
9. **International Science Achievement:** Has the state reduced the gap between the percentage of public school 8th graders and the percentage of 13-year-olds in the highest-scoring country who meet the Goals Panel's performance standard in science?	—	—	
10. **Adult Literacy:** Has the state increased the percentage of adults who score at or above Level 3 in prose literacy? *(1992)* ■	—	—	
11. **Participation in Adult Education:** Has the state reduced the gap in adult education participation between adults who have a high school diploma or less, and those who have additional post-secondary education or technical training?	—	—	
12. **Participation in Higher Education:** Has the state reduced the gap between White and minority high school graduates who:			
• enroll in college?	—	—	
• complete a college degree?	—	—	
13. **Overall Student Drug and Alcohol Use:** Has the state reduced the percentage of public high school students reporting doing the following during the past 30 days: ■			
• using marijuana at least once? *(1990, 1993)*	—	—	
• having 5 or more drinks in a row? *(1990, 1993)*	—	—	
14. **Sale of Drugs at School:** Has the state reduced the percentage of public high school students reporting that someone offered, sold, or gave them an illegal drug on school property during the past 12 months? *(1993)* ■	—	—	
15. **Student and Teacher Victimization:** Has the state reduced the percentage of students and teachers reporting that they were threatened or injured on school property during the past 12 months?			
• public high school students *(1993)* ■	—	—	
• public school teachers	—	—	
16. **Disruptions in Class by Students:** Has the state reduced the percentage of students and teachers reporting that disruptions often interfere with teaching and learning?			
• high school students	—	—	
• high school teachers	—	—	

— Data not available.
ns Interpret with caution. Change was not statistically significant.

▲ See technical note on page 133.
▼ See technical note on pages 134-135.

■ See technical note on page 136.
■ See technical note on page 137.

MINNESOTA

	Baseline	Most Recent Update	Overall Progress

1. **Children's Health Index:** Has the state reduced the percentage of infants born with 2 or more health and developmental risks? *(1990, 1991)* ▲ — 12% / 12% / ↔

2. **Immunizations:** Has the state increased the percentage of 2-year-olds who have been fully immunized against preventable childhood diseases? — — / —

3. **Family-Child Reading and Storytelling:** Has the state increased the percentage of 3- to 5-year-olds whose parents read to them or tell them stories regularly? — — / —

4. **Preschool Participation:** Has the state reduced the gap in preschool participation between 3- to 5-year-olds from high- and low-income families? — — / —

5. **High School Completion:** Has the state increased the percentage of 19- to 20-year-olds who have a high school credential? *(1990)* — 92% / —

6. **Mathematics Achievement:** Has the state increased the percentage of public school students who meet the Goals Panel's performance standard in mathematics? ▼
   - Grade 4 *(1992)* — 27% / —
   - Grade 8 *(1990, 1992)* — 29% / 37% / ↑
   - Grade 12 — — / —

7. **Reading Achievement:** Has the state increased the percentage of public school students who meet the Goals Panel's performance standard in reading? ▼
   - Grade 4 *(1992)* — 28% / —
   - Grade 8 — — / —
   - Grade 12 — — / —

8. **International Mathematics Achievement:** Has the state reduced the gap between the percentage of public school 8th graders and the percentage of 13-year-olds in the highest-scoring country who meet the Goals Panel's performance standard in mathematics? *(1991 and 1992)* — 4 percentage points / —

9. **International Science Achievement:** Has the state reduced the gap between the percentage of public school 8th graders and the percentage of 13-year-olds in the highest-scoring country who meet the Goals Panel's performance standard in science? — — / —

10. **Adult Literacy:** Has the state increased the percentage of adults who score at or above Level 3 in prose literacy? *(1992)* ■ — — / —

11. **Participation in Adult Education:** Has the state reduced the gap in adult education participation between adults who have a high school diploma or less, and those who have additional post-secondary education or technical training? — — / —

12. **Participation in Higher Education:** Has the state reduced the gap between White and minority high school graduates who:
    - enroll in college? — — / —
    - complete a college degree? — — / —

13. **Overall Student Drug and Alcohol Use:** Has the state reduced the percentage of public high school students reporting doing the following during the past 30 days: ■
    - using marijuana at least once? *(1990, 1993)* — — / —
    - having 5 or more drinks in a row? *(1990, 1993)* — — / —

14. **Sale of Drugs at School:** Has the state reduced the percentage of public high school students reporting that someone offered, sold, or gave them an illegal drug on school property during the past 12 months? *(1993)* ■ — — / —

15. **Student and Teacher Victimization:** Has the state reduced the percentage of students and teachers reporting that they were threatened or injured on school property during the past 12 months?
    - public high school students *(1993)* ■ — — / —
    - public school teachers — — / —

16. **Disruptions in Class by Students:** Has the state reduced the percentage of students and teachers reporting that disruptions often interfere with teaching and learning?
    - high school students — — / —
    - high school teachers — — / —

— Data not available.
ns Interpret with caution. Change was not statistically significant.

▲ See technical note on page 133.
▼ See technical note on pages 134-135.

■ See technical note on page 136.
■ See technical note on page 137.

MISSISSIPPI

	Baseline	Most Recent Update	Overall Progress
1. Children's Health Index: Has the state reduced the percentage of infants born with 2 or more health and developmental risks? *(1990, 1991)* ▲	15%	14%	↑
2. Immunizations: Has the state increased the percentage of 2-year-olds who have been fully immunized against preventable childhood diseases?	—	—	
3. Family-Child Reading and Storytelling: Has the state increased the percentage of 3- to 5-year-olds whose parents read to them or tell them stories regularly?	—	—	
4. Preschool Participation: Has the state reduced the gap in preschool participation between 3- to 5-year-olds from high- and low-income families?	—	—	
5. High School Completion: Has the state increased the percentage of 19- to 20-year-olds who have a high school credential? *(1990)*	83%	—	
6. Mathematics Achievement: Has the state increased the percentage of public school students who meet the Goals Panel's performance standard in mathematics? ▼ • Grade 4 *(1992)* • Grade 8 *(1992)* • Grade 12	7% 8% —	— — —	
7. Reading Achievement: Has the state increased the percentage of public school students who meet the Goals Panel's performance standard in reading? ▼ • Grade 4 *(1992)* • Grade 8 • Grade 12	12% — —	— — —	
8. International Mathematics Achievement: Has the state reduced the gap between the percentage of public school 8th graders and the percentage of 13-year-olds in the highest-scoring country who meet the Goals Panel's performance standard in mathematics? *(1991 and 1992)*	33 percentage points	—	
9. International Science Achievement: Has the state reduced the gap between the percentage of public school 8th graders and the percentage of 13-year-olds in the highest-scoring country who meet the Goals Panel's performance standard in science?	—	—	
10. Adult Literacy: Has the state increased the percentage of adults who score at or above Level 3 in prose literacy? *(1992)* ■	—	—	
11. Participation in Adult Education: Has the state reduced the gap in adult education participation between adults who have a high school diploma or less, and those who have additional post-secondary education or technical training?	—	—	
12. Participation in Higher Education: Has the state reduced the gap between White and minority high school graduates who: • enroll in college? • complete a college degree?	— —	— —	
13. Overall Student Drug and Alcohol Use: Has the state reduced the percentage of public high school students reporting doing the following during the past 30 days: ■ • using marijuana at least once? *(1990, 1993)* • having 5 or more drinks in a row? *(1990, 1993)*	11% 37%	9% ns 27%	↔ ↑
14. Sale of Drugs at School: Has the state reduced the percentage of public high school students reporting that someone offered, sold, or gave them an illegal drug on school property during the past 12 months? *(1993)* ■	16%	—	
15. Student and Teacher Victimization: Has the state reduced the percentage of students and teachers reporting that they were threatened or injured on school property during the past 12 months? • public high school students *(1993)* ■ • public school teachers	8% —	— —	
16. Disruptions in Class by Students: Has the state reduced the percentage of students and teachers reporting that disruptions often interfere with teaching and learning? • high school students • high school teachers	— —	— —	

— Data not available.
ns Interpret with caution. Change was not statistically significant.

▲ See technical note on page 133.
▼ See technical note on pages 134-135.

■ See technical note on page 136.
■ See technical note on page 137.

MISSOURI

	Baseline	Most Recent Update	Overall Progress
1. **Children's Health Index:** Has the state reduced the percentage of infants born with 2 or more health and developmental risks? *(1990, 1991)* ▲	16%	15%	↑
2. **Immunizations:** Has the state increased the percentage of 2-year-olds who have been fully immunized against preventable childhood diseases?	—	—	
3. **Family-Child Reading and Storytelling:** Has the state increased the percentage of 3- to 5-year-olds whose parents read to them or tell them stories regularly?	—	—	
4. **Preschool Participation:** Has the state reduced the gap in preschool participation between 3- to 5-year-olds from high- and low-income families?	—	—	
5. **High School Completion:** Has the state increased the percentage of 19- to 20-year-olds who have a high school credential? *(1990)*	85%	—	
6. **Mathematics Achievement:** Has the state increased the percentage of public school students who meet the Goals Panel's performance standard in mathematics? ▼			
• Grade 4 *(1992)*	19%	—	
• Grade 8 *(1992)*	24%	—	
• Grade 12	—	—	
7. **Reading Achievement:** Has the state increased the percentage of public school students who meet the Goals Panel's performance standard in reading? ▼			
• Grade 4 *(1992)*	26%	—	
• Grade 8	—	—	
• Grade 12	—	—	
8. **International Mathematics Achievement:** Has the state reduced the gap between the percentage of public school 8th graders and the percentage of 13-year-olds in the highest-scoring country who meet the Goals Panel's performance standard in mathematics? *(1991 and 1992)*	17 percentage points	—	
9. **International Science Achievement:** Has the state reduced the gap between the percentage of public school 8th graders and the percentage of 13-year-olds in the highest-scoring country who meet the Goals Panel's performance standard in science?	—	—	
10. **Adult Literacy:** Has the state increased the percentage of adults who score at or above Level 3 in prose literacy? *(1992)* ■	—	—	
11. **Participation in Adult Education:** Has the state reduced the gap in adult education participation between adults who have a high school diploma or less, and those who have additional post-secondary education or technical training?	—	—	
12. **Participation in Higher Education:** Has the state reduced the gap between White and minority high school graduates who:			
• enroll in college?	—	—	
• complete a college degree?	—	—	
13. **Overall Student Drug and Alcohol Use:** Has the state reduced the percentage of public high school students reporting doing the following during the past 30 days: ■			
• using marijuana at least once? *(1990, 1993)*	—	—	
• having 5 or more drinks in a row? *(1990, 1993)*	—	—	
14. **Sale of Drugs at School:** Has the state reduced the percentage of public high school students reporting that someone offered, sold, or gave them an illegal drug on school property during the past 12 months? *(1993)* ■	—	—	
15. **Student and Teacher Victimization:** Has the state reduced the percentage of students and teachers reporting that they were threatened or injured on school property during the past 12 months?			
• public high school students *(1993)* ■	—	—	
• public school teachers	—	—	
16. **Disruptions in Class by Students:** Has the state reduced the percentage of students and teachers reporting that disruptions often interfere with teaching and learning?			
• high school students	—	—	
• high school teachers	—	—	

— Data not available.
ns Interpret with caution. Change was not statistically significant.

▲ See technical note on page 133.
▼ See technical note on pages 134-135.

■ See technical note on page 136.
■ See technical note on page 137.

MONTANA

	Baseline	Most Recent Update	Overall Progress

1. **Children's Health Index:** Has the state reduced the percentage of infants born with 2 or more health and developmental risks? *(1990, 1991)* ▲ — 17% — 14% — ↑

2. **Immunizations:** Has the state increased the percentage of 2-year-olds who have been fully immunized against preventable childhood diseases? — —

3. **Family-Child Reading and Storytelling:** Has the state increased the percentage of 3- to 5-year-olds whose parents read to them or tell them stories regularly? — —

4. **Preschool Participation:** Has the state reduced the gap in preschool participation between 3- to 5-year-olds from high- and low-income families? — —

5. **High School Completion:** Has the state increased the percentage of 19- to 20-year-olds who have a high school credential? *(1990)* — 89% — —

6. **Mathematics Achievement:** Has the state increased the percentage of public school students who meet the Goals Panel's performance standard in mathematics? ▼
   - Grade 4 *(1992)* — —
   - Grade 8 *(1990, 1992)* — —
   - Grade 12 — —

7. **Reading Achievement:** Has the state increased the percentage of public school students who meet the Goals Panel's performance standard in reading? ▼
   - Grade 4 *(1992)* — —
   - Grade 8 — —
   - Grade 12 — —

8. **International Mathematics Achievement:** Has the state reduced the gap between the percentage of public school 8th graders and the percentage of 13-year-olds in the highest-scoring country who meet the Goals Panel's performance standard in mathematics? *(1991 and 1992)* — —

9. **International Science Achievement:** Has the state reduced the gap between the percentage of public school 8th graders and the percentage of 13-year-olds in the highest-scoring country who meet the Goals Panel's performance standard in science? — —

10. **Adult Literacy:** Has the state increased the percentage of adults who score at or above Level 3 in prose literacy? *(1992)* ■ — —

11. **Participation in Adult Education:** Has the state reduced the gap in adult education participation between adults who have a high school diploma or less, and those who have additional post-secondary education or technical training? — —

12. **Participation in Higher Education:** Has the state reduced the gap between White and minority high school graduates who:
    - enroll in college? — —
    - complete a college degree? — —

13. **Overall Student Drug and Alcohol Use:** Has the state reduced the percentage of public high school students reporting doing the following during the past 30 days: ■
    - using marijuana at least once? *(1993)* — 14% — —
    - having 5 or more drinks in a row? *(1993)* — 41% — —

14. **Sale of Drugs at School:** Has the state reduced the percentage of public high school students reporting that someone offered, sold, or gave them an illegal drug on school property during the past 12 months? *(1993)* ■ — 22% — —

15. **Student and Teacher Victimization:** Has the state reduced the percentage of students and teachers reporting that they were threatened or injured on school property during the past 12 months?
    - public high school students *(1993)* ■ — 7% — —
    - public school teachers — —

16. **Disruptions in Class by Students:** Has the state reduced the percentage of students and teachers reporting that disruptions often interfere with teaching and learning?
    - high school students — —
    - high school teachers — —

— Data not available.
ns Interpret with caution. Change was not statistically significant.

▲ See technical note on page 133.
▼ See technical note on pages 134-135.

■ See technical note on page 136.
■ See technical note on page 137.

NEBRASKA

	Baseline	Most Recent Update	Overall Progress
1. Children's Health Index: Has the state reduced the percentage of infants born with 2 or more health and developmental risks? *(1990, 1991)* ▲	15%	14%	↑
2. Immunizations: Has the state increased the percentage of 2-year-olds who have been fully immunized against preventable childhood diseases?	—	—	
3. Family-Child Reading and Storytelling: Has the state increased the percentage of 3- to 5-year-olds whose parents read to them or tell them stories regularly?	—	—	
4. Preschool Participation: Has the state reduced the gap in preschool participation between 3- to 5-year-olds from high- and low-income families?	—	—	
5. High School Completion: Has the state increased the percentage of 19- to 20-year-olds who have a high school credential? *(1990)*	92%	—	
6. Mathematics Achievement: Has the state increased the percentage of public school students who meet the Goals Panel's performance standard in mathematics? ▼			
• Grade 4 *(1992)*	23%	—	
• Grade 8 *(1990, 1992)*	30%	32% ns	↔
• Grade 12	—	—	
7. Reading Achievement: Has the state increased the percentage of public school students who meet the Goals Panel's performance standard in reading? ▼			
• Grade 4 *(1992)*	27%	—	
• Grade 8	—	—	
• Grade 12	—	—	
8. International Mathematics Achievement: Has the state reduced the gap between the percentage of public school 8th graders and the percentage of 13-year-olds in the highest-scoring country who meet the Goals Panel's performance standard in mathematics? *(1991 and 1992)*	9 percentage points	—	
9. International Science Achievement: Has the state reduced the gap between the percentage of public school 8th graders and the percentage of 13-year-olds in the highest-scoring country who meet the Goals Panel's performance standard in science?	—	—	
10. Adult Literacy: Has the state increased the percentage of adults who score at or above Level 3 in prose literacy? *(1992)* ■	—	—	
11. Participation in Adult Education: Has the state reduced the gap in adult education participation between adults who have a high school diploma or less, and those who have additional post-secondary education or technical training?	—	—	
12. Participation in Higher Education: Has the state reduced the gap between White and minority high school graduates who:			
• enroll in college?	—	—	
• complete a college degree?	—	—	
13. Overall Student Drug and Alcohol Use: Has the state reduced the percentage of public high school students reporting doing the following during the past 30 days: ■			
• using marijuana at least once? *(1991, 1993)*	10%	9% ns	↔
• having 5 or more drinks in a row? *(1991, 1993)*	37%	36% ns	↔
14. Sale of Drugs at School: Has the state reduced the percentage of public high school students reporting that someone offered, sold, or gave them an illegal drug on school property during the past 12 months? *(1993)* ■	11%	—	
15. Student and Teacher Victimization: Has the state reduced the percentage of students and teachers reporting that they were threatened or injured on school property during the past 12 months?			
• public high school students *(1993)* ■	6%	—	
• public school teachers	—	—	
16. Disruptions in Class by Students: Has the state reduced the percentage of students and teachers reporting that disruptions often interfere with teaching and learning?			
• high school students	—	—	
• high school teachers	—	—	

— Data not available.
ns Interpret with caution. Change was not statistically significant.

▲ See technical note on page 133.
▼ See technical note on pages 134-135.

■ See technical note on page 136.
■ See technical note on page 137.

NEVADA

	Baseline	Most Recent Update	Overall Progress
1. Children's Health Index: Has the state reduced the percentage of infants born with 2 or more health and developmental risks? *(1990, 1991)* ▲	16%	15% ns	⟷
2. Immunizations: Has the state increased the percentage of 2-year-olds who have been fully immunized against preventable childhood diseases?	—	—	
3. Family-Child Reading and Storytelling: Has the state increased the percentage of 3- to 5-year-olds whose parents read to them or tell them stories regularly?	—	—	
4. Preschool Participation: Has the state reduced the gap in preschool participation between 3- to 5-year-olds from high- and low-income families?	—	—	
5. High School Completion: Has the state increased the percentage of 19- to 20-year-olds who have a high school credential? *(1990)*	78%	—	
6. Mathematics Achievement: Has the state increased the percentage of public school students who meet the Goals Panel's performance standard in mathematics? ▼ • Grade 4 *(1992)* • Grade 8 *(1990, 1992)* • Grade 12	— — —	— — —	
7. Reading Achievement: Has the state increased the percentage of public school students who meet the Goals Panel's performance standard in reading? ▼ • Grade 4 *(1992)* • Grade 8 • Grade 12	— — —	— — —	
8. International Mathematics Achievement: Has the state reduced the gap between the percentage of public school 8th graders and the percentage of 13-year-olds in the highest-scoring country who meet the Goals Panel's performance standard in mathematics? *(1991 and 1992)*	—	—	
9. International Science Achievement: Has the state reduced the gap between the percentage of public school 8th graders and the percentage of 13-year-olds in the highest-scoring country who meet the Goals Panel's performance standard in science?	—	—	
10. Adult Literacy: Has the state increased the percentage of adults who score at or above Level 3 in prose literacy? *(1992)* ■	—	—	
11. Participation in Adult Education: Has the state reduced the gap in adult education participation between adults who have a high school diploma or less, and those who have additional post-secondary education or technical training?	—	—	
12. Participation in Higher Education: Has the state reduced the gap between White and minority high school graduates who: • enroll in college? • complete a college degree?	— —	— —	
13. Overall Student Drug and Alcohol Use: Has the state reduced the percentage of public high school students reporting doing the following during the past 30 days: ■ • using marijuana at least once? *(1993)* • having 5 or more drinks in a row? *(1993)*	19% 32%	— —	
14. Sale of Drugs at School: Has the state reduced the percentage of public high school students reporting that someone offered, sold, or gave them an illegal drug on school property during the past 12 months? *(1993)* ■	30%	—	
15. Student and Teacher Victimization: Has the state reduced the percentage of students and teachers reporting that they were threatened or injured on school property during the past 12 months? • public high school students *(1993)* ■ • public school teachers	10% —	— —	
16. Disruptions in Class by Students: Has the state reduced the percentage of students and teachers reporting that disruptions often interfere with teaching and learning? • high school students • high school teachers	— —	— —	

— Data not available.
ns Interpret with caution. Change was not statistically significant.

▲ See technical note on page 133.
▼ See technical note on pages 134-135.

■ See technical note on page 136.
■ See technical note on page 137.

103

	Baseline	Most Recent Update	Overall Progress
1. Children's Health Index: Has the state reduced the percentage of infants born with 2 or more health and developmental risks? *(1990, 1991)* ▲	12%	12%	↔
2. Immunizations: Has the state increased the percentage of 2-year-olds who have been fully immunized against preventable childhood diseases?	—	—	
3. Family-Child Reading and Storytelling: Has the state increased the percentage of 3- to 5-year-olds whose parents read to them or tell them stories regularly?	—	—	
4. Preschool Participation: Has the state reduced the gap in preschool participation between 3- to 5-year-olds from high- and low-income families?	—	—	
5. High School Completion: Has the state increased the percentage of 19- to 20-year-olds who have a high school credential? *(1990)*	87%	—	
6. Mathematics Achievement: Has the state increased the percentage of public school students who meet the Goals Panel's performance standard in mathematics? ▼			
• Grade 4 *(1992)*	26%	—	
• Grade 8 *(1990, 1992)*	25%	30%	↑
• Grade 12	—	—	
7. Reading Achievement: Has the state increased the percentage of public school students who meet the Goals Panel's performance standard in reading? ▼			
• Grade 4 *(1992)*	34%	—	
• Grade 8	—	—	
• Grade 12	—	—	
8. International Mathematics Achievement: Has the state reduced the gap between the percentage of public school 8th graders and the percentage of 13-year-olds in the highest-scoring country who meet the Goals Panel's performance standard in mathematics? *(1991 and 1992)*	11 percentage points	—	
9. International Science Achievement: Has the state reduced the gap between the percentage of public school 8th graders and the percentage of 13-year-olds in the highest-scoring country who meet the Goals Panel's performance standard in science?	—	—	
10. Adult Literacy: Has the state increased the percentage of adults who score at or above Level 3 in prose literacy? *(1992)* ■	—	—	
11. Participation in Adult Education: Has the state reduced the gap in adult education participation between adults who have a high school diploma or less, and those who have additional post-secondary education or technical training?	—	—	
12. Participation in Higher Education: Has the state reduced the gap between White and minority high school graduates who:			
• enroll in college?	—	—	
• complete a college degree?	—	—	
13. Overall Student Drug and Alcohol Use: Has the state reduced the percentage of public high school students reporting doing the following during the past 30 days: ■			
• using marijuana at least once? *(1993)*	21%	—	
• having 5 or more drinks in a row? *(1993)*	31%	—	
14. Sale of Drugs at School: Has the state reduced the percentage of public high school students reporting that someone offered, sold, or gave them an illegal drug on school property during the past 12 months? *(1993)* ■	26%	—	
15. Student and Teacher Victimization: Has the state reduced the percentage of students and teachers reporting that they were threatened or injured on school property during the past 12 months?			
• public high school students *(1993)* ■	7%	—	
• public school teachers	—	—	
16. Disruptions in Class by Students: Has the state reduced the percentage of students and teachers reporting that disruptions often interfere with teaching and learning?			
• high school students	—	—	
• high school teachers	—	—	

— Data not available.
ns Interpret with caution. Change was not statistically significant.

▲ See technical note on page 133.
▼ See technical note on pages 134-135.

■ See technical note on page 136.
■ See technical note on page 137.

	Baseline	Most Recent Update	Overall Progress
1. Children's Health Index: Has the state reduced the percentage of infants born with 2 or more health and developmental risks? *(1990, 1991)* ▲	11%	10% ns	⟷
2. Immunizations: Has the state increased the percentage of 2-year-olds who have been fully immunized against preventable childhood diseases?	—	—	
3. Family-Child Reading and Storytelling: Has the state increased the percentage of 3- to 5-year-olds whose parents read to them or tell them stories regularly?	—	—	
4. Preschool Participation: Has the state reduced the gap in preschool participation between 3- to 5-year-olds from high- and low-income families?	—	—	
5. High School Completion: Has the state increased the percentage of 19- to 20-year-olds who have a high school credential? *(1990)*	86%	—	
6. Mathematics Achievement: Has the state increased the percentage of public school students who meet the Goals Panel's performance standard in mathematics? ▼			
• Grade 4 *(1992)*	25%	—	
• Grade 8 *(1990, 1992)*	25%	28% ns	⟷
• Grade 12	—	—	
7. Reading Achievement: Has the state increased the percentage of public school students who meet the Goals Panel's performance standard in reading? ▼			
• Grade 4 *(1992)*	31%	—	
• Grade 8	—	—	
• Grade 12	—	—	
8. International Mathematics Achievement: Has the state reduced the gap between the percentage of public school 8th graders and the percentage of 13-year-olds in the highest-scoring country who meet the Goals Panel's performance standard in mathematics? *(1991 and 1992)*	13 percentage points	—	
9. International Science Achievement: Has the state reduced the gap between the percentage of public school 8th graders and the percentage of 13-year-olds in the highest-scoring country who meet the Goals Panel's performance standard in science?	—	—	
10. Adult Literacy: Has the state increased the percentage of adults who score at or above Level 3 in prose literacy? *(1992)* ■	53%	—	
11. Participation in Adult Education: Has the state reduced the gap in adult education participation between adults who have a high school diploma or less, and those who have additional post-secondary education or technical training?	—	—	
12. Participation in Higher Education: Has the state reduced the gap between White and minority high school graduates who:			
• enroll in college?	—	—	
• complete a college degree?	—	—	
13. Overall Student Drug and Alcohol Use: Has the state reduced the percentage of public high school students reporting doing the following during the past 30 days: ■			
• using marijuana at least once? *(1990, 1993)*	—	—	
• having 5 or more drinks in a row? *(1990, 1993)*	—	—	
14. Sale of Drugs at School: Has the state reduced the percentage of public high school students reporting that someone offered, sold, or gave them an illegal drug on school property during the past 12 months? *(1993)* ■	—	—	
15. Student and Teacher Victimization: Has the state reduced the percentage of students and teachers reporting that they were threatened or injured on school property during the past 12 months?			
• public high school students *(1993)* ■	—	—	
• public school teachers	—	—	
16. Disruptions in Class by Students: Has the state reduced the percentage of students and teachers reporting that disruptions often interfere with teaching and learning?			
• high school students	—	—	
• high school teachers	—	—	

— Data not available.
ns Interpret with caution. Change was not statistically significant.

▲ See technical note on page 133.
▼ See technical note on pages 134-135.

■ See technical note on page 136.
■ See technical note on page 137.

NEW MEXICO

	Baseline	Most Recent Update	Overall Progress
1. Children's Health Index: Has the state reduced the percentage of infants born with 2 or more health and developmental risks? *(1990, 1991)* ▲	15%	13%	↑
2. Immunizations: Has the state increased the percentage of 2-year-olds who have been fully immunized against preventable childhood diseases?	—	—	
3. Family-Child Reading and Storytelling: Has the state increased the percentage of 3- to 5-year-olds whose parents read to them or tell them stories regularly?	—	—	
4. Preschool Participation: Has the state reduced the gap in preschool participation between 3- to 5-year-olds from high- and low-income families?	—	—	
5. High School Completion: Has the state increased the percentage of 19- to 20-year-olds who have a high school credential? *(1990)*	82%	—	
6. Mathematics Achievement: Has the state increased the percentage of public school students who meet the Goals Panel's performance standard in mathematics? ▼ • Grade 4 *(1992)* • Grade 8 *(1990, 1992)* • Grade 12	 11% 13% —	 — 14% ns —	 ↔
7. Reading Achievement: Has the state increased the percentage of public school students who meet the Goals Panel's performance standard in reading? ▼ • Grade 4 *(1992)* • Grade 8 • Grade 12	 20% — —	 — — —	
8. International Mathematics Achievement: Has the state reduced the gap between the percentage of public school 8th graders and the percentage of 13-year-olds in the highest-scoring country who meet the Goals Panel's performance standard in mathematics? *(1991 and 1992)*	27 percentage points	—	
9. International Science Achievement: Has the state reduced the gap between the percentage of public school 8th graders and the percentage of 13-year-olds in the highest-scoring country who meet the Goals Panel's performance standard in science?	—	—	
10. Adult Literacy: Has the state increased the percentage of adults who score at or above Level 3 in prose literacy? *(1992)* ■	—	—	
11. Participation in Adult Education: Has the state reduced the gap in adult education participation between adults who have a high school diploma or less, and those who have additional post-secondary education or technical training?	—	—	
12. Participation in Higher Education: Has the state reduced the gap between White and minority high school graduates who: • enroll in college? • complete a college degree?	 — —	 — —	
13. Overall Student Drug and Alcohol Use: Has the state reduced the percentage of public high school students reporting doing the following during the past 30 days: ■ • using marijuana at least once? *(1990, 1991)* • having 5 or more drinks in a row? *(1990, 1991)*	 11% 45%	 18% 43% ns	 ↓ ↔
14. Sale of Drugs at School: Has the state reduced the percentage of public high school students reporting that someone offered, sold, or gave them an illegal drug on school property during the past 12 months? *(1993)* ■	—	—	
15. Student and Teacher Victimization: Has the state reduced the percentage of students and teachers reporting that they were threatened or injured on school property during the past 12 months? • public high school students *(1993)* ■ • public school teachers	 — —	 — —	
16. Disruptions in Class by Students: Has the state reduced the percentage of students and teachers reporting that disruptions often interfere with teaching and learning? • high school students • high school teachers	 — —	 — —	

— Data not available.
ns Interpret with caution. Change was not statistically significant.

▲ See technical note on page 133.
▼ See technical note on pages 134-135.

■ See technical note on page 136.
■ See technical note on page 137.

NEW YORK

	Baseline	Most Recent Update	Overall Progress

1. **Children's Health Index:** Has the state reduced the percentage of infants born with 2 or more health and developmental risks? *(1990, 1991)* ▲ — | — | —

2. **Immunizations:** Has the state increased the percentage of 2-year-olds who have been fully immunized against preventable childhood diseases? — | —

3. **Family-Child Reading and Storytelling:** Has the state increased the percentage of 3- to 5-year-olds whose parents read to them or tell them stories regularly? — | —

4. **Preschool Participation:** Has the state reduced the gap in preschool participation between 3- to 5-year-olds from high- and low-income families? — | —

5. **High School Completion:** Has the state increased the percentage of 19- to 20-year-olds who have a high school credential? *(1990)* — 86% | —

6. **Mathematics Achievement:** Has the state increased the percentage of public school students who meet the Goals Panel's performance standard in mathematics? ▼
   - Grade 4 *(1992)* — 17% | —
   - Grade 8 *(1990, 1992)* — 19% | 24% | ↑
   - Grade 12 — — | —

7. **Reading Achievement:** Has the state increased the percentage of public school students who meet the Goals Panel's performance standard in reading? ▼
   - Grade 4 *(1992)* — 23% | —
   - Grade 8 — — | —
   - Grade 12 — — | —

8. **International Mathematics Achievement:** Has the state reduced the gap between the percentage of public school 8th graders and the percentage of 13-year-olds in the highest-scoring country who meet the Goals Panel's performance standard in mathematics? *(1991 and 1992)* — 17 percentage points | —

9. **International Science Achievement:** Has the state reduced the gap between the percentage of public school 8th graders and the percentage of 13-year-olds in the highest-scoring country who meet the Goals Panel's performance standard in science? — | —

10. **Adult Literacy:** Has the state increased the percentage of adults who score at or above Level 3 in prose literacy? *(1992)* ■ — 46% | —

11. **Participation in Adult Education:** Has the state reduced the gap in adult education participation between adults who have a high school diploma or less, and those who have additional post-secondary education or technical training? — | —

12. **Participation in Higher Education:** Has the state reduced the gap between White and minority high school graduates who:
   - enroll in college? — | —
   - complete a college degree? — | —

13. **Overall Student Drug and Alcohol Use:** Has the state reduced the percentage of public high school students reporting doing the following during the past 30 days: ■
   - using marijuana at least once? *(1991, 1993)* — 16% | 19% ns | ↔
   - having 5 or more drinks in a row? *(1991, 1993)* — 36% | 32% ns | ↔

14. **Sale of Drugs at School:** Has the state reduced the percentage of public high school students reporting that someone offered, sold, or gave them an illegal drug on school property during the past 12 months? *(1993)* ■ — 28% | —

15. **Student and Teacher Victimization:** Has the state reduced the percentage of students and teachers reporting that they were threatened or injured on school property during the past 12 months?
   - public high school students *(1993)* ■ — 8% | —
   - public school teachers — — | —

16. **Disruptions in Class by Students:** Has the state reduced the percentage of students and teachers reporting that disruptions often interfere with teaching and learning?
   - high school students — — | —
   - high school teachers — — | —

— Data not available.
ns Interpret with caution. Change was not statistically significant.

▲ See technical note on page 133.
▼ See technical note on pages 134-135.

■ See technical note on page 136.
■ See technical note on page 137.

NORTH CAROLINA

	Baseline	Most Recent Update	Overall Progress
1. Children's Health Index: Has the state reduced the percentage of infants born with 2 or more health and developmental risks? *(1990, 1991)* ▲	15%	13%	↑
2. Immunizations: Has the state increased the percentage of 2-year-olds who have been fully immunized against preventable childhood diseases?	—	—	
3. Family-Child Reading and Storytelling: Has the state increased the percentage of 3- to 5-year-olds whose parents read to them or tell them stories regularly?	—	—	
4. Preschool Participation: Has the state reduced the gap in preschool participation between 3- to 5-year-olds from high- and low-income families?	—	—	
5. High School Completion: Has the state increased the percentage of 19- to 20-year-olds who have a high school credential? *(1990)*	85%	—	
6. Mathematics Achievement: Has the state increased the percentage of public school students who meet the Goals Panel's performance standard in mathematics? ▼			
• Grade 4 *(1992)*	13%	—	
• Grade 8 *(1990, 1992)*	11%	15%	↑
• Grade 12	—	—	
7. Reading Achievement: Has the state increased the percentage of public school students who meet the Goals Panel's performance standard in reading? ▼			
• Grade 4 *(1992)*	22%	—	
• Grade 8	—	—	
• Grade 12	—	—	
8. International Mathematics Achievement: Has the state reduced the gap between the percentage of public school 8th graders and the percentage of 13-year-olds in the highest-scoring country who meet the Goals Panel's performance standard in mathematics? *(1991 and 1992)*	26 percentage points	—	
9. International Science Achievement: Has the state reduced the gap between the percentage of public school 8th graders and the percentage of 13-year-olds in the highest-scoring country who meet the Goals Panel's performance standard in science?	—	—	
10. Adult Literacy: Has the state increased the percentage of adults who score at or above Level 3 in prose literacy? *(1992)* ■	—	—	
11. Participation in Adult Education: Has the state reduced the gap in adult education participation between adults who have a high school diploma or less, and those who have additional post-secondary education or technical training?	—	—	
12. Participation in Higher Education: Has the state reduced the gap between White and minority high school graduates who:			
• enroll in college?	—	—	
• complete a college degree?	—	—	
13. Overall Student Drug and Alcohol Use: Has the state reduced the percentage of public high school students reporting doing the following during the past 30 days: ■			
• using marijuana at least once? *(1993)*	15%	—	
• having 5 or more drinks in a row? *(1993)*	23%	—	
14. Sale of Drugs at School: Has the state reduced the percentage of public high school students reporting that someone offered, sold, or gave them an illegal drug on school property during the past 12 months? *(1993)* ■	29%	—	
15. Student and Teacher Victimization: Has the state reduced the percentage of students and teachers reporting that they were threatened or injured on school property during the past 12 months?			
• public high school students *(1993)* ■	10%	—	
• public school teachers	—	—	
16. Disruptions in Class by Students: Has the state reduced the percentage of students and teachers reporting that disruptions often interfere with teaching and learning?			
• high school students	—	—	
• high school teachers	—	—	

— Data not available.
ns Interpret with caution. Change was not statistically significant.

▲ See technical note on page 133.
▼ See technical note on pages 134-135.

■ See technical note on page 136.
■ See technical note on page 137.

NORTH DAKOTA

	Baseline	Most Recent Update	Overall Progress

1. **Children's Health Index:** Has the state reduced the percentage of infants born with 2 or more health and developmental risks? *(1990, 1991)* ▲ — 14% — 14% — ↔

2. **Immunizations:** Has the state increased the percentage of 2-year-olds who have been fully immunized against preventable childhood diseases? — —

3. **Family-Child Reading and Storytelling:** Has the state increased the percentage of 3- to 5-year-olds whose parents read to them or tell them stories regularly? — —

4. **Preschool Participation:** Has the state reduced the gap in preschool participation between 3- to 5-year-olds from high- and low-income families? — —

5. **High School Completion:** Has the state increased the percentage of 19- to 20-year-olds who have a high school credential? *(1990)* — 95% —

6. **Mathematics Achievement:** Has the state increased the percentage of public school students who meet the Goals Panel's performance standard in mathematics? ▼
   - Grade 4 *(1992)* — 23% — —
   - Grade 8 *(1990, 1992)* — 34% — 36% ns — ↔
   - Grade 12 — —

7. **Reading Achievement:** Has the state increased the percentage of public school students who meet the Goals Panel's performance standard in reading? ▼
   - Grade 4 *(1992)* — 31% — —
   - Grade 8 — —
   - Grade 12 — —

8. **International Mathematics Achievement:** Has the state reduced the gap between the percentage of public school 8th graders and the percentage of 13-year-olds in the highest-scoring country who meet the Goals Panel's performance standard in mathematics? *(1991 and 1992)* — 5 percentage points — —

9. **International Science Achievement:** Has the state reduced the gap between the percentage of public school 8th graders and the percentage of 13-year-olds in the highest-scoring country who meet the Goals Panel's performance standard in science? — —

10. **Adult Literacy:** Has the state increased the percentage of adults who score at or above Level 3 in prose literacy? *(1992)* ■ — —

11. **Participation in Adult Education:** Has the state reduced the gap in adult education participation between adults who have a high school diploma or less, and those who have additional post-secondary education or technical training? — —

12. **Participation in Higher Education:** Has the state reduced the gap between White and minority high school graduates who:
    - enroll in college? — —
    - complete a college degree? — —

13. **Overall Student Drug and Alcohol Use:** Has the state reduced the percentage of public high school students reporting doing the following during the past 30 days: ■
    - using marijuana at least once? *(1990, 1993)* — —
    - having 5 or more drinks in a row? *(1990, 1993)* — —

14. **Sale of Drugs at School:** Has the state reduced the percentage of public high school students reporting that someone offered, sold, or gave them an illegal drug on school property during the past 12 months? *(1993)* ■ — —

15. **Student and Teacher Victimization:** Has the state reduced the percentage of students and teachers reporting that they were threatened or injured on school property during the past 12 months?
    - public high school students *(1993)* ■ — —
    - public school teachers — —

16. **Disruptions in Class by Students:** Has the state reduced the percentage of students and teachers reporting that disruptions often interfere with teaching and learning?
    - high school students — —
    - high school teachers — —

— Data not available.
ns Interpret with caution. Change was not statistically significant.

▲ See technical note on page 133.
▼ See technical note on pages 134-135.

■ See technical note on page 136.
■ See technical note on page 137.

OHIO

	Baseline	Most Recent Update	Overall Progress
1. Children's Health Index: Has the state reduced the percentage of infants born with 2 or more health and developmental risks? *(1990, 1991)* ▲	16%	15%	↑
2. Immunizations: Has the state increased the percentage of 2-year-olds who have been fully immunized against preventable childhood diseases?	—	—	
3. Family-Child Reading and Storytelling: Has the state increased the percentage of 3- to 5-year-olds whose parents read to them or tell them stories regularly?	—	—	
4. Preschool Participation: Has the state reduced the gap in preschool participation between 3- to 5-year-olds from high- and low-income families?	—	—	
5. High School Completion: Has the state increased the percentage of 19- to 20-year-olds who have a high school credential? *(1990)*	87%	—	
6. Mathematics Achievement: Has the state increased the percentage of public school students who meet the Goals Panel's performance standard in mathematics? ▼			
• Grade 4 *(1992)*	17%	—	
• Grade 8 *(1990, 1992)*	19%	22% ns	↔
• Grade 12	—	—	
7. Reading Achievement: Has the state increased the percentage of public school students who meet the Goals Panel's performance standard in reading? ▼			
• Grade 4 *(1992)*	24%	—	
• Grade 8	—	—	
• Grade 12	—	—	
8. International Mathematics Achievement: Has the state reduced the gap between the percentage of public school 8th graders and the percentage of 13-year-olds in the highest-scoring country who meet the Goals Panel's performance standard in mathematics? *(1991 and 1992)*	19 percentage points	—	
9. International Science Achievement: Has the state reduced the gap between the percentage of public school 8th graders and the percentage of 13-year-olds in the highest-scoring country who meet the Goals Panel's performance standard in science?	—	—	
10. Adult Literacy: Has the state increased the percentage of adults who score at or above Level 3 in prose literacy? *(1992)* ■	55%	—	
11. Participation in Adult Education: Has the state reduced the gap in adult education participation between adults who have a high school diploma or less, and those who have additional post-secondary education or technical training?	—	—	
12. Participation in Higher Education: Has the state reduced the gap between White and minority high school graduates who:			
• enroll in college?	—	—	
• complete a college degree?	—	—	
13. Overall Student Drug and Alcohol Use: Has the state reduced the percentage of public high school students reporting doing the following during the past 30 days: ■			
• using marijuana at least once? *(1993)*	16%	—	
• having 5 or more drinks in a row? *(1993)*	30%	—	
14. Sale of Drugs at School: Has the state reduced the percentage of public high school students reporting that someone offered, sold, or gave them an illegal drug on school property during the past 12 months? *(1993)* ■	20%	—	
15. Student and Teacher Victimization: Has the state reduced the percentage of students and teachers reporting that they were threatened or injured on school property during the past 12 months?			
• public high school students *(1993)* ■	8%	—	
• public school teachers	—	—	
16. Disruptions in Class by Students: Has the state reduced the percentage of students and teachers reporting that disruptions often interfere with teaching and learning?			
• high school students	—	—	
• high school teachers	—	—	

— Data not available.
ns Interpret with caution. Change was not statistically significant.

▲ See technical note on page 133.
▼ See technical note on pages 134-135.

■ See technical note on page 136.
■ See technical note on page 137.

OKLAHOMA

	Baseline	Most Recent Update	Overall Progress

1. **Children's Health Index:** Has the state reduced the percentage of infants born with 2 or more health and developmental risks? *(1991)* ▲ — Baseline: 14% — Most Recent Update: —

2. **Immunizations:** Has the state increased the percentage of 2-year-olds who have been fully immunized against preventable childhood diseases? — —

3. **Family-Child Reading and Storytelling:** Has the state increased the percentage of 3- to 5-year-olds whose parents read to them or tell them stories regularly? — —

4. **Preschool Participation:** Has the state reduced the gap in preschool participation between 3- to 5-year-olds from high- and low-income families? — —

5. **High School Completion:** Has the state increased the percentage of 19- to 20-year-olds who have a high school credential? *(1990)* — Baseline: 86% — Most Recent Update: —

6. **Mathematics Achievement:** Has the state increased the percentage of public school students who meet the Goals Panel's performance standard in mathematics? ▼
   - Grade 4 *(1992)* — Baseline: 14% — Most Recent Update: —
   - Grade 8 *(1990, 1992)* — Baseline: 17% — Most Recent Update: 21% — Overall Progress: ▲
   - Grade 12 — —

7. **Reading Achievement:** Has the state increased the percentage of public school students who meet the Goals Panel's performance standard in reading? ▼
   - Grade 4 *(1992)* — Baseline: 25% — Most Recent Update: —
   - Grade 8 — —
   - Grade 12 — —

8. **International Mathematics Achievement:** Has the state reduced the gap between the percentage of public school 8th graders and the percentage of 13-year-olds in the highest-scoring country who meet the Goals Panel's performance standard in mathematics? *(1991 and 1992)* — Baseline: 20 percentage points — Most Recent Update: —

9. **International Science Achievement:** Has the state reduced the gap between the percentage of public school 8th graders and the percentage of 13-year-olds in the highest-scoring country who meet the Goals Panel's performance standard in science? — —

10. **Adult Literacy:** Has the state increased the percentage of adults who score at or above Level 3 in prose literacy? *(1992)* ■ — —

11. **Participation in Adult Education:** Has the state reduced the gap in adult education participation between adults who have a high school diploma or less, and those who have additional post-secondary education or technical training? — —

12. **Participation in Higher Education:** Has the state reduced the gap between White and minority high school graduates who:
    - enroll in college? — —
    - complete a college degree? — —

13. **Overall Student Drug and Alcohol Use:** Has the state reduced the percentage of public high school students reporting doing the following during the past 30 days: ■
    - using marijuana at least once? *(1990, 1993)* — —
    - having 5 or more drinks in a row? *(1990, 1993)* — —

14. **Sale of Drugs at School:** Has the state reduced the percentage of public high school students reporting that someone offered, sold, or gave them an illegal drug on school property during the past 12 months? *(1993)* ■ — —

15. **Student and Teacher Victimization:** Has the state reduced the percentage of students and teachers reporting that they were threatened or injured on school property during the past 12 months?
    - public high school students *(1993)* ■ — —
    - public school teachers — —

16. **Disruptions in Class by Students:** Has the state reduced the percentage of students and teachers reporting that disruptions often interfere with teaching and learning?
    - high school students — —
    - high school teachers — —

— Data not available.
ns Interpret with caution. Change was not statistically significant.

▲ See technical note on page 133.
▼ See technical note on pages 134-135.

■ See technical note on page 136.
■ See technical note on page 137.

OREGON

	Baseline	Most Recent Update	Overall Progress

1. **Children's Health Index:** Has the state reduced the percentage of infants born with 2 or more health and developmental risks? *(1990, 1991)* ▲ — 16% — 14% — ↑

2. **Immunizations:** Has the state increased the percentage of 2-year-olds who have been fully immunized against preventable childhood diseases? — —

3. **Family-Child Reading and Storytelling:** Has the state increased the percentage of 3- to 5-year-olds whose parents read to them or tell them stories regularly? — —

4. **Preschool Participation:** Has the state reduced the gap in preschool participation between 3- to 5-year-olds from high- and low-income families? — —

5. **High School Completion:** Has the state increased the percentage of 19- to 20-year-olds who have a high school credential? *(1990)* — 83% — —

6. **Mathematics Achievement:** Has the state increased the percentage of public school students who meet the Goals Panel's performance standard in mathematics? ▼
   - Grade 4 *(1992)* — —
   - Grade 8 *(1990, 1992)* — —
   - Grade 12 — —

7. **Reading Achievement:** Has the state increased the percentage of public school students who meet the Goals Panel's performance standard in reading? ▼
   - Grade 4 *(1992)* — —
   - Grade 8 — —
   - Grade 12 — —

8. **International Mathematics Achievement:** Has the state reduced the gap between the percentage of public school 8th graders and the percentage of 13-year-olds in the highest-scoring country who meet the Goals Panel's performance standard in mathematics? *(1991 and 1992)* — —

9. **International Science Achievement:** Has the state reduced the gap between the percentage of public school 8th graders and the percentage of 13-year-olds in the highest-scoring country who meet the Goals Panel's performance standard in science? — —

10. **Adult Literacy:** Has the state increased the percentage of adults who score at or above Level 3 in prose literacy? *(1990)* ■ — 77% — —

11. **Participation in Adult Education:** Has the state reduced the gap in adult education participation between adults who have a high school diploma or less, and those who have additional post-secondary education or technical training? — —

12. **Participation in Higher Education:** Has the state reduced the gap between White and minority high school graduates who:
    - enroll in college? — —
    - complete a college degree? — —

13. **Overall Student Drug and Alcohol Use:** Has the state reduced the percentage of public high school students reporting doing the following during the past 30 days: ■
    - using marijuana at least once? *(1990, 1993)* — —
    - having 5 or more drinks in a row? *(1990, 1993)* — —

14. **Sale of Drugs at School:** Has the state reduced the percentage of public high school students reporting that someone offered, sold, or gave them an illegal drug on school property during the past 12 months? *(1993)* ■ — —

15. **Student and Teacher Victimization:** Has the state reduced the percentage of students and teachers reporting that they were threatened or injured on school property during the past 12 months?
    - public high school students *(1993)* ■ — —
    - public school teachers — —

16. **Disruptions in Class by Students:** Has the state reduced the percentage of students and teachers reporting that disruptions often interfere with teaching and learning?
    - high school students — —
    - high school teachers — —

— Data not available.
ns Interpret with caution. Change was not statistically significant.

▲ See technical note on page 133.
▼ See technical note on pages 134-135.

■ See technical note on page 136.
■ See technical note on page 137.

PENNSYLVANIA

	Baseline	Most Recent Update	Overall Progress
1. Children's Health Index: Has the state reduced the percentage of infants born with 2 or more health and developmental risks? *(1990, 1991)* ▲	15%	15%	⟷
2. Immunizations: Has the state increased the percentage of 2-year-olds who have been fully immunized against preventable childhood diseases?	—	—	
3. Family-Child Reading and Storytelling: Has the state increased the percentage of 3- to 5-year-olds whose parents read to them or tell them stories regularly?	—	—	
4. Preschool Participation: Has the state reduced the gap in preschool participation between 3- to 5-year-olds from high- and low-income families?	—	—	
5. High School Completion: Has the state increased the percentage of 19- to 20-year-olds who have a high school credential? *(1990)*	89%	—	
6. Mathematics Achievement: Has the state increased the percentage of public school students who meet the Goals Panel's performance standard in mathematics? ▼			
• Grade 4 *(1992)*	23%	—	
• Grade 8 *(1990, 1992)*	21%	26% ns	⟷
• Grade 12	—	—	
7. Reading Achievement: Has the state increased the percentage of public school students who meet the Goals Panel's performance standard in reading? ▼			
• Grade 4 *(1992)*	28%	—	
• Grade 8	—	—	
• Grade 12	—	—	
8. International Mathematics Achievement: Has the state reduced the gap between the percentage of public school 8th graders and the percentage of 13-year-olds in the highest-scoring country who meet the Goals Panel's performance standard in mathematics? *(1991 and 1992)*	15 percentage points	—	
9. International Science Achievement: Has the state reduced the gap between the percentage of public school 8th graders and the percentage of 13-year-olds in the highest-scoring country who meet the Goals Panel's performance standard in science?	—	—	
10. Adult Literacy: Has the state increased the percentage of adults who score at or above Level 3 in prose literacy? *(1992)* ■	54%	—	
11. Participation in Adult Education: Has the state reduced the gap in adult education participation between adults who have a high school diploma or less, and those who have additional post-secondary education or technical training?	—	—	
12. Participation in Higher Education: Has the state reduced the gap between White and minority high school graduates who:			
• enroll in college?	—	—	
• complete a college degree?	—	—	
13. Overall Student Drug and Alcohol Use: Has the state reduced the percentage of public high school students reporting doing the following during the past 30 days: ■			
• using marijuana at least once? *(1990, 1993)*	—	—	
• having 5 or more drinks in a row? *(1990, 1993)*	—	—	
14. Sale of Drugs at School: Has the state reduced the percentage of public high school students reporting that someone offered, sold, or gave them an illegal drug on school property during the past 12 months? *(1993)* ■	—	—	
15. Student and Teacher Victimization: Has the state reduced the percentage of students and teachers reporting that they were threatened or injured on school property during the past 12 months?			
• public high school students *(1993)* ■	—	—	
• public school teachers	—	—	
16. Disruptions in Class by Students: Has the state reduced the percentage of students and teachers reporting that disruptions often interfere with teaching and learning?			
• high school students	—	—	
• high school teachers	—	—	

— Data not available.
ns Interpret with caution. Change was not statistically significant.

▲ See technical note on page 133.
▼ See technical note on pages 134-135.

■ See technical note on page 136.
■ See technical note on page 137.

RHODE ISLAND

	Baseline	Most Recent Update	Overall Progress
1. Children's Health Index: Has the state reduced the percentage of infants born with 2 or more health and developmental risks? *(1990, 1991)*▲	13%	13%	⟷
2. Immunizations: Has the state increased the percentage of 2-year-olds who have been fully immunized against preventable childhood diseases?	—	—	
3. Family-Child Reading and Storytelling: Has the state increased the percentage of 3- to 5-year-olds whose parents read to them or tell them stories regularly?	—	—	
4. Preschool Participation: Has the state reduced the gap in preschool participation between 3- to 5-year-olds from high- and low-income families?	—	—	
5. High School Completion: Has the state increased the percentage of 19- to 20-year-olds who have a high school credential? *(1990)*	87%	—	
6. Mathematics Achievement: Has the state increased the percentage of public school students who meet the Goals Panel's performance standard in mathematics? ▼			
• Grade 4 *(1992)*	14%	—	
• Grade 8 *(1990, 1992)*	18%	20% ns	⟷
• Grade 12	—	—	
7. Reading Achievement: Has the state increased the percentage of public school students who meet the Goals Panel's performance standard in reading? ▼			
• Grade 4 *(1992)*	24%	—	
• Grade 8	—	—	
• Grade 12	—	—	
8. International Mathematics Achievement: Has the state reduced the gap between the percentage of public school 8th graders and the percentage of 13-year-olds in the highest-scoring country who meet the Goals Panel's performance standard in mathematics? *(1991 and 1992)*	21 percentage points	—	
9. International Science Achievement: Has the state reduced the gap between the percentage of public school 8th graders and the percentage of 13-year-olds in the highest-scoring country who meet the Goals Panel's performance standard in science?	—	—	
10. Adult Literacy: Has the state increased the percentage of adults who score at or above Level 3 in prose literacy? *(1992)*■	—	—	
11. Participation in Adult Education: Has the state reduced the gap in adult education participation between adults who have a high school diploma or less, and those who have additional post-secondary education or technical training?	—	—	
12. Participation in Higher Education: Has the state reduced the gap between White and minority high school graduates who:			
• enroll in college?	—	—	
• complete a college degree?	—	—	
13. Overall Student Drug and Alcohol Use: Has the state reduced the percentage of public high school students reporting doing the following during the past 30 days: ■			
• using marijuana at least once? *(1990, 1993)*	—	—	
• having 5 or more drinks in a row? *(1990, 1993)*	—	—	
14. Sale of Drugs at School: Has the state reduced the percentage of public high school students reporting that someone offered, sold, or gave them an illegal drug on school property during the past 12 months? *(1993)*■	—	—	
15. Student and Teacher Victimization: Has the state reduced the percentage of students and teachers reporting that they were threatened or injured on school property during the past 12 months?			
• public high school students *(1993)*■	—	—	
• public school teachers	—	—	
16. Disruptions in Class by Students: Has the state reduced the percentage of students and teachers reporting that disruptions often interfere with teaching and learning?			
• high school students	—	—	
• high school teachers	—	—	

— Data not available.
ns Interpret with caution. Change was not statistically significant.

▲ See technical note on page 133.
▼ See technical note on pages 134-135.

■ See technical note on page 136.
■ See technical note on page 137.

SOUTH CAROLINA

	Baseline	Most Recent Update	Overall Progress

1. Children's Health Index: Has the state reduced the percentage of infants born with 2 or more health and developmental risks? *(1990, 1991)*▲ — 16% — 14% — ↑

2. Immunizations: Has the state increased the percentage of 2-year-olds who have been fully immunized against preventable childhood diseases? — — — —

3. Family-Child Reading and Storytelling: Has the state increased the percentage of 3- to 5-year-olds whose parents read to them or tell them stories regularly? — — — —

4. Preschool Participation: Has the state reduced the gap in preschool participation between 3- to 5-year-olds from high- and low-income families? — — — —

5. High School Completion: Has the state increased the percentage of 19- to 20-year-olds who have a high school credential? *(1990)* — 84% — —

6. Mathematics Achievement: Has the state increased the percentage of public school students who meet the Goals Panel's performance standard in mathematics? ▼
- Grade 4 *(1992)* — 13% — —
- Grade 8 *(1992)* — 18% — —
- Grade 12 — — — —

7. Reading Achievement: Has the state increased the percentage of public school students who meet the Goals Panel's performance standard in reading? ▼
- Grade 4 *(1992)* — 19% — —
- Grade 8 — — — —
- Grade 12 — — — —

8. International Mathematics Achievement: Has the state reduced the gap between the percentage of public school 8th graders and the percentage of 13-year-olds in the highest-scoring country who meet the Goals Panel's performance standard in mathematics? *(1991 and 1992)* — 23 percentage points — —

9. International Science Achievement: Has the state reduced the gap between the percentage of public school 8th graders and the percentage of 13-year-olds in the highest-scoring country who meet the Goals Panel's performance standard in science? — — — —

10. Adult Literacy: Has the state increased the percentage of adults who score at or above Level 3 in prose literacy? *(1992)*■ — — — —

11. Participation in Adult Education: Has the state reduced the gap in adult education participation between adults who have a high school diploma or less, and those who have additional post-secondary education or technical training? — — — —

12. Participation in Higher Education: Has the state reduced the gap between White and minority high school graduates who:
- enroll in college? — — — —
- complete a college degree? — — — —

13. Overall Student Drug and Alcohol Use: Has the state reduced the percentage of public high school students reporting doing the following during the past 30 days: ■
- using marijuana at least once? *(1991, 1993)* — 12% — 13% [ns] — ↔
- having 5 or more drinks in a row? *(1991, 1993)* — 27% — 25% [ns] — ↔

14. Sale of Drugs at School: Has the state reduced the percentage of public high school students reporting that someone offered, sold, or gave them an illegal drug on school property during the past 12 months? *(1993)*■ — 25% — —

15. Student and Teacher Victimization: Has the state reduced the percentage of students and teachers reporting that they were threatened or injured on school property during the past 12 months?
- public high school students *(1993)*■ — 10% — —
- public school teachers — — — —

16. Disruptions in Class by Students: Has the state reduced the percentage of students and teachers reporting that disruptions often interfere with teaching and learning?
- high school students — — — —
- high school teachers — — — —

— Data not available.
ns Interpret with caution. Change was not statistically significant.

▲ See technical note on page 133.
▼ See technical note on pages 134-135.

■ See technical note on page 136.
■ See technical note on page 137.

SOUTH DAKOTA

	Baseline	Most Recent Update	Overall Progress

1. **Children's Health Index:** Has the state reduced the percentage of infants born with 2 or more health and developmental risks? *(1990, 1991)* ▲ | — | — |

2. **Immunizations:** Has the state increased the percentage of 2-year-olds who have been fully immunized against preventable childhood diseases? | — | — |

3. **Family-Child Reading and Storytelling:** Has the state increased the percentage of 3- to 5-year-olds whose parents read to them or tell them stories regularly? | — | — |

4. **Preschool Participation:** Has the state reduced the gap in preschool participation between 3- to 5-year-olds from high- and low-income families? | — | — |

5. **High School Completion:** Has the state increased the percentage of 19- to 20-year-olds who have a high school credential? *(1990)* | 91% | — |

6. **Mathematics Achievement:** Has the state increased the percentage of public school students who meet the Goals Panel's performance standard in mathematics? ▼
   - Grade 4 *(1992)* | — | — |
   - Grade 8 *(1990, 1992)* | — | — |
   - Grade 12 | — | — |

7. **Reading Achievement:** Has the state increased the percentage of public school students who meet the Goals Panel's performance standard in reading? ▼
   - Grade 4 *(1992)* | — | — |
   - Grade 8 | — | — |
   - Grade 12 | — | — |

8. **International Mathematics Achievement:** Has the state reduced the gap between the percentage of public school 8th graders and the percentage of 13-year-olds in the highest-scoring country who meet the Goals Panel's performance standard in mathematics? *(1991 and 1992)* | — | — |

9. **International Science Achievement:** Has the state reduced the gap between the percentage of public school 8th graders and the percentage of 13-year-olds in the highest-scoring country who meet the Goals Panel's performance standard in science? | — | — |

10. **Adult Literacy:** Has the state increased the percentage of adults who score at or above Level 3 in prose literacy? *(1992)* ■ | — | — |

11. **Participation in Adult Education:** Has the state reduced the gap in adult education participation between adults who have a high school diploma or less, and those who have additional post-secondary education or technical training? | — | — |

12. **Participation in Higher Education:** Has the state reduced the gap between White and minority high school graduates who:
    - enroll in college? | — | — |
    - complete a college degree? | — | — |

13. **Overall Student Drug and Alcohol Use:** Has the state reduced the percentage of public high school students reporting doing the following during the past 30 days: ■
    - using marijuana at least once? *(1990, 1993)* | 12% | 10% [ns] | ◄►
    - having 5 or more drinks in a row? *(1990, 1993)* | 42% | 44% [ns] | ◄►

14. **Sale of Drugs at School:** Has the state reduced the percentage of public high school students reporting that someone offered, sold, or gave them an illegal drug on school property during the past 12 months? *(1993)* ■ | 19% | — |

15. **Student and Teacher Victimization:** Has the state reduced the percentage of students and teachers reporting that they were threatened or injured on school property during the past 12 months?
    - public high school students *(1993)* ■ | 6% | — |
    - public school teachers | — | — |

16. **Disruptions in Class by Students:** Has the state reduced the percentage of students and teachers reporting that disruptions often interfere with teaching and learning?
    - high school students | — | — |
    - high school teachers | — | — |

— Data not available.
ns Interpret with caution. Change was not statistically significant.

▲ See technical note on page 133.
▼ See technical note on pages 134-135.

■ See technical note on page 136.
■ See technical note on page 137.

TENNESSEE

	Baseline	Most Recent Update	Overall Progress
1. **Children's Health Index:** Has the state reduced the percentage of infants born with 2 or more health and developmental risks? *(1990, 1991)* ▲	14%	13%	↑
2. **Immunizations:** Has the state increased the percentage of 2-year-olds who have been fully immunized against preventable childhood diseases?	—	—	
3. **Family-Child Reading and Storytelling:** Has the state increased the percentage of 3- to 5-year-olds whose parents read to them or tell them stories regularly?	—	—	
4. **Preschool Participation:** Has the state reduced the gap in preschool participation between 3- to 5-year-olds from high- and low-income families?	—	—	
5. **High School Completion:** Has the state increased the percentage of 19- to 20-year-olds who have a high school credential? *(1990)*	81%	—	
6. **Mathematics Achievement:** Has the state increased the percentage of public school students who meet the Goals Panel's performance standard in mathematics? ▼			
• Grade 4 *(1992)*	10%	—	
• Grade 8 *(1992)*	15%	—	
• Grade 12	—	—	
7. **Reading Achievement:** Has the state increased the percentage of public school students who meet the Goals Panel's performance standard in reading? ▼			
• Grade 4 *(1992)*	20%	—	
• Grade 8	—	—	
• Grade 12	—	—	
8. **International Mathematics Achievement:** Has the state reduced the gap between the percentage of public school 8th graders and the percentage of 13-year-olds in the highest-scoring country who meet the Goals Panel's performance standard in mathematics? *(1991 and 1992)*	26 percentage points	—	
9. **International Science Achievement:** Has the state reduced the gap between the percentage of public school 8th graders and the percentage of 13-year-olds in the highest-scoring country who meet the Goals Panel's performance standard in science?	—	—	
10. **Adult Literacy:** Has the state increased the percentage of adults who score at or above Level 3 in prose literacy? *(1992)* ■	—	—	
11. **Participation in Adult Education:** Has the state reduced the gap in adult education participation between adults who have a high school diploma or less, and those who have additional post-secondary education or technical training?	—	—	
12. **Participation in Higher Education:** Has the state reduced the gap between White and minority high school graduates who:			
• enroll in college?	—	—	
• complete a college degree?	—	—	
13. **Overall Student Drug and Alcohol Use:** Has the state reduced the percentage of public high school students reporting doing the following during the past 30 days: ■			
• using marijuana at least once? *(1993)*	17%	—	
• having 5 or more drinks in a row? *(1993)*	28%	—	
14. **Sale of Drugs at School:** Has the state reduced the percentage of public high school students reporting that someone offered, sold, or gave them an illegal drug on school property during the past 12 months? *(1993)* ■	22%	—	
15. **Student and Teacher Victimization:** Has the state reduced the percentage of students and teachers reporting that they were threatened or injured on school property during the past 12 months?			
• public high school students *(1993)* ■	9%	—	
• public school teachers	—	—	
16. **Disruptions in Class by Students:** Has the state reduced the percentage of students and teachers reporting that disruptions often interfere with teaching and learning?			
• high school students	—	—	
• high school teachers	—	—	

— Data not available.
ns Interpret with caution. Change was not statistically significant.

▲ See technical note on page 133.
▼ See technical note on pages 134-135.

■ See technical note on page 136.
■ See technical note on page 137.

TEXAS

	Baseline	Most Recent Update	Overall Progress
1. **Children's Health Index:** Has the state reduced the percentage of infants born with 2 or more health and developmental risks? *(1990, 1991)* ▲	12%	11%	▲
2. **Immunizations:** Has the state increased the percentage of 2-year-olds who have been fully immunized against preventable childhood diseases?	—	—	
3. **Family-Child Reading and Storytelling:** Has the state increased the percentage of 3- to 5-year-olds whose parents read to them or tell them stories regularly?	—	—	
4. **Preschool Participation:** Has the state reduced the gap in preschool participation between 3- to 5-year-olds from high- and low-income families?	—	—	
5. **High School Completion:** Has the state increased the percentage of 19- to 20-year-olds who have a high school credential? *(1990)*	80%	—	
6. **Mathematics Achievement:** Has the state increased the percentage of public school students who meet the Goals Panel's performance standard in mathematics? ▼ • Grade 4 *(1992)* • Grade 8 *(1990, 1992)* • Grade 12	16% 16% —	— 21% —	▲
7. **Reading Achievement:** Has the state increased the percentage of public school students who meet the Goals Panel's performance standard in reading? ▼ • Grade 4 *(1992)* • Grade 8 • Grade 12	20% — —	— — —	
8. **International Mathematics Achievement:** Has the state reduced the gap between the percentage of public school 8th graders and the percentage of 13-year-olds in the highest-scoring country who meet the Goals Panel's performance standard in mathematics? *(1991 and 1992)*	20 percentage points	—	
9. **International Science Achievement:** Has the state reduced the gap between the percentage of public school 8th graders and the percentage of 13-year-olds in the highest-scoring country who meet the Goals Panel's performance standard in science?	—	—	
10. **Adult Literacy:** Has the state increased the percentage of adults who score at or above Level 3 in prose literacy? *(1992)* ■	47%	—	
11. **Participation in Adult Education:** Has the state reduced the gap in adult education participation between adults who have a high school diploma or less, and those who have additional post-secondary education or technical training?	—	—	
12. **Participation in Higher Education:** Has the state reduced the gap between White and minority high school graduates who: • enroll in college? • complete a college degree?	— —	— —	
13. **Overall Student Drug and Alcohol Use:** Has the state reduced the percentage of public high school students reporting doing the following during the past 30 days: ■ • using marijuana at least once? *(1990, 1993)* • having 5 or more drinks in a row? *(1990, 1993)*	— —	— —	
14. **Sale of Drugs at School:** Has the state reduced the percentage of public high school students reporting that someone offered, sold, or gave them an illegal drug on school property during the past 12 months? *(1993)* ■	—	—	
15. **Student and Teacher Victimization:** Has the state reduced the percentage of students and teachers reporting that they were threatened or injured on school property during the past 12 months? • public high school students *(1993)* ■ • public school teachers	— —	— —	
16. **Disruptions in Class by Students:** Has the state reduced the percentage of students and teachers reporting that disruptions often interfere with teaching and learning? • high school students • high school teachers	— —	— —	

— Data not available.
ns Interpret with caution. Change was not statistically significant.

▲ See technical note on page 133.
▼ See technical note on pages 134-135.

■ See technical note on page 136.
■ See technical note on page 137.

UTAH

	Baseline	Most Recent Update	Overall Progress

1. **Children's Health Index:** Has the state reduced the percentage of infants born with 2 or more health and developmental risks? *(1990, 1991)* ▲ — 13% — 12% — ↑

2. **Immunizations:** Has the state increased the percentage of 2-year-olds who have been fully immunized against preventable childhood diseases? — —

3. **Family-Child Reading and Storytelling:** Has the state increased the percentage of 3- to 5-year-olds whose parents read to them or tell them stories regularly? — —

4. **Preschool Participation:** Has the state reduced the gap in preschool participation between 3- to 5-year-olds from high- and low-income families? — —

5. **High School Completion:** Has the state increased the percentage of 19- to 20-year-olds who have a high school credential? *(1990)* — 87% — —

6. **Mathematics Achievement:** Has the state increased the percentage of public school students who meet the Goals Panel's performance standard in mathematics? ▼
   - Grade 4 *(1992)* — 20% — —
   - Grade 8 *(1992)* — 27% — —
   - Grade 12 — — —

7. **Reading Achievement:** Has the state increased the percentage of public school students who meet the Goals Panel's performance standard in reading? ▼
   - Grade 4 *(1992)* — 26% — —
   - Grade 8 — — —
   - Grade 12 — — —

8. **International Mathematics Achievement:** Has the state reduced the gap between the percentage of public school 8th graders and the percentage of 13-year-olds in the highest-scoring country who meet the Goals Panel's performance standard in mathematics? *(1991 and 1992)* — 14 percentage points — —

9. **International Science Achievement:** Has the state reduced the gap between the percentage of public school 8th graders and the percentage of 13-year-olds in the highest-scoring country who meet the Goals Panel's performance standard in science? — —

10. **Adult Literacy:** Has the state increased the percentage of adults who score at or above Level 3 in prose literacy? *(1992)* ■ — —

11. **Participation in Adult Education:** Has the state reduced the gap in adult education participation between adults who have a high school diploma or less, and those who have additional post-secondary education or technical training? — —

12. **Participation in Higher Education:** Has the state reduced the gap between White and minority high school graduates who:
    - enroll in college? — —
    - complete a college degree? — —

13. **Overall Student Drug and Alcohol Use:** Has the state reduced the percentage of public high school students reporting doing the following during the past 30 days: ■
    - using marijuana at least once? *(1990, 1993)* — 8% — 7% ns — ↔
    - having 5 or more drinks in a row? *(1990, 1993)* — 19% — 17% ns — ↔

14. **Sale of Drugs at School:** Has the state reduced the percentage of public high school students reporting that someone offered, sold, or gave them an illegal drug on school property during the past 12 months? *(1993)* ■ — 19% — —

15. **Student and Teacher Victimization:** Has the state reduced the percentage of students and teachers reporting that they were threatened or injured on school property during the past 12 months?
    - public high school students *(1993)* ■ — 8% — —
    - public school teachers — — —

16. **Disruptions in Class by Students:** Has the state reduced the percentage of students and teachers reporting that disruptions often interfere with teaching and learning?
    - high school students — —
    - high school teachers — —

— Data not available.
ns Interpret with caution. Change was not statistically significant.

▲ See technical note on page 133.
▼ See technical note on pages 134-135.

■ See technical note on page 136.
■ See technical note on page 137.

VERMONT

	Baseline	Most Recent Update	Overall Progress

1. **Children's Health Index:** Has the state reduced the percentage of infants born with 2 or more health and developmental risks? *(1990, 1991)* ▲ — 14% — 13% ns — ↔

2. **Immunizations:** Has the state increased the percentage of 2-year-olds who have been fully immunized against preventable childhood diseases? — —

3. **Family-Child Reading and Storytelling:** Has the state increased the percentage of 3- to 5-year-olds whose parents read to them or tell them stories regularly? — —

4. **Preschool Participation:** Has the state reduced the gap in preschool participation between 3- to 5-year-olds from high- and low-income families? — —

5. **High School Completion:** Has the state increased the percentage of 19- to 20-year-olds who have a high school credential? *(1990)* — 90% — —

6. **Mathematics Achievement:** Has the state increased the percentage of public school students who meet the Goals Panel's performance standard in mathematics? ▼
   - Grade 4 *(1992)* — —
   - Grade 8 *(1990, 1992)* — —
   - Grade 12 — —

7. **Reading Achievement:** Has the state increased the percentage of public school students who meet the Goals Panel's performance standard in reading? ▼
   - Grade 4 *(1992)* — —
   - Grade 8 — —
   - Grade 12 — —

8. **International Mathematics Achievement:** Has the state reduced the gap between the percentage of public school 8th graders and the percentage of 13-year-olds in the highest-scoring country who meet the Goals Panel's performance standard in mathematics? *(1991 and 1992)* — —

9. **International Science Achievement:** Has the state reduced the gap between the percentage of public school 8th graders and the percentage of 13-year-olds in the highest-scoring country who meet the Goals Panel's performance standard in science? — —

10. **Adult Literacy:** Has the state increased the percentage of adults who score at or above Level 3 in prose literacy? *(1992)* ■ — —

11. **Participation in Adult Education:** Has the state reduced the gap in adult education participation between adults who have a high school diploma or less, and those who have additional post-secondary education or technical training? — —

12. **Participation in Higher Education:** Has the state reduced the gap between White and minority high school graduates who:
   - enroll in college? — —
   - complete a college degree? — —

13. **Overall Student Drug and Alcohol Use:** Has the state reduced the percentage of public high school students reporting doing the following during the past 30 days: ▪
   - using marijuana at least once? *(1993)* — 19% — —
   - having 5 or more drinks in a row? *(1993)* — 31% — —

14. **Sale of Drugs at School:** Has the state reduced the percentage of public high school students reporting that someone offered, sold, or gave them an illegal drug on school property during the past 12 months? *(1993)* ▪ — —

15. **Student and Teacher Victimization:** Has the state reduced the percentage of students and teachers reporting that they were threatened or injured on school property during the past 12 months?
   - public high school students *(1993)* ▪ — —
   - public school teachers — —

16. **Disruptions in Class by Students:** Has the state reduced the percentage of students and teachers reporting that disruptions often interfere with teaching and learning?
   - high school students — —
   - high school teachers — —

— Data not available.
ns Interpret with caution. Change was not statistically significant.

▲ See technical note on page 133.
▼ See technical note on pages 134-135.

■ See technical note on page 136.
▪ See technical note on page 137.

VIRGINIA

	Baseline	Most Recent Update	Overall Progress

1. **Children's Health Index:** Has the state reduced the percentage of infants born with 2 or more health and developmental risks? *(1990, 1991)* ▲ — 12% / 11% / ↑

	Baseline	Most Recent Update	Overall Progress
1. **Children's Health Index:** Has the state reduced the percentage of infants born with 2 or more health and developmental risks? *(1990, 1991)* ▲	12%	11%	↑
2. **Immunizations:** Has the state increased the percentage of 2-year-olds who have been fully immunized against preventable childhood diseases?	—	—	
3. **Family-Child Reading and Storytelling:** Has the state increased the percentage of 3- to 5-year-olds whose parents read to them or tell them stories regularly?	—	—	
4. **Preschool Participation:** Has the state reduced the gap in preschool participation between 3- to 5-year-olds from high- and low-income families?	—	—	
5. **High School Completion:** Has the state increased the percentage of 19- to 20-year-olds who have a high school credential? *(1990)*	86%	—	
6. **Mathematics Achievement:** Has the state increased the percentage of public school students who meet the Goals Panel's performance standard in mathematics? ▼			
• Grade 4 *(1992)*	19%	—	
• Grade 8 *(1990, 1992)*	21%	23% ns	↔
• Grade 12	—	—	
7. **Reading Achievement:** Has the state increased the percentage of public school students who meet the Goals Panel's performance standard in reading? ▼			
• Grade 4 *(1992)*	28%	—	
• Grade 8	—	—	
• Grade 12	—	—	
8. **International Mathematics Achievement:** Has the state reduced the gap between the percentage of public school 8th graders and the percentage of 13-year-olds in the highest-scoring country who meet the Goals Panel's performance standard in mathematics? *(1991 and 1992)*	18 percentage points	—	
9. **International Science Achievement:** Has the state reduced the gap between the percentage of public school 8th graders and the percentage of 13-year-olds in the highest-scoring country who meet the Goals Panel's performance standard in science?	—	—	
10. **Adult Literacy:** Has the state increased the percentage of adults who score at or above Level 3 in prose literacy? *(1992)* ■	—	—	
11. **Participation in Adult Education:** Has the state reduced the gap in adult education participation between adults who have a high school diploma or less, and those who have additional post-secondary education or technical training?	—	—	
12. **Participation in Higher Education:** Has the state reduced the gap between White and minority high school graduates who:			
• enroll in college?	—	—	
• complete a college degree?	—	—	
13. **Overall Student Drug and Alcohol Use:** Has the state reduced the percentage of public high school students reporting doing the following during the past 30 days: ■			
• using marijuana at least once? *(1990, 1993)*	—	—	
• having 5 or more drinks in a row? *(1990, 1993)*	—	—	
14. **Sale of Drugs at School:** Has the state reduced the percentage of public high school students reporting that someone offered, sold, or gave them an illegal drug on school property during the past 12 months? *(1993)* ■	—	—	
15. **Student and Teacher Victimization:** Has the state reduced the percentage of students and teachers reporting that they were threatened or injured on school property during the past 12 months?			
• public high school students *(1993)* ■	—	—	
• public school teachers	—	—	
16. **Disruptions in Class by Students:** Has the state reduced the percentage of students and teachers reporting that disruptions often interfere with teaching and learning?			
• high school students	—	—	
• high school teachers	—	—	

— Data not available.
ns Interpret with caution. Change was not statistically significant.

▲ See technical note on page 133.
▼ See technical note on pages 134-135.

■ See technical note on page 136.
■ See technical note on page 137.

WASHINGTON

	Baseline	Most Recent Update	Overall Progress
1. **Children's Health Index:** Has the state reduced the percentage of infants born with 2 or more health and developmental risks? *(1990, 1991)* ▲	13%	12%	↑
2. **Immunizations:** Has the state increased the percentage of 2-year-olds who have been fully immunized against preventable childhood diseases?	—	—	
3. **Family-Child Reading and Storytelling:** Has the state increased the percentage of 3- to 5-year-olds whose parents read to them or tell them stories regularly?	—	—	
4. **Preschool Participation:** Has the state reduced the gap in preschool participation between 3- to 5-year-olds from high- and low-income families?	—	—	
5. **High School Completion:** Has the state increased the percentage of 19- to 20-year-olds who have a high school credential? *(1990)*	85%	—	
6. **Mathematics Achievement:** Has the state increased the percentage of public school students who meet the Goals Panel's performance standard in mathematics? ▼			
• Grade 4 *(1992)*	—	—	
• Grade 8 *(1990, 1992)*	—	—	
• Grade 12	—	—	
7. **Reading Achievement:** Has the state increased the percentage of public school students who meet the Goals Panel's performance standard in reading? ▼			
• Grade 4 *(1992)*	—	—	
• Grade 8	—	—	
• Grade 12	—	—	
8. **International Mathematics Achievement:** Has the state reduced the gap between the percentage of public school 8th graders and the percentage of 13-year-olds in the highest-scoring country who meet the Goals Panel's performance standard in mathematics? *(1991 and 1992)*	—	—	
9. **International Science Achievement:** Has the state reduced the gap between the percentage of public school 8th graders and the percentage of 13-year-olds in the highest-scoring country who meet the Goals Panel's performance standard in science?	—	—	
10. **Adult Literacy:** Has the state increased the percentage of adults who score at or above Level 3 in prose literacy? *(1992)* ■	69%	—	
11. **Participation in Adult Education:** Has the state reduced the gap in adult education participation between adults who have a high school diploma or less, and those who have additional post-secondary education or technical training?	—	—	
12. **Participation in Higher Education:** Has the state reduced the gap between White and minority high school graduates who:			
• enroll in college?	—	—	
• complete a college degree?	—	—	
13. **Overall Student Drug and Alcohol Use:** Has the state reduced the percentage of public high school students reporting doing the following during the past 30 days: ■			
• using marijuana at least once? *(1990, 1993)*	—	—	
• having 5 or more drinks in a row? *(1990, 1993)*	—	—	
14. **Sale of Drugs at School:** Has the state reduced the percentage of public high school students reporting that someone offered, sold, or gave them an illegal drug on school property during the past 12 months? *(1993)* ■	—	—	
15. **Student and Teacher Victimization:** Has the state reduced the percentage of students and teachers reporting that they were threatened or injured on school property during the past 12 months?			
• public high school students *(1993)* ■	—	—	
• public school teachers	—	—	
16. **Disruptions in Class by Students:** Has the state reduced the percentage of students and teachers reporting that disruptions often interfere with teaching and learning?			
• high school students	—	—	
• high school teachers	—	—	

— Data not available.
ns Interpret with caution. Change was not statistically significant.

▲ See technical note on page 133.
▼ See technical note on pages 134-135.

■ See technical note on page 136.
■ See technical note on page 137.

WEST VIRGINIA

	Baseline	Most Recent Update	Overall Progress
1. Children's Health Index: Has the state reduced the percentage of infants born with 2 or more health and developmental risks? *(1990, 1991)* ▲	16%	15%	↑
2. Immunizations: Has the state increased the percentage of 2-year-olds who have been fully immunized against preventable childhood diseases?	—	—	
3. Family-Child Reading and Storytelling: Has the state increased the percentage of 3- to 5-year-olds whose parents read to them or tell them stories regularly?	—	—	
4. Preschool Participation: Has the state reduced the gap in preschool participation between 3- to 5-year-olds from high- and low-income families?	—	—	
5. High School Completion: Has the state increased the percentage of 19- to 20-year-olds who have a high school credential? *(1990)*	85%	—	
6. Mathematics Achievement: Has the state increased the percentage of public school students who meet the Goals Panel's performance standard in mathematics? ▼			
• Grade 4 *(1992)*	13%	—	
• Grade 8 *(1990, 1992)*	12%	13% ns	↔
• Grade 12	—	—	
7. Reading Achievement: Has the state increased the percentage of public school students who meet the Goals Panel's performance standard in reading? ▼			
• Grade 4 *(1992)*	22%	—	
• Grade 8	—	—	
• Grade 12	—	—	
8. International Mathematics Achievement: Has the state reduced the gap between the percentage of public school 8th graders and the percentage of 13-year-olds in the highest-scoring country who meet the Goals Panel's performance standard in mathematics? *(1991 and 1992)*	28 percentage points	—	
9. International Science Achievement: Has the state reduced the gap between the percentage of public school 8th graders and the percentage of 13-year-olds in the highest-scoring country who meet the Goals Panel's performance standard in science?	—	—	
10. Adult Literacy: Has the state increased the percentage of adults who score at or above Level 3 in prose literacy? *(1992)* ■	—	—	
11. Participation in Adult Education: Has the state reduced the gap in adult education participation between adults who have a high school diploma or less, and those who have additional post-secondary education or technical training?	—	—	
12. Participation in Higher Education: Has the state reduced the gap between White and minority high school graduates who:			
• enroll in college?	—	—	
• complete a college degree?	—	—	
13. Overall Student Drug and Alcohol Use: Has the state reduced the percentage of public high school students reporting doing the following during the past 30 days: ■			
• using marijuana at least once? *(1990, 1993)*	17%	18% ns	↔
• having 5 or more drinks in a row? *(1990, 1993)*	42%	39% ns	↔
14. Sale of Drugs at School: Has the state reduced the percentage of public high school students reporting that someone offered, sold, or gave them an illegal drug on school property during the past 12 months? *(1993)* ■	26%	—	
15. Student and Teacher Victimization: Has the state reduced the percentage of students and teachers reporting that they were threatened or injured on school property during the past 12 months?			
• public high school students *(1993)* ■	8%	—	
• public school teachers	—	—	
16. Disruptions in Class by Students: Has the state reduced the percentage of students and teachers reporting that disruptions often interfere with teaching and learning?			
• high school students	—	—	
• high school teachers	—	—	

— Data not available.
ns Interpret with caution. Change was not statistically significant.

▲ See technical note on page 133.
▼ See technical note on pages 134-135.

■ See technical note on page 136.
■ See technical note on page 137.

WISCONSIN

	Baseline	Most Recent Update	Overall Progress

1. **Children's Health Index:** Has the state reduced the percentage of infants born with 2 or more health and developmental risks? *(1990, 1991)* ▲ — Baseline 18%, Most Recent Update 17%, Overall Progress ↑

2. **Immunizations:** Has the state increased the percentage of 2-year-olds who have been fully immunized against preventable childhood diseases? — —

3. **Family-Child Reading and Storytelling:** Has the state increased the percentage of 3- to 5-year-olds whose parents read to them or tell them stories regularly? — —

4. **Preschool Participation:** Has the state reduced the gap in preschool participation between 3- to 5-year-olds from high- and low-income families? — —

5. **High School Completion:** Has the state increased the percentage of 19- to 20-year-olds who have a high school credential? *(1990)* — Baseline 90%, —

6. **Mathematics Achievement:** Has the state increased the percentage of public school students who meet the Goals Panel's performance standard in mathematics? ▼
   - Grade 4 *(1992)* — Baseline 25%, —
   - Grade 8 *(1990, 1992)* — Baseline 29%, Most Recent Update 32% ns, Overall Progress ↔
   - Grade 12 — —

7. **Reading Achievement:** Has the state increased the percentage of public school students who meet the Goals Panel's performance standard in reading? ▼
   - Grade 4 *(1992)* — Baseline 29%, —
   - Grade 8 — —
   - Grade 12 — —

8. **International Mathematics Achievement:** Has the state reduced the gap between the percentage of public school 8th graders and the percentage of 13-year-olds in the highest-scoring country who meet the Goals Panel's performance standard in mathematics? *(1991 and 1992)* — Baseline 9 percentage points, —

9. **International Science Achievement:** Has the state reduced the gap between the percentage of public school 8th graders and the percentage of 13-year-olds in the highest-scoring country who meet the Goals Panel's performance standard in science? — —

10. **Adult Literacy:** Has the state increased the percentage of adults who score at or above Level 3 in prose literacy? *(1992)* ■ — —

11. **Participation in Adult Education:** Has the state reduced the gap in adult education participation between adults who have a high school diploma or less, and those who have additional post-secondary education or technical training? — —

12. **Participation in Higher Education:** Has the state reduced the gap between White and minority high school graduates who:
   - enroll in college? — —
   - complete a college degree? — —

13. **Overall Student Drug and Alcohol Use:** Has the state reduced the percentage of public high school students reporting doing the following during the past 30 days: ■
   - using marijuana at least once? *(1993)* — Baseline 11%, —
   - having 5 or more drinks in a row? *(1993)* — Baseline 29%, —

14. **Sale of Drugs at School:** Has the state reduced the percentage of public high school students reporting that someone offered, sold, or gave them an illegal drug on school property during the past 12 months? *(1993)* ■ — Baseline 20%, —

15. **Student and Teacher Victimization:** Has the state reduced the percentage of students and teachers reporting that they were threatened or injured on school property during the past 12 months?
   - public high school students *(1993)* ■ — Baseline 8%, —
   - public school teachers — —

16. **Disruptions in Class by Students:** Has the state reduced the percentage of students and teachers reporting that disruptions often interfere with teaching and learning?
   - high school students — —
   - high school teachers — —

— Data not available.
ns Interpret with caution. Change was not statistically significant.

▲ See technical note on page 133.
▼ See technical note on pages 134-135.

■ See technical note on page 136.
■ See technical note on page 137.

124

	Baseline	Most Recent Update	Overall Progress
1. Children's Health Index: Has the state reduced the percentage of infants born with 2 or more health and developmental risks? *(1990, 1991)* ▲	17%	16% ns	↔
2. Immunizations: Has the state increased the percentage of 2-year-olds who have been fully immunized against preventable childhood diseases?	—	—	
3. Family-Child Reading and Storytelling: Has the state increased the percentage of 3- to 5-year-olds whose parents read to them or tell them stories regularly?	—	—	
4. Preschool Participation: Has the state reduced the gap in preschool participation between 3- to 5-year-olds from high- and low-income families?	—	—	
5. High School Completion: Has the state increased the percentage of 19- to 20-year-olds who have a high school credential? *(1990)*	90%	—	
6. Mathematics Achievement: Has the state increased the percentage of public school students who meet the Goals Panel's performance standard in mathematics? ▼			
• Grade 4 *(1992)*	19%	—	
• Grade 8 *(1990, 1992)*	24%	26% ns	↔
• Grade 12	—	—	
7. Reading Achievement: Has the state increased the percentage of public school students who meet the Goals Panel's performance standard in reading? ▼			
• Grade 4 *(1992)*	28%	—	
• Grade 8	—	—	
• Grade 12	—	—	
8. International Mathematics Achievement: Has the state reduced the gap between the percentage of public school 8th graders and the percentage of 13-year-olds in the highest-scoring country who meet the Goals Panel's performance standard in mathematics? *(1991 and 1992)*	15 percentage points	—	
9. International Science Achievement: Has the state reduced the gap between the percentage of public school 8th graders and the percentage of 13-year-olds in the highest-scoring country who meet the Goals Panel's performance standard in science?	—	—	
10. Adult Literacy: Has the state increased the percentage of adults who score at or above Level 3 in prose literacy? *(1992)* ■	—	—	
11. Participation in Adult Education: Has the state reduced the gap in adult education participation between adults who have a high school diploma or less, and those who have additional post-secondary education or technical training?	—	—	
12. Participation in Higher Education: Has the state reduced the gap between White and minority high school graduates who:			
• enroll in college?	—	—	
• complete a college degree?	—	—	
13. Overall Student Drug and Alcohol Use: Has the state reduced the percentage of public high school students reporting doing the following during the past 30 days: ■			
• using marijuana at least once? *(1990, 1993)*	—	—	
• having 5 or more drinks in a row? *(1990, 1993)*	—	—	
14. Sale of Drugs at School: Has the state reduced the percentage of public high school students reporting that someone offered, sold, or gave them an illegal drug on school property during the past 12 months? *(1993)* ■	—	—	
15. Student and Teacher Victimization: Has the state reduced the percentage of students and teachers reporting that they were threatened or injured on school property during the past 12 months?			
• public high school students *(1993)* ■	—	—	
• public school teachers	—	—	
16. Disruptions in Class by Students: Has the state reduced the percentage of students and teachers reporting that disruptions often interfere with teaching and learning?			
• high school students	—	—	
• high school teachers	—	—	

— Data not available.
ns Interpret with caution. Change was not statistically significant.

▲ See technical note on page 133.
▼ See technical note on pages 134-135.

■ See technical note on page 136.
■ See technical note on page 137.

AMERICAN SAMOA

	Baseline	Most Recent Update	Overall Progress

1. **Children's Health Index:** Has the territory reduced the percentage of infants born with 2 or more health and developmental risks? *(1990, 1991)* ▲ — —

2. **Immunizations:** Has the territory increased the percentage of 2-year-olds who have been fully immunized against preventable childhood diseases? — —

3. **Family-Child Reading and Storytelling:** Has the territory increased the percentage of 3- to 5-year-olds whose parents read to them or tell them stories regularly? — —

4. **Preschool Participation:** Has the territory reduced the gap in preschool participation between 3- to 5-year-olds from high- and low-income families? — —

5. **High School Completion:** Has the territory increased the percentage of 19- to 20-year-olds who have a high school credential? *(1990)* — —

6. **Mathematics Achievement:** Has the territory increased the percentage of public school students who meet the Goals Panel's performance standard in mathematics? ▼
   - Grade 4 *(1992)* — —
   - Grade 8 *(1990, 1992)* — —
   - Grade 12 — —

7. **Reading Achievement:** Has the territory increased the percentage of public school students who meet the Goals Panel's performance standard in reading? ▼
   - Grade 4 *(1992)* — —
   - Grade 8 — —
   - Grade 12 — —

8. **International Mathematics Achievement:** Has the territory reduced the gap between the percentage of public school 8th graders and the percentage of 13-year-olds in the highest-scoring country who meet the Goals Panel's performance standard in mathematics? *(1991 and 1992)* — —

9. **International Science Achievement:** Has the territory reduced the gap between the percentage of public school 8th graders and the percentage of 13-year-olds in the highest-scoring country who meet the Goals Panel's performance standard in science? — —

10. **Adult Literacy:** Has the territory increased the percentage of adults who score at or above Level 3 in prose literacy? *(1992)* ■ — —

11. **Participation in Adult Education:** Has the territory reduced the gap in adult education participation between adults who have a high school diploma or less, and those who have additional post-secondary education or technical training? — —

12. **Participation in Higher Education:** Has the territory reduced the gap between White and minority high school graduates who:
   - enroll in college? — —
   - complete a college degree? — —

13. **Overall Student Drug and Alcohol Use:** Has the territory reduced the percentage of public high school students reporting doing the following during the past 30 days: ■
   - using marijuana at least once? *(1993)* 14% —
   - having 5 or more drinks in a row? *(1993)* 23% —

14. **Sale of Drugs at School:** Has the territory reduced the percentage of public high school students reporting that someone offered, sold, or gave them an illegal drug on school property during the past 12 months? *(1993)* ■ 14% —

15. **Student and Teacher Victimization:** Has the territory reduced the percentage of students and teachers reporting that they were threatened or injured on school property during the past 12 months?
   - public high school students *(1993)* ■ 15% —
   - public school teachers — —

16. **Disruptions in Class by Students:** Has the territory reduced the percentage of students and teachers reporting that disruptions often interfere with teaching and learning?
   - high school students — —
   - high school teachers — —

— Data not available.
ns Interpret with caution. Change was not statistically significant.

▲ See technical note on page 133.
▼ See technical note on pages 134-135.

■ See technical note on page 136.
■ See technical note on page 137.

GUAM

	Baseline	Most Recent Update	Overall Progress

1. Children's Health Index: Has the territory reduced the percentage of infants born with 2 or more health and developmental risks? *(1990, 1991)* ▲ — 18% — 18% — ↔

2. Immunizations: Has the territory increased the percentage of 2-year-olds who have been fully immunized against preventable childhood diseases? — —

3. Family-Child Reading and Storytelling: Has the territory increased the percentage of 3- to 5-year-olds whose parents read to them or tell them stories regularly? — —

4. Preschool Participation: Has the territory reduced the gap in preschool participation between 3- to 5-year-olds from high- and low-income families? — —

5. High School Completion: Has the territory increased the percentage of 19- to 20-year-olds who have a high school credential? *(1990)* — —

6. Mathematics Achievement: Has the territory increased the percentage of public school students who meet the Goals Panel's performance standard in mathematics? ▼
- Grade 4 *(1992)* — 5% — —
- Grade 8 *(1990, 1992)* — 5% — 7% ns — ↔
- Grade 12 — —

7. Reading Achievement: Has the territory increased the percentage of public school students who meet the Goals Panel's performance standard in reading? ▼
- Grade 4 *(1992)* — 6% — —
- Grade 8 — —
- Grade 12 — —

8. International Mathematics Achievement: Has the territory reduced the gap between the percentage of public school 8th graders and the percentage of 13-year-olds in the highest-scoring country who meet the Goals Panel's performance standard in mathematics? *(1991 and 1992)* — 34 percentage points — —

9. International Science Achievement: Has the territory reduced the gap between the percentage of public school 8th graders and the percentage of 13-year-olds in the highest-scoring country who meet the Goals Panel's performance standard in science? — —

10. Adult Literacy: Has the territory increased the percentage of adults who score at or above Level 3 in prose literacy? *(1992)* ■ — —

11. Participation in Adult Education: Has the territory reduced the gap in adult education participation between adults who have a high school diploma or less, and those who have additional post-secondary education or technical training? — —

12. Participation in Higher Education: Has the territory reduced the gap between White and minority high school graduates who:
- enroll in college? — —
- complete a college degree? — —

13. Overall Student Drug and Alcohol Use: Has the territory reduced the percentage of public high school students reporting doing the following during the past 30 days: ■
- using marijuana at least once? *(1990, 1993)* — —
- having 5 or more drinks in a row? *(1990, 1993)* — —

14. Sale of Drugs at School: Has the territory reduced the percentage of public high school students reporting that someone offered, sold, or gave them an illegal drug on school property during the past 12 months? *(1993)* ■ — —

15. Student and Teacher Victimization: Has the territory reduced the percentage of students and teachers reporting that they were threatened or injured on school property during the past 12 months?
- public high school students *(1993)* ■ — —
- public school teachers — —

16. Disruptions in Class by Students: Has the territory reduced the percentage of students and teachers reporting that disruptions often interfere with teaching and learning?
- high school students — —
- high school teachers — —

— Data not available.
ns Interpret with caution. Change was not statistically significant.

▲ See technical note on page 133.
▼ See technical note on pages 134-135.

■ See technical note on page 136.
■ See technical note on page 137.

	Baseline	Most Recent Update	Overall Progress

1. **Children's Health Index:** Has the territory reduced the percentage of infants born with 2 or more health and developmental risks? *(1990, 1991)* ▲ — —

2. **Immunizations:** Has the territory increased the percentage of 2-year-olds who have been fully immunized against preventable childhood diseases? — —

3. **Family-Child Reading and Storytelling:** Has the territory increased the percentage of 3- to 5-year-olds whose parents read to them or tell them stories regularly? — —

4. **Preschool Participation:** Has the territory reduced the gap in preschool participation between 3- to 5-year-olds from high- and low-income families? — —

5. **High School Completion:** Has the territory increased the percentage of 19- to 20-year-olds who have a high school credential? *(1990)* — —

6. **Mathematics Achievement:** Has the territory increased the percentage of public school students who meet the Goals Panel's performance standard in mathematics? ▼
   - Grade 4 *(1992)* — —
   - Grade 8 *(1990, 1992)* — —
   - Grade 12 — —

7. **Reading Achievement:** Has the territory increased the percentage of public school students who meet the Goals Panel's performance standard in reading? ▼
   - Grade 4 *(1992)* — —
   - Grade 8 — —
   - Grade 12 — —

8. **International Mathematics Achievement:** Has the territory reduced the gap between the percentage of public school 8th graders and the percentage of 13-year-olds in the highest-scoring country who meet the Goals Panel's performance standard in mathematics? *(1991 and 1992)* — —

9. **International Science Achievement:** Has the territory reduced the gap between the percentage of public school 8th graders and the percentage of 13-year-olds in the highest-scoring country who meet the Goals Panel's performance standard in science? — —

10. **Adult Literacy:** Has the territory increased the percentage of adults who score at or above Level 3 in prose literacy? *(1992)* ■ — —

11. **Participation in Adult Education:** Has the territory reduced the gap in adult education participation between adults who have a high school diploma or less, and those who have additional post-secondary education or technical training? — —

12. **Participation in Higher Education:** Has the territory reduced the gap between White and minority high school graduates who:
    - enroll in college? — —
    - complete a college degree? — —

13. **Overall Student Drug and Alcohol Use:** Has the territory reduced the percentage of public high school students reporting doing the following during the past 30 days: ■
    - using marijuana at least once? *(1990, 1993)* — —
    - having 5 or more drinks in a row? *(1990, 1993)* — —

14. **Sale of Drugs at School:** Has the territory reduced the percentage of public high school students reporting that someone offered, sold, or gave them an illegal drug on school property during the past 12 months? *(1993)* ■ — —

15. **Student and Teacher Victimization:** Has the territory reduced the percentage of students and teachers reporting that they were threatened or injured on school property during the past 12 months?
    - public high school students *(1993)* ■ — —
    - public school teachers — —

16. **Disruptions in Class by Students:** Has the territory reduced the percentage of students and teachers reporting that disruptions often interfere with teaching and learning?
    - high school students — —
    - high school teachers — —

— Data not available.
ns Interpret with caution. Change was not statistically significant.

▲ See technical note on page 133.
▼ See technical note on pages 134-135.

■ See technical note on page 136.
■ See technical note on page 137.

	Baseline	Most Recent Update	Overall Progress
1. Children's Health Index: Has the Commonwealth reduced the percentage of infants born with 2 or more health and developmental risks? *(1990, 1991)* ▲	17%	16%	↑
2. Immunizations: Has the Commonwealth increased the percentage of 2-year-olds who have been fully immunized against preventable childhood diseases?	—	—	
3. Family-Child Reading and Storytelling: Has the Commonwealth increased the percentage of 3- to 5-year-olds whose parents read to them or tell them stories regularly?	—	—	
4. Preschool Participation: Has the Commonwealth reduced the gap in preschool participation between 3- to 5-year-olds from high- and low-income families?	—	—	
5. High School Completion: Has the Commonwealth increased the percentage of 19- to 20-year-olds who have a high school credential? *(1990)*	—	—	
6. Mathematics Achievement: Has the Commonwealth increased the percentage of public school students who meet the Goals Panel's performance standard in mathematics? ▼			
• Grade 4 *(1992)*	—	—	
• Grade 8 *(1990, 1992)*	—	—	
• Grade 12	—	—	
7. Reading Achievement: Has the Commonwealth increased the percentage of public school students who meet the Goals Panel's performance standard in reading? ▼			
• Grade 4 *(1992)*	—	—	
• Grade 8	—	—	
• Grade 12	—	—	
8. International Mathematics Achievement: Has the Commonwealth reduced the gap between the percentage of public school 8th graders and the percentage of 13-year-olds in the highest-scoring country who meet the Goals Panel's performance standard in mathematics? *(1991 and 1992)*	—	—	
9. International Science Achievement: Has the Commonwealth reduced the gap between the percentage of public school 8th graders and the percentage of 13-year-olds in the highest-scoring country who meet the Goals Panel's performance standard in science?	—	—	
10. Adult Literacy: Has the Commonwealth increased the percentage of adults who score at or above Level 3 in prose literacy? *(1992)* ■	—	—	
11. Participation in Adult Education: Has the Commonwealth reduced the gap in adult education participation between adults who have a high school diploma or less, and those who have additional post-secondary education or technical training?	—	—	
12. Participation in Higher Education: Has the Commonwealth reduced the gap between White and minority high school graduates who:			
• enroll in college?	—	—	
• complete a college degree?	—	—	
13. Overall Student Drug and Alcohol Use: Has the Commonwealth reduced the percentage of public high school students reporting doing the following during the past 30 days: ■			
• using marijuana at least once? *(1991, 1993)*	4%	—	
• having 5 or more drinks in a row? *(1991, 1993)*	18%	—	
14. Sale of Drugs at School: Has the Commonwealth reduced the percentage of public high school students reporting that someone offered, sold, or gave them an illegal drug on school property during the past 12 months? *(1993)* ■	—	—	
15. Student and Teacher Victimization: Has the Commonwealth reduced the percentage of students and teachers reporting that they were threatened or injured on school property during the past 12 months?			
• public high school students *(1993)* ■	—	—	
• public school teachers	—	—	
16. Disruptions in Class by Students: Has the Commonwealth reduced the percentage of students and teachers reporting that disruptions often interfere with teaching and learning?			
• high school students	—	—	
• high school teachers	—	—	

— Data not available.
ns Interpret with caution. Change was not statistically significant.

▲ See technical note on page 133.
▼ See technical note on pages 134-135.

■ See technical note on page 136.
■ See technical note on page 137.

VIRGIN ISLANDS

	Baseline	Most Recent Update	Overall Progress

1. **Children's Health Index:** Has the territory reduced the percentage of infants born with 2 or more health and developmental risks? *(1990, 1991)* ▲ — —

2. **Immunizations:** Has the territory increased the percentage of 2-year-olds who have been fully immunized against preventable childhood diseases? — —

3. **Family-Child Reading and Storytelling:** Has the territory increased the percentage of 3- to 5-year-olds whose parents read to them or tell them stories regularly? — —

4. **Preschool Participation:** Has the territory reduced the gap in preschool participation between 3- to 5-year-olds from high- and low-income families? — —

5. **High School Completion:** Has the territory increased the percentage of 19- to 20-year-olds who have a high school credential? *(1990)* — —

6. **Mathematics Achievement:** Has the territory increased the percentage of public school students who meet the Goals Panel's performance standard in mathematics? ▼
   - Grade 4 *(1992)* — —
   - Grade 8 *(1990, 1992)* — 1% — 1% — ↔
   - Grade 12 — —

7. **Reading Achievement:** Has the territory increased the percentage of public school students who meet the Goals Panel's performance standard in reading? ▼
   - Grade 4 *(1992)* — —
   - Grade 8 — —
   - Grade 12 — —

8. **International Mathematics Achievement:** Has the territory reduced the gap between the percentage of public school 8th graders and the percentage of 13-year-olds in the highest-scoring country who meet the Goals Panel's performance standard in mathematics? *(1991 and 1992)* — 40 percentage points — —

9. **International Science Achievement:** Has the territory reduced the gap between the percentage of public school 8th graders and the percentage of 13-year-olds in the highest-scoring country who meet the Goals Panel's performance standard in science? — —

10. **Adult Literacy:** Has the territory increased the percentage of adults who score at or above Level 3 in prose literacy? *(1992)* ■ — —

11. **Participation in Adult Education:** Has the territory reduced the gap in adult education participation between adults who have a high school diploma or less, and those who have additional post-secondary education or technical training? — —

12. **Participation in Higher Education:** Has the territory reduced the gap between White and minority high school graduates who:
    - enroll in college? — —
    - complete a college degree? — —

13. **Overall Student Drug and Alcohol Use:** Has the territory reduced the percentage of public high school students reporting doing the following during the past 30 days: ■
    - using marijuana at least once? *(1990, 1993)* — —
    - having 5 or more drinks in a row? *(1993)* — 9% —

14. **Sale of Drugs at School:** Has the territory reduced the percentage of public high school students reporting that someone offered, sold, or gave them an illegal drug on school property during the past 12 months? *(1993)* ■ — 27% —

15. **Student and Teacher Victimization:** Has the territory reduced the percentage of students and teachers reporting that they were threatened or injured on school property during the past 12 months?
    - public high school students *(1993)* ■ — 12% —
    - public school teachers — —

16. **Disruptions in Class by Students:** Has the territory reduced the percentage of students and teachers reporting that disruptions often interfere with teaching and learning?
    - high school students — —
    - high school teachers — —

— Data not available.
ns Interpret with caution. Change was not statistically significant.

▲ See technical note on page 133.
▼ See technical note on pages 134-135.

■ See technical note on page 136.
■ See technical note on page 137.

Appendix B: Technical Notes and Sources

General Information

Accuracy of Data

The accuracy of any statistic is determined by the joint effects of "sampling" and "nonsampling" errors. Estimates based on a sample will differ somewhat from the figures that would have been obtained if a complete census had been taken using the same survey instruments, instructions, and procedures. In addition to such sampling errors, all surveys, both universe and sample, are subject to design, reporting, and processing errors and errors due to nonresponse. To the extent possible, these nonsampling errors are kept to a minimum by methods built into the survey procedures. In general, however, the effects of nonsampling errors are more difficult to gauge than those produced by sampling variability.

Sampling Errors

The samples used in surveys are selected from a large number of possible samples of the same size that could have been selected using the same sample design. Estimates derived from the different samples would differ from each other. The difference between a sample estimate and the average of all possible samples is called the sampling deviation. The standard or sampling error of a survey estimate is a measure of the variation among the estimates from all possible samples and, thus, is a measure of the precision with which an estimate from a particular sample approximates the average result of all possible samples.

The sample estimate and an estimate of its standard error permit us to construct interval estimates with prescribed confidence that the interval includes the average result of all possible samples. If all possible samples were selected under essentially the same conditions and an estimate and its estimated standard error were calculated from each sample, then: 1) approximately 2/3 of the intervals from one standard error below the estimate to one standard error above the estimate would include the average value of the possible samples; and 2) approximately 19/20 of the intervals from two standard errors above the estimate to two standard errors below the estimate would include the average value of all possible samples. We call an interval from two standard errors below the estimate to two standard errors above the estimate a 95 percent confidence interval.

Analysis of standard errors can help assess how valid a comparison between two estimates might be. The standard error of a difference between two independent sample estimates is equal to the square root of the sum of the squared standard errors of the estimates. The standard error (se) of the difference between independent sample estimates "a" and "b" is:

$$se_{a,b} = \sqrt{se_a^2 + se_b^2}$$

To compare changes in between-group differences (groups "a" and "b") over time (years "1" and "2"), we approximate the standard error of the difference as:

$$se_{a,b} = \sqrt{se_a^2 + se_b^2}$$

This method overestimates the standard error because it does not account for covariance (the covariance figures were not available). Because of this overestimation, the approach is conservative; that is, one is less likely to obtain significant results.

Nonsampling Errors

Universe and sample surveys are subject to nonsampling errors. Nonsampling errors may arise when respondents or interviewers interpret questions differently; when respondents must estimate values; when coders, keyers, and other processors handle answers differently; when persons who should be included in the universe are not;

or when persons fail to respond (completely or partially). Nonsampling errors usually, but not always, result in an understatement of total survey error and thus an overstatement of the precision of survey estimates. Since estimating the magnitude of nonsampling errors often would require special experiments or access to independent data, these magnitudes are seldom available.

1. Children's Health Index (for the U.S. and for the states)

The percentages of infants at risk are based on the number of births used to calculate the health index, not the actual number of births. The percentage of complete and usable birth records used to calculate the health index varied from a high of 99.93 to a low of 73.18. Four states (California, Indiana, New York, and South Dakota) did not collect information on all six risks in 1990 and 1991. Oklahoma provided 1991 data only. These states and the territories are not included in the U.S. total. New Hampshire was included in the U.S. total but not in the race/ethnicity totals because the state does not collect information on Hispanic origin. Minority populations may be underrepresented due to the exclusion of the four states in 1991 (and five states in 1990), particularly California and New York; therefore, the risk factors by race/ethnicity should be interpreted with caution.

Source: Nicholas Zill and Christine Winquist Nord of Westat, Inc. developed the concept of the Children's Health Index. Stephanie Ventura and Sally Clarke of the National Center for Health Statistics provided the special tabulations of the 1990 and 1991 birth certificate data needed to produce the index.

2. Immunizations (for the U.S. only)

Source: Data from the 1992 National Health Interview Survey of Child Health, National Center for Health Statistics and National Immunization Programs, Centers for Disease Control and Prevention, 1994.

3. Family-Child Reading and Storytelling (for the U.S. only)

The population estimates for the National Household Education Survey (NHES) data on family activities cover 3- to 5-year-old children who are not yet enrolled in kindergarten. Age from the NHES:93 was established as of January 1, 1993.

In the NHES:93, information on daily reading was collected using two approaches with split-half samples. The two approaches did not result in significantly different estimates for daily reading among 3- to 5-year-old

preschoolers. A combined measure using both items is included in this Report.

Source: U.S. Department of Education, National Center for Education Statistics, National Household Education Survey: 1993 School Readiness Interview, unpublished tabulations prepared by Westat, Inc., August 1994.

4. Preschool Participation (for the U.S. only)

The population estimates for the National Household Education Survey (NHES) data on preschool participation cover 3- to 5-year-old children who are not yet enrolled in kindergarten. Preschool participation includes children enrolled in any center-based program. Age from the NHES:91 was established as of January 1, 1991. Age from the NHES:93 was established as of January 1, 1993.

In both surveys, the bottom quintile of the income distribution consisted of families whose total family cash income before taxes was $10,000 or less. The top quintile of the income distribution consisted of families whose total income was over $50,000.

Sources: U.S. Department of Education, National Center for Education Statistics, National Household Education Survey: 1991 Early Childhood Component, unpublished tabulations prepared by Westat, Inc., August 1994.

U.S. Department of Education, National Center for Education Statistics, National Household Education Survey: 1993 School Readiness Interview, unpublished tabulations prepared by Westat, Inc., August 1994.

5. High School Completion (for the U.S.)

There are two major paths to high school completion. Most students receive a regular high school diploma after completing the requisite secondary school coursework; other students, regardless of the number of high school courses they have completed, receive an alternative credential such as a General Educational Development (GED) certificate, Individual Education Plan (IEP) credential, or certificate of attendance. The high school completion rate for this Report was calculated by combining data for students receiving regular high school diplomas with data for students receiving alternative credentials.

For this Report, completion rates were calculated for 19- to 20-year-olds. Persons still enrolled in high school were not included in the calculation.

Source: Marilyn M. McMillen, Phillip Kaufman, and Summer D. Whitener, *Dropout Rates in the United States: 1993* (Washington, D.C.: U.S. Department of Education, National Center for Education Statistics, 1994), and unpublished tabulations from the October 1993 Current Population Survey, prepared by Management Planning Research Associates, Inc., 1994.

5. High School Completion (for the states)

The 1990 Decennial Census data used in computing state high school completion rates are from special tabulations of the Census sample detail file. That file included data on current high school enrollment and high school graduation status. Those data were used in conjunction with Census single-year of-age population data. By definition, the high school completion rates for 19- to 20-year-olds were computed as a percentage of the non-high school enrolled population at that age who possess a high school credential (either a high school diploma or an alternative credential).

Source: U.S. Department of Commerce, Bureau of the Census, 1990 Census of Population and Housing, unpublished tables, July 1992.

6. Mathematics Achievement (for the U.S. and the states)

National Assessment of Educational Progress (NAEP)

NAEP is a survey of the educational achievement of American students and changes in that achievement across time. Since 1969, NAEP has assessed the achievement of national samples of 9-, 13-, and 17-year-old students in public and private schools. In 1983, it expanded the samples so that grade-level results could be reported.

The assessments, conducted annually until the 1979-80 school year and biennially since then, have included periodic measures of student performance in reading, mathematics, science, writing, U.S. history, civics, geography, and other subject areas. NAEP also collects demographic, curricular, and instructional background information from students, teachers, and school administrators.

In 1988, Congress added a new dimension to NAEP by authorizing, on a trial basis, voluntary participation of public schools in state-level assessments in 1990 and 1992. Forty jurisdictions (states and territories) participated in the 1990 trial mathematics assessment. In 1992, 44 jurisdictions participated in the state mathematics assessments of 4th and 8th graders and 43 participated in the 4th grade reading assessments.

National Assessment Governing Board (NAGB) Achievement Levels

The NAEP data should be interpreted with caution. The Goals Panel's performance standard classifies student performance according to achievement levels devised by the National Assessment Governing Board (NAGB). These achievement level data have been previously reported by the National Center for Education Statistics (NCES). Students with NAEP scores falling below the Goals Panel's performance standard have been classified by NAGB as "Basic" or below; those above have been classified as "Proficient" or "Advanced."

The NAGB achievement levels represent a reasonable way of categorizing overall performance on the NAEP. They are also consistent with the Panel's efforts to report such performance against a high criterion standard. However, the methods used to derive the NAGB achievement "cut points" (i.e., the points distinguishing the percentage of students scoring at the different achievement levels) have been questioned and are still under review.

NAGB has established standards for reporting the results of the National Assessment of Educational Progress. This effort has resulted in three achievement levels: basic, proficient, and advanced. The NAGB achievement levels are reasoned judgements of what students should know and be able to do. They are attempts to characterize overall student performance in particular subject matter. Readers should exercise caution, however, in making particular inferences about what students at each level actually know and can do. A NAEP assessment is a complex picture of student achievement and applying external standards for performance is a difficult task. Evaluation studies completed and under way have raised questions about the degree to which the standards in the NAGB achievement levels are actually reflected in an assessment and, hence, the degree to which inferences about actual performance can be made from these achievement levels. The Goal Panel acknowledges these limitations but believes that, used with caution, these levels convey important information about how American students are faring in reaching Goal 3.

Basic: *This level, below proficient, denotes partial mastery of knowledge and skills that are fundamental for proficient work at each grade — 4, 8, and 12. For twelfth grade, this is higher than minimum competency skills (which are normally taught in elementary and junior high school) and covers significant elements of standard high-school-level work.*

Proficient: *This central level represents solid academic performance for each grade tested — 4, 8, and 12.* It reflects a consensus that students reaching this level have demonstrated competency over challenging subject matter and are well prepared for the next level of schooling. At grade 12, the proficient level encompasses a body of subject-matter knowledge and analytical skills, of cultural literacy and insight, that all high school graduates should have for democratic citizenship, responsible adulthood, and productive work.

Advanced: *This higher level signifies superior performance beyond proficient grade-level mastery at grades 4, 8, and 12.* For twelfth grade, the advanced level shows readiness for rigorous college courses, advanced training, or employment requiring advanced academic achievement.

Sources: Mary Lyn Bourque and Howard H. Garrison, *The Levels of Mathematics Achievement: Initial Performance Standards for the 1990 NAEP Mathematics Assessment.* Vol. 1, National and State Summaries (Washington D.C.: National Assessment Governing Board, 1991).

Ina V.S. Mullis, John A. Dossey, Eugene H. Owen, and Gary W. Phillips, *NAEP 1992 Mathematics Report Card for the Nation and the States: Data from the National and Trial State Assessments* (Washington, D.C.: U.S. Department of Education, National Center for Education Statistics, April 1993).

7. Reading Achievement (for the U.S. and for the states)

See technical notes regarding NAEP and the NAGB achievement levels under the notes for core indicator 6.

Source: Ina V.S. Mullis, Jay Campbell, and Alan Farstrup, *NAEP 1992 Reading Report Card for the Nation and the States: Data from the National and Trial State Assessments* (Washington, D.C.: U.S. Department of Education, National Center for Education Statistics, 1993).

8. International Mathematics Achievement (for the U.S.)

International Assessment of Educational Progress (IAEP)

Twenty countries assessed the mathematics and science achievement of 13-year-old students and 14 assessed 9-year-old students in these same subjects. In some cases, participants assessed virtually all age-eligible children in their countries, and in other cases they confined samples to certain geographic regions, language groups, or grade levels. In some countries, significant proportions of age-eligible children were not represented because they did not attend school. Also, in some countries, low rates of school or student participation mean that results may be biased. The countries participating in the IAEP were: Brazil, Canada, China, England, France, Hungary, Ireland, Israel, Italy, Jordan, Korea, Mozambique (mathematics only), Portugal, Scotland, Slovenia, the former Soviet Union, Spain, Switzerland, Taiwan, and the United States. For this Report, the five countries chosen to be compared with the United States had comprehensive populations (France, Hungary, Korea, Switzerland, and Taiwan).

Mathematics achievement was assessed in five areas — numbers and operations; measurement; geometry; data analysis, probability and statistics; and algebra and functions. The U.S. was below 5 out of 5 countries in more than half of these areas.

Source: Archie E. LaPointe, Janice M. Askew, and Nancy A. Mead, *Learning Mathematics* (Princeton, NJ: Educational Testing Service, Center for the Assessment of Educational Progress, 1992).

8. International Mathematics Achievement (for the states)

International comparisons have been drawn between countries participating in the 1991 International Assessment of Educational Progress (IAEP) and states participating in the 1992 NAEP. Representative samples of 9- and 13-year old students were tested in mathematics in 20 countries. Those countries decided to adopt the 1990 NAEP objectives in mathematics as a blueprint for the construction of the IAEP mathematics assessment. Even with differences in the target population and timing, there was substantial overlap between the NAEP and the IAEP. By linking the IAEP scale to the NAEP scale, it is possible to predict the percentages of 13-year-olds in each of the 20 countries that participated in the 1991 IAEP in mathematics who would have performed at or above each of the three achievement levels established by the NAGB for U.S. students (see technical notes for core indicator 6). These predictions can then be compared with actual performance of U.S. eighth graders in public schools in the 1992 mathematics assessment with respect to these same criteria. For this Report, Taiwan, the highest-scoring country, was selected for comparison to the United States.

Source: Peter Pashley and Gary W. Phillips, *Toward World-Class Standards: A Research Study Linking International and National Assessments* (Princeton, NJ: Educational Testing Service, June 1993).

9. International Science Achievement (for the U.S. only)

For a description of the International Assessment of Educational Progress (IAEP), see technical note for core indicator 8.

Science achievement was assessed in four areas — life science, physical science, earth science, and nature of science. The U.S. was below 3 out of 5 countries in more than half of these areas.

Source: Archie E. LaPointe, Janice M. Askew, and Nancy A. Mead, *Learning Science* (Princeton, NJ: Educational Testing Service, Center for the Assessment of Educational Progress, 1992).

10. Adult Literacy (for the U.S. and the states)

The Department of Education (ED) and the Educational Testing Service (ETS) characterized the literacy of America's adults in terms of three "literacy scales" representing distinct and important aspects of literacy: prose, document, and quantitative literacy.

Prose literacy, selected as a core indicator for this Report, is defined as the knowledge and skills needed to understand and use information from texts that include editorials, news stories, poems, and fiction; for example, finding a piece of information in a newspaper article, interpreting instructions from a warranty, inferring a theme from a poem, or contrasting views expressed in an editorial.

Level 1 – Most of the tasks in this level require the reader to read relatively short text to locate a single piece of information which is identical to or synonymous with the information given in the question or directive. If plausible but incorrect information is present in the text, it tends not to be located near the correct information.

Level 2 – Some tasks in this level require readers to locate a single piece of information in the text; however, several distractors or plausible but incorrect pieces of information may be present, or low-level inferences may be required. Other tasks require the reader to integrate two or more pieces of information or to compare and contrast easily identifiable information based on a criterion provided in the question or directive.

Level 3 – Tasks in this level tend to require readers to make literal or synonymous matches between the text and information given in the task, or to make matches that require low-level inferences. Other tasks ask readers to integrate information from dense or lengthy text that contains no organizational aids such as headings. Readers may also be asked to generate a response based on information that can be easily identified in the text. Distracting information is present, but is not located near the correct information.

Level 4 – These tasks require readers to perform multiple-feature matches and to integrate or synthesize information from complex or lengthy passages. More complex inferences are needed to perform successfully. Conditional information is frequently present in tasks at this level and must be taken into consideration by the reader.

Level 5 – Some tasks in this level require the reader to search for information in dense text which contains a number of plausible distractors. Others ask readers to make high-level inferences or use specialized background knowledge. Some tasks ask readers to contrast complex information.

For definitions of document and quantitative literacy, and for descriptions of their five levels, see the accompanying *Data Volumes*.

Twelve states (California, Florida, Illinois, Indiana, Iowa, Louisiana, New Jersey, New York, Ohio, Pennsylvania, Texas, and Washington) participated in the 1992 State Adult Literacy Survey. California's data were not available for this Report. The Oregon Progress Board conducted an independent study in 1990, which was validated by the Educational Testing Service. Adults aged 16-65 participated in the 1990 Oregon study; in other states which participated in 1992, the sample included adults aged 16 and older.

Source (for the U.S.): Irwin S. Kirsch, Ann Jungeblut, Lynn Jenkins, and Andrew Kolstad, *Adult Literacy in America: A First Look at the Results of the National Adult Literacy Survey* (Washington, D.C.: U.S. Department of Education, National Center for Education Statistics, September 1993).

Source (for the states): Educational Testing Service, unpublished tabulations from the 1992 State Adult Literacy Survey, August, 1993; the Oregon Progress Board conducted an independent study in 1990 which was validated by the Educational Testing Service.

11. Participation in Adult Education (for the U.S. only)

The population estimates for the National Household Education Survey data on participation in adult education cover adults 17 years and older, excluding those engaged in full-time study.

Source: U.S. Department of Education, National Center for Education Statistics, National Household Education Survey: 1991 Adult Education Component, unpublished tabulations prepared by Westat, Inc., August 1994.

12. Participation in Higher Education (for the U.S. only)

Source: U.S. Department of Commerce, Bureau of the Census, October and March Current Population Surveys, 1991, 1992, 1993, unpublished tabulations from the National Center for Education Statistics, prepared by Pinkerton Computer Consultants, Inc., August 1994.

13. Overall Student Drug and Alcohol Use (for the U.S.)

Use of "any illicit drug" includes any use of marijuana, inhalants, hallucinogens, cocaine, and heroin, or any use of stimulants or tranquilizers not under a doctor's orders.

Source: Lloyd D. Johnston, Patrick M. O'Malley, and Jerald G. Bachman, *Selected 1993 Outcome Measures from the Monitoring the Future Study for Goal 7 of the National Education Goals: A Special Report for the National Education Goals Panel* (Ann Arbor: University of Michigan's Institute for Social Research, July 1994).

13. Overall Student Drug and Alcohol Use (for the states)

The information from the Youth Risk Behavior Survey includes only states with weighted data. The wording in the survey questions changed between 1990 and 1991, which may account for any significant differences from 1990 to 1991 and from 1990 to 1993.

Sources: Centers for Disease Control and Prevention, *Current Tobacco, Alcohol, Marijuana, and Cocaine Use Among High School Students - United States, 1990* (Atlanta, GA: 1991).

Centers for Disease Control and Prevention, *Current Tobacco, Alcohol, Marijuana, and Cocaine Use Among High School Students - United States, 1991* (Atlanta, GA: 1992).

Centers for Disease Control and Prevention, *Current Tobacco, Alcohol, Marijuana, and Cocaine Use Among High School Students - United States, 1993* (Atlanta, GA: 1994).

14. Sale of Drugs at School (for the U.S.)

Source: Lloyd D. Johnston, Patrick M. O'Malley, and Jerald G. Bachman, *Selected 1993 Outcome Measures from the Monitoring the Future Study for Goal 7 of the National Education Goals: A Special Report for the National Education Goals Panel* (Ann Arbor: University of Michigan's Institute for Social Research, July 1994).

14. Sale of Drugs at School (for the states)

The information from the Youth Risk Behavior Survey includes only states with weighted data.

Source: Centers for Disease Control and Prevention, *Current Tobacco, Alcohol, Marijuana, and Cocaine Use Among High School Students - United States, 1993* (Atlanta, GA: 1994).

15. Student and Teacher Victimization

Student Victimization:

Source (for the U.S.): Lloyd D. Johnston, Patrick M. O'Malley, and Jerald G. Bachman, *Selected 1993 Outcome Measures from the Monitoring the Future Study for Goal 7 of the National Education Goals: A Special Report for the National Education Goals Panel* (Ann Arbor: University of Michigan's Institute for Social Research, July 1994).

The information from the Youth Risk Behavior Survey includes only states with weighted data.

Source (for the states): Centers for Disease Control and Prevention, *Current Tobacco, Alcohol, Marijuana, and Cocaine Use Among High School Students - United States, 1993* (Atlanta, GA: 1994).

Teacher Victimization (for the U.S. only):

Victimization at-school includes victimization inside the school building, on school grounds, or on a school bus.

Source: U.S. Department of Education, National Center for Education Statistics, Fast Response Survey System, Teacher Survey on Safe, Disciplined, and Drug-free Schools, FRSS 42, unpublished tabulations prepared by Westat, Inc., August 1994.

16. Disruptions in Class by Students (for the U.S. only)

Student Reports

Source: Lloyd D. Johnston, Patrick M. O'Malley, and Jerald G. Bachman, *Selected 1993 Outcome Measures from the Monitoring the Future Study for Goal 7 of the National Education Goals: A Special Report for the National Education Goals Panel* (Ann Arbor: University of Michigan's Institute for Social Research, July 1994).

Teacher Reports

Source: U.S. Department of Education, National Center for Education Statistics, 1990-91 Teacher Survey of the Schools and Staffing Survey (SASS), unpublished tabulations, August 1992.

Readers interested in further information from data sources presented in the *1994 Goals Report* and accompanying *National* and *State Data Volumes* can contact the sponsoring agencies, as follows:

Data Source	Sponsoring Agency	Contact
Advanced Placement Program	The College Board	Wade Curry (212) 713-8000
Children's Health Index	National Center for Health Statistics (NCHS)	Sally Clarke (301) 436-8500
The Condition of Education	National Center for Education Statistics (NCES)	Nabeel Alsalam (202) 219-2252
Fast Response Survey System (FRSS)	NCES	Judi Carpenter (202) 219-1333
High School and Beyond (HS&B)	NCES	Aurora D'Amico (202) 219-1365
Integrated Postsecondary Education Data System (IPEDS)	NCES	Roslyn Korb (202) 219-1587
International Education Surveys	NCES	Eugene Owen (202) 219-1746
Meaning of Work Study	Cornell University	Antonio Ruiz Quintanilla (607) 255-2742
Monitoring the Future	University of Michigan, Institute for Social Research	Lloyd Johnston (313) 763-5043
National Adult Literacy Survey (NALS)	NCES	Andrew Kolstad (202) 219-1773
National Assessment of Educational Progress (NAEP)	NCES	Gary Phillips (202) 219-1761
National Education Longitudinal Study of 1988 (NELS: 88)	NCES	Jeff Owings (202) 219-1777
National Health Interview Survey Immunization Section	Centers for Disease Control and Prevention	Elizabeth Zell (404) 639-3311
National Household Education Survey (NHES)	NCES	Kathryn Chandler (202) 219-1767
NHES Adult Education Component	NCES	Peter Stowe (202) 219-1363
National Longitudinal Study of the High School Class of 1972 (NLS:72)	NCES	Aurora D'Amico (202) 219-1365

Data Source	Sponsoring Agency	Contact
NCES items in the Current Population Survey (CPS)	NCES	Elvira Hausken (202) 219-1623
Schools and Staffing Survey (SASS)	NCES	Daniel Kasprzyk (202) 219-1588
SASS Teacher Followup Survey	NCES	Sharon Bobbitt (202) 219-1461
Survey of Earned Doctorates Awarded in the United States	NCES	Nancy Schantz (202) 219-1590
Youth Risk Behavior Survey (YRBS)	Centers for Disease Control and Prevention	Laura Kann (404) 639-3311

Readers interested in further analyses from NCES data sources can contact the National Data Resource Center (NDRC) at the National Center for Education Statistics. NCES has established the NDRC to enable state education personnel, education researchers, and others to obtain special statistical tabulations and analyses of data sets maintained by NCES. Researchers and others can ask the Data Center to perform specific tabulations or analyses, or they can work on-site directly with confidential files upon signing a confidentiality pledge. This service currently is provided free of charge by NCES.

The Data Center has files available from the:

> Common Core of Data (CCD),
> Integrated Postsecondary Education Data System (IPEDS),
> National Education Longitudinal Study (NELS:88),
> National Household Education Survey (NHES),
> National Postsecondary Student Aid Study (NPSAS),
> National Study of Postsecondary Faculty, and
> Schools and Staffing Survey (SASS).

In the future, the Data Center plans to add additional databases to its inventory.

To contact the National Data Resource Center, write or call:

> Carl Schmitt
> Elementary and Secondary Education Statistics Division
> National Center for Education Statistics
> 555 New Jersey Ave, NW
> Washington, DC 20208-5651
> (202) 219-1642

Appendix C: Acknowledgements

The National Education Goals Panel and staff gratefully acknowledge the contributions of many thoughtful and knowledgeable people to the development of the *1994 National Education Goals Report*. Some served on the Panel's Working Group as staff to Goals Panel members or on advisory groups convened to recommend core indicators or to identify actions that federal, state, and local governments should take to achieve the National Education Goals. Others were invaluable consultants offering their expertise on data acquisition and analysis or report production and release. We extend a special thanks to W. Davis Lackey and Leo Martin, representatives of the 1993-94 Chair of the Panel, Governor John R. McKernan, Jr., of Maine, for their contributions. We remain appreciative of the good counsel and support we received from all.

REPORT PRODUCTION

Justin Boesel, Westat, Inc.
Babette Gutmann, Westat, Inc.
Allison Henderson, Westat, Inc.
Anne Lewis, free-lance writer
Scott Miller, Editorial Experts, Inc.
Jim Page, Impact Design, Inc.
Kelli Sechrist, Impact Design, Inc.
Patricia Treichel, U.S. Department of Education
Agnes Tyer, U.S. Department of Education

REPORTING COMMITTEE

Patricia Brown, National Governors' Association
John Burkett, U.S. Department of Education,
   National Center for Education Statistics
Alison Englund, Office of the Governor of Minnesota
Lori Gremel, Office of the Governor of Michigan
W. Davis Lackey, Office of the Governor of Maine

Leo Martin, Office of the Governor of Maine
Mary Rollefson, U.S. Department of Education,
   National Center for Education Statistics
Marjorie Steinberg, U.S. Senate, Office of
   Senator Bingaman
Susan Traiman, National Governors' Association
Georgia Jackson VanAdestine, Office of the Governor
   of Michigan

WORKING GROUP

Governors' Representatives

Daniel Austin, Office of the Governor of Maine
Treeby Brown, Office of the Governor of
   North Carolina
Danielle Buente, Office of the Governor of Illinois
William Christopher, Office of the Governor of
   Indiana
Nancy Cobb, Office of the Governor of Indiana
Andrew Cunningham, Office of the Governor of
   Nebraska
Alison Englund, Office of the Governor of
   Minnesota
Joy Fitzgerald, Office of the Governor of Colorado
Richard Gordon, Office of the Governor of Indiana
Lori Gremel, Office of the Governor of Michigan
Corrine Hill, Office of the Governor of Utah
Thomas Houlihan, Office of the Governor of
   North Carolina
Curt Johnson, Office of the Governor of Minnesota
W. Davis Lackey, Office of the Governor of Maine
Thomas Litjen, Office of the Governor of Nebraska
Kay Logan, Office of the Governor of Colorado
Mary Majorowicz, Office of the Governor of Maine
Leo Martin, Office of the Governor of Maine
Terri Moreland, Office of the Governor of Illinois

Joanne Snow Neumann, Office of the Governor of Utah
William Porter, Office of the Governor of Colorado
Rachelle Roberson, Office of the Governor of Illinois
Stephen Schapiro, Office of the Governor of New Jersey
Marguerite Sullivan, Office of the Governor of New Jersey
Georgia Jackson VanAdestine, Office of the Governor of Michigan
Linda Wilson, Office of the Governor of New Jersey

Administration Representatives

John Burkett, U.S. Department of Education, National Center for Education Statistics
John Christensen, U.S. Department of Education, Office of Educational Research and Improvement
Mike Cohen, U.S. Department of Education, Office of the Secretary
Jennifer Davis, U.S. Department of Education, Office of the Secretary
Edward Fuentes, U.S. Department of Education, Office of Educational Research and Improvement
Catherine Jovicich, U.S. Department of Education, Office of the Secretary
William Galston, The White House, Office of Domestic Policy
Patrick Lester, The White House, Office of Domestic Policy
Mary Rollefson, U.S. Department of Education, National Center for Education Statistics
Kimberly Ross, U.S. Department of Education, Office of Intergovernmental and Interagency Affairs
Henry Smith, U.S. Department of Education, Office of Intergovernmental and Interagency Affairs

Congressional Representatives

John Barth, U.S. House of Representatives, Office of Representative Goodling
Elizabeth Beck, U.S. Senate, Office of Senator Bingaman
Doris Dixon, U.S. Senate, Office of Senator Cochran
Andrew Hartman, U.S. House of Representatives, Office of Representative Goodling
Vic Klatt, U.S. House of Representatives, Office of Representative Goodling
Jeff McFarland, U.S. House of Representatives, Office of Representative Kildee
Greg McGinity, U.S. Senate, Office of Senator Cochran
Marjorie Steinberg, U.S. Senate, Office of Senator Bingaman

Susan Wilhelm, U.S. House of Representatives, Office of Representative Kildee

State Legislators' Representatives

Angela Bruce-Raeburn, Wisconsin State Legislature, Office of State Representative Coggs
Jean Diener, Delaware State Legislature, Office of State Senator Connor
James Watts, North Carolina State Legislature, Office of State Representative Barnes

Other Working Group Contributors

Aaron Bell, National Conference of State Legislatures
Patty Sullivan, National Governors' Association
Susan Traiman, National Governors' Association
Bayla White, Office of Management and Budget

RESOURCE GROUP ON FEDERAL, STATE, AND LOCAL ACTIONS TO ACHIEVE THE GOALS

Resource Group Convener: Susan Fuhrman, Rutgers University

Members:
Sharon Brumbaugh, Pennsylvania School Boards Association
Gene Carter, Association for Supervision and Curriculum Development
Michael Casserly, The Council of the Great City Schools
Chester Finn, Jr., Edison Project
Frank Newman, Education Commission of the States
Ramsay Selden, Council of Chief State School Officers
Peggy Siegel, National Alliance of Business

Working Group Representatives:
Aaron Bell, National Conference of State Legislatures
Patty Sullivan, National Governors' Association

ADVISORS ON CORE INDICATORS

C. Leonard Anderson, Portland Public Schools
Janet Baldwin, General Education Development Testing Service
Paul Barton, Educational Testing Service
Rolf Blank, Council of Chief State School Officers
Barbara Clements, Council of Chief State School Officers
Peter Ewell, National Center for Higher Education Management Systems

Chester Finn, Jr., Edison Project
Sarah Greene, National Head Start Association
Michael Guerra, National Catholic Education
  Association
J. David Hawkins, Social Development Research Group
Anne Heald, University of Maryland
Barbara Huff, Federation of Families for Children's
  Mental Health
Lloyd Johnston, University of Michigan
Sharon Lynn Kagan, Yale University
Shirley Malcom, American Association for the
  Advancement of Science
Richard Mills, Vermont Department of Education
Evelyn Moore, National Black Child Development
  Institute
Mark Musick, Southern Regional Education Board
Michael Nettles, University of Michigan
Aaron Pallas, Michigan State University
Claire Pelton, San Jose Unified School District
John Porter, Urban Education Alliance, Inc.
Senta Raizen, National Center for Improving Science
  Education
Chester Richmond, Oak Ridge National Laboratory
William Schmidt, Michigan State University
Ramsay Selden, Council of Chief State School Officers
Thomas Sticht, Applied, Behavioral, and Cognitive
  Sciences, Inc.
Ronda Talley, American Psychological Association
Rafael Valdivieso, Academy for Educational
  Development, Inc.
Nicholas Zill, Westat, Inc.

DATA ACQUISITION

Nabeel Alsalam, U.S. Department of Education
Jim Bethel, Westat, Inc.
Marilyn Binkley, U.S. Department of Education
Rolf Blank, Council of Chief State School Officers
Justin Boesel, Westat, Inc.
Marsha Brauen, Westat, Inc.
Susan Broyles, U.S. Department of Education
Joyce Buchanon, University of Michigan
John Burkett, U.S. Department of Education
Amy Cellini, Educational Testing Service
Sally Clarke, U.S. Department of Health and
  Human Services
Janet Collins, Centers for Disease Control
  and Prevention
Mary Collins, Westat, Inc.

Jude Corina, Pinkerton Computer Consultants, Inc.
Elaine Cousino, University of Michigan
Wade Curry, The College Board
Julie Daft, Westat, Inc.
Margaret Daly, Westat, Inc.
Lou Danielson, U.S. Department of Education
Emerson Elliott, U.S. Department of Education
Elizabeth Farris, Westat, Inc.
Claudia Gentile, Educational Testing Service
Steven Gorman, U.S. Department of Education
Doreen Gruebel, Council of Chief State School
  Officers
Babette Gutmann, Westat, Inc.
Elvie Germino Hausken, U.S. Department of
  Education
Allison Henderson, Westat, Inc.
Susan Hill, National Science Foundation
Ron Hirschhorn, Westat, Inc.
J.G. Huckenpohler, National Science Foundation
Lloyd Johnston, University of Michigan
Laura Kann, Centers for Disease Control
  and Prevention
Phillip Kaufman, Management Planning Research
  Associates, Inc.
Walter MacDonald, Educational Testing Service
Ginger Maggio, University of Michigan
Joyce Martin, U.S. Department of Health and
  Human Services
Marilyn McMillan, U.S. Department of Education
Christine Winquist Nord, Westat, Inc.
George Nozicka, Quantum Research Corporation
Patrick O'Malley, University of Michigan
Jeffrey Owings, U.S. Department of Education
Linda Penn, Quantum Research Company
Douglas Rhodes, Educational Testing Service
Ethel Sanniez, Westat, Inc.
Elizabeth Sinclair, Westat, Inc.
Thomas Smith, U.S. Department of Education
Stephanie Ventura, U.S. Department of Health and
  Human Services
Elizabeth Zell, Centers for Disease Control
  and Prevention
Nicholas Zill, Westat, Inc.

REPORT RELEASE

Ogilvy, Adams and Rinehart, Inc.
Tricom Associates, Inc.
Widmeyer Group, Inc.

The Goals Panel also wishes to thank the following individuals who continue to serve as advisors to the Panel on a wide variety of educational policy, practice, and research issues, including data collection and analysis, measurement and assessment, standards-setting, basic and applied research, promising and effective practices, and opportunities to learn. Two new Resource Groups will be convened during the coming year to recommend indicators for Goal 4: Teacher Education and Professional Development, and Goal 8: Parental Participation, so that national and state progress toward these new Goals can be measured in future reports.

RESOURCE AND TECHNICAL PLANNING GROUPS

GOAL 1: READY TO LEARN

Resource Group Convener: Ernest Boyer, The Carnegie Foundation for the Advancement of Teaching

Members:
James Comer, Yale University
Donna Foglia, Evergreen School District, California
Peter Gerber, MacArthur Foundation
Sarah Greene, National Head Start Association
Sharon Lynn Kagan, Yale University
William Kolberg, National Alliance of Business
Luís Laosa, Educational Testing Service
Michael Levine, Carnegie Corporation of New York
Samuel Meisels, University of Michigan
Evelyn Moore, National Black Child Development Institute
Lucile Newman, Brown University
Douglas Powell, Purdue University
Julius Richmond, Harvard Medical School
Marilyn Smith, National Association for the Education of Young Children
James Wilsford, Jim Wilsford Associates, Inc.
Nicholas Zill, Westat, Inc.

Technical Planning Group on Readiness for School
Leader: Sharon Lynn Kagan, Yale University

Members:
Ernest Boyer, The Carnegie Foundation for the Advancement of Teaching
Sue Bredekamp, National Association for the Education of Young Children
M. Elizabeth Graue, University of Wisconsin
Luís Laosa, Educational Testing Service

Samuel Meisels, University of Michigan
Evelyn Moore, National Black Child Development Institute
Lucile Newman, Brown University
Lorrie Shepard, University of Colorado
Valora Washington, The Kellogg Foundation
Nicholas Zill, Westat, Inc.

GOAL 2: SCHOOL COMPLETION

Resource Group Convener: Rafael Valdivieso, Academy for Educational Development, Inc.

Members:
Janet Baldwin, General Education Development Testing Service
José Cardenas, The Intercultural Development Research Association
Barbara Clements, Council of Chief State School Officers
Edmond Gordon, City College of New York
Noreen López, Illinois State Board of Education
Pamela Keating, University of Washington
Steven Neilson, Milliman and Robertson, Inc.
Bill Padia, California Department of Education
Aaron Pallas, Michigan State University
Richard Wallace, University of Pittsburgh

Technical Planning Subgroup on Core Data Elements
Leader: Barbara Clements, Council of Chief State School Officers

Members:
Linda Baker, Maryland State Department of Education
Paul Barton, Educational Testing Service
Matthew Cohen, Ohio Department of Education
Dennis Jones, National Center for Higher Education Management Systems
Glynn Ligon, Evaluation Software Publication
John Porter, Urban Education Alliance, Inc.
Ramsay Selden, Council of Chief State School Officers
Nicholas Zill, Westat, Inc.

GOAL 3: STUDENT ACHIEVEMENT AND CITIZENSHIP

Resource Group Convener: Lauren Resnick, University of Pittsburgh

Members:
Gordon Ambach, Council of Chief State School Officers

Chester Finn, Jr., Edison Project
Asa Hilliard, Georgia State University
David Hornbeck, Philadelphia Public Schools
Richard Mills, Vermont Department of Education
Claire Pelton, San Jose Unified School District

Goal 3/5 NAEP Technical Advisory Subgroup
Leader: Ramsay Selden, Council of Chief State
   School Officers

Members:
Eva Baker, University of California, Los Angeles
Dorothy Gilford, National Academy of Sciences
Robert Glaser, University of Pittsburgh
Steven Leinwand, Connecticut State Department
   of Education
Robert Linn, University of Colorado
Michael Nettles, University of Michigan
Senta Raizen, National Center for Improving
   Science Education
William Schmidt, Michigan State University
Elizabeth Stage, National Research Council
Uri Treisman, University of Texas, Austin
James Wilsford, Jim Wilsford Associates, Inc.

GOAL 4: TEACHER EDUCATION AND PROFESSIONAL DEVELOPMENT

(Resource Group will be formed during 1994-95.)

GOAL 5: MATHEMATICS AND SCIENCE

Resource Group Convener: Alvin Trivelpiece, Oak
   Ridge National Laboratory

Members:
Iris Carl, National Council of Teachers of Mathematics
Steven Leinwand, Connecticut State Department of
   Education
Michael Nettles, University of Michigan
Alba Ortiz, University of Texas, Austin
Senta Raizen, National Center for Improving Science
   Education
Ramsay Selden, Council of Chief State School Officers

Goal 3/5 Standards Review Technical Planning
Subgroup Leader: Shirley Malcom, American
   Association for the Advancement of Science

Members:
Iris Carl, National Council of Teachers of Mathematics

Thomas Crawford, U.S. Olympic Committee
Mihaly Csikszentmihalyi, University of Chicago
Phillip Daro, University of California
Chester Finn, Jr., Edison Project
Anne Heald, University of Maryland
David Hornbeck, Philadelphia Public Schools
David Kearns, Xerox Corporation
Richard Mills, Vermont Department of Education
Harold Noah, Teachers College, Columbia University
Claire Pelton, San Jose Unified School District
James Renier, Honeywell Corporation
Sidney Smith, Coalition of Essential Schools/Atlas
James Wilsford, Jim Wilsford Associates, Inc.

Goal 3/5: Higher Education Advisory Group on
Standards Leader: Michael Timpane, Teachers
   College, Columbia University

Members:
Bob Albright, Educational Testing Service
Michael Behnke, Massachusetts Institute of Technology
Kenneth Boutte, Xavier University
David Conley, University of Oregon
Jon Fuller, National Association of Independent
   Colleges and Universities
Claire Gaudiani, Connecticut College
Terry Hartle, American Council of Education
Doris Helms, Clemson University
Bob McCabe, Miami-Dade Community College
Arturo Pacheco, University of Texas–El Paso
Paul Ruiz, American Association of Higher Education
Donald Stewart, The College Board
Art Wise, National Council for Accreditation of
   Teacher Education

GOAL 6: ADULT LITERACY AND LIFELONG LEARNING

Resource Group Convener: Mark Musick, Southern
   Regional Education Board

Members:
Paul Barton, Educational Testing Service
Forest Chisman, Southport Institute for Policy Analysis
Peter Ewell, National Center for Higher Education
   Management Systems
Joy McLarty, American College Testing
William Spring, Federal Reserve Bank of Boston
Thomas Sticht, Applied, Behavioral, and Cognitive
   Sciences, Inc.
Marc Tucker, National Center on Education and
   the Economy

GOAL 7: SAFE, DISCIPLINED, AND ALCOHOL- AND DRUG-FREE SCHOOLS

Resource Group Convener: John Porter, Urban Education Alliance

Members:
C. Leonard Anderson, Portland Public Schools
Michael Guerra, National Catholic Education Association
J. David Hawkins, Social Development Research Group
Fred Hechinger, Carnegie Corporation of New York
Barbara Huff, Federation of Families for Children's Mental Health
Lloyd Johnston, University of Michigan
Ronda Talley, American Psychological Association

Consultants for Resource Group on Safe, Disciplined, Alcohol- and Drug-free Schools:
Janet Collins, Centers for Disease Control and Prevention
Vincent Giordano, New York City Public Schools
Oliver Moles, U.S. Department of Education
Ed Zubrow, Independent Consultant

Task Force on Disciplined Environments Conducive to Learning Leader: Ronda Tally, American Psychological Association

Members:
C. Leonard Anderson, Portland Public Schools
Michael Guerra, National Catholic Education Association
J. David Hawkins, Social Development Research Group
Fred Hechinger, Carnegie Corporation of New York
Barbara Huff, Federation of Families for Children's Mental Health

Consultants for Task Force on Disciplined Environments Conducive to Learning:
Oliver Moles, U.S. Department of Education
Ed Zubrow, Independent Consultant

GOAL 8: PARENTAL PARTICIPATION

(Resource Group will be formed during 1994-95.)

TASK FORCE ON EDUCATION NETWORK TECHNOLOGY

Leader: Robert Palaich, Education Commission of the States

Members:
Laura Breeden, U.S. Department of Commerce
John Clement, National Science Foundation
Jan Hawkins, Bank Street College of Education
Robert Kansky, National Academy of Sciences
Pamela Keating, University of Washington
Glenn Kessler, Fairfax County Public Schools, Virginia
Mark Musick, Southern Regional Education Board
Bill Padia, California Department of Education
Nora Sabelli, National Science Foundation
Rafael Valdivieso, Academy for Educational Development, Inc.

Task Force Advisors:
Steven Gould, Congressional Research Service
Gerald Malitz, U.S. Department of Education
Linda Roberts, U.S. Department of Education

National Education Goals Panel Staff

Ken Nelson
Executive Director

Cynthia D. Prince
Associate Director for Analysis and Reporting

Ruth Whitman Chacon
Associate Director for Communications

Martin E. Orland
Associate Director for Analysis and Reporting – through July 9, 1994
Acting Director – through December 1993

PROGRAM STAFF

Leslie A. Lawrence
Education Associate

Emily O. Wurtz
Senior Education Associate

ADMINISTRATIVE STAFF

Tia M. Cosey
Receptionist and Office Automation Assistant

Cynthia M. Dixon
Program Assistant

Charles J. Walter
Executive Officer

with assistance from

Hilary M. Cairns
Bryan J. Flynn
Ramesh Ganeshram
Geri Anderson Nielsen
Julie O'Brian
Barbara A. Pape
Cristina Ritchie

ISBN 0-16-045194-9

9 780160 451942

90000

The National Education Goals Panel values your response to the *1994 Goals Report* and the *National* and *State Data Volumes*. Please take a few moments to fill out and return this questionnaire so that we can continue to improve future reports. Mail or FAX to:

National Education Goals Panel
1850 M Street, NW, Suite 270, Washington, DC 20036
PHONE (202) 632-0952
FAX (202) 632-0957

Name: _____

Organization: _____

Title/Position: _____

Address: _____

Phone: _____ **Fax:** _____

Please Circle As Many As Apply:
Student / Parent / Educator / Business or Community Leader /
Federal, State, or Local Policymaker / Concerned Citizen

1. Do you have any general comments about the Report (e.g., clarity of the data and text, new focus on sixteen core indicators, graphics, etc.)?

_____

_____

_____

2. How do you rate the usefulness of the Report? (1 = not very useful and 5 = very useful)

1994 National Education Goals Report

    1   2   3   4   5

1994 Volume One: National Data

    1   2   3   4   5

1994 Volume Two: State Data

    1   2   3   4   5

3. How are you or your organization using the information in the Report (e.g., in speeches, local/state data reports, etc.)?

_____

_____

4. How can the Goals Panel make the information more useful to you or your organization?

_____

_____

5. Do you use electronic or on-line services? If so, which ones? Would you make use of the Goals Panel's data and publications if they were available on that service?

_____

_____

6. How did you receive this Report (please circle)?
   • automatically mailed me
   • I requested it
   • other (please explain)_____

7. Would you like additional copies of the:

1994 National Education Goals Report	Yes	How Many? _____
1994 Volume One: National Data	Yes	How Many? _____
1994 Volume Two: State Data	Yes	How Many? _____

8. Would you like further information about the Community Action Toolkit? _____

9. Would you like an order form which lists the Goals Panel's other publications? _____

The National Education Goals Panel thanks you for your interest.

Place First Class Postage Here or Fax to: (202) 6__-____

National Education Goals Panel
1850 M Street, NW, Suite 270
Washington, DC 20036-7590

NATIONAL
EDUCATION
GOALS
PANEL

Tape or staple here